Passions of the Sign

PARALLAX RE-VISIONS OF CULTURE
AND SOCIETY

Stephen G. Nichols, Gerald Prince, and Wendy Steiner
SERIES EDITORS

Passions of the Sign

Revolution and Language in
Kant, Goethe, and Kleist

Andreas Gailus

The Johns Hopkins University Press
Baltimore

The Johns Hopkins University Press
2715 North Charles Street
Baltimore, Maryland 21218-4363
www.press.jhu.edu

Library of Congress Cataloging-in-Publication Data

Gailus, Andreas.
    Passions of the sign : revolution and language in Kant,
Goethe, and Kleist / Andreas Gailus.
        p.   cm. — (Parallax, re-visions of culture and society)
    Includes bibliographical references and index.
    ISBN 0-8018-8277-X (hardcover : alk. paper)
    1. Semiotics—Germany—History. 2. German language—
Rhetoric—History.   3. Kleist, Heinrich von, 1777–1811.
Michael Kohlhaas.   4. Kant, Immanuel, 1724–1804—
Criticism and interpretation.   5. Goethe, Johann Wolfgang
von, 1749–1832. Unterhaltungen deutscher Ausgewanderten.
6. France—Revolution, 1789–1799—Influence.   7. France—
Revolution, 1789–1799—Literature and the revolution.
8. Subjectivity—History—19th centuury.   9. Subjectivity
in literature. I. Title. II. Parallax (Baltimore, Md.)
    P99.37.G3G35 2006
    830.9′0001′4—dc22   2005014176

A catalog record for this book is available from the
British Library.

To Christine and Russell

Contents

▐ *Abbreviations*

AA   Kant, *Gesammelte Schriften*, ed. Königlich Preußischen
Akademie der Wissenschaften (Berlin: De Gruyter, 1922–)

AV   Kleist, "Über die allmähliche Verfertigung der Gedanken
beim Reden," in id., *Sämtliche Werke und Briefe*, vol. 3:
Erzählungen; Anekdoten; Gedichte; Schriften, ed. Klaus
Müller-Salget, 534–40 (Frankfurt a/M: Deutscher Klassiker
Verlag, 1990)

CAF   Goethe, *Campagne in Frankreich,* in id., *Sämtliche Werke:
Briefe, Tagebücher und Gespräche*, part 1, vol. 16, *Campagne
in Frankreich; Belagerung von Mainz; Reiseschriften*, ed.
Klaus-Detlef Müller, 386–573 (Frankfurt a/M: Deutscher
Klassiker Verlag, 1994)

CF   Kant, *The Conflict of the Faculties / Der Streit der
Fakultäten*, trans. Mary J. Gregor (Lincoln: University of
Nebraska Press, 1992)

CJ   Kant, *Critique of Judgment*, trans. Werner Pluhar
(Indianapolis: Hackett, 1987)

CPR   Kant, *Critique of Pure Reason,* trans. and ed. Paul Guyer
and Allen W. Wood (New York: Cambridge University
Press, 1998)

CprR   Kant, *Critique of Practical Reason*, trans. Lewis White Beck
(New York: Macmillan, 1993)

CR   Goethe, *Conversations of German Refugees,* trans. Jan van
Heurck, ed. Jane K. Brown (New York: Suhrkamp, 1991)

EDD   Goethe, "Über epische und dramatische Dichtung. Von
Goethe und Schiller." in id., *Sämtliche Werke: Briefe,
Tagebücher und Gespräche*, part 1, vol. 22, *Ästhetische
Schriften, 1824–1832,* ed. Anne Bohnenkamp, 295–306
(Frankfurt a/M: Deutscher Klassiker Verlag, 1999)

EDP   Goethe, "On Epic and Dramatic Poetry." In id., *Essays on*

Art and Literature, trans. Elleen von Nardroff and Ernest H. von Nardroff, ed. John Gearey, 192–194 (New York: Suhrkamp, 1986)

GMM Kant, *Groundwork of the Metaphysic of Morals,* trans. H. J. Paton (New York: Harper & Row, 1964)

GMS Kant, *Grundlegung zur Metaphysik der Sitten,* ed. Karl Vorländer (Hamburg: Meiner, 1994)

GP Kleist, "On the Gradual Production of Thoughts Whilst Speaking," in id., *Selected Writings,* trans. David Constantine, 405–9 (London: J. M. Dent, 1997)

GW Freud, *Gesammelte Werke* (London: Imago, 1940)

IUH Kant, "Idea for a Universal History from a Cosmopolitan Point of View." In id., *On History,* trans. and ed. Lewis White Beck, 11–26 (Indianapolis: Bobbs-Merrill, 1963)

KpV Kant, *Kritik der praktischen Vernunft,* ed. Karl Vorländer (Hamburg: Meiner, 1990)

KrV Kant, *Kritik der reinen Vernunft,* ed. Raymund Schmid (Hamburg: Meiner, 1956)

KU Kant, *Kritik der Urteilskraft,* ed. Karl Vorländer (Hamburg: Meiner, 1990)

M Goethe, *Zur Morphologie,* in id., *Sämtliche Werke nach Epochen seines Schaffens,* vol. 12: *Zur Naturwissenschaft überhaupt, besonders zur Morphologie,* ed. Hans J. Becker et al., 9–386 (Munich: Carl Hanser, 1989)

MK Kleist, *Michael Kohlhaas,* in id., *Sämtliche Werke und Briefe,* vol. 3: *Erzählungen; Anekdoten; Gedichte; Schriften,* ed. Klaus Müller-Salget, 11–142 (Frankfurt a/M: Deutscher Klassiker Verlag, 1990)

MK/G Kleist, *Michael Kohlhaas,* in id., *The Marquise of O—and Other Stories,* trans. and ed. Martin Greenberg (New York: Frederick Ungar, 1960)

MM Kant, *The Metaphysics of Morals,* in *The Cambridge Edition of the Works of Immanuel Kant: Practical Philosophy,* trans. and ed. Mary J. Gregor, 353–605 (Cambridge: Cambridge University Press, 1996)

OBS Kant, *Observations on the Feeling of the Beautiful and Sublime,* trans. John T. Goldthwait (Berkeley: University of California Press, 1960)

PP   Kant, "Perpetual Peace: A Philosophical Sketch," in *Kant's Political Writings*, trans. H. B. Nisbet, ed. Hans Reiss, 93–130 (Cambridge: Cambridge University Press, 1970)

RGV   Kant, *Die Religion innerhalb der Grenzen der Vernunft* (Hamburg: Meiner, 1990)

RLR   Kant, *Religion Within the Limits of Reason Alone*, trans. Theodore M. Greene and Hoyt H. Hudson (Chicago: Open Court, 1934)

RSM   Goethe, "Reise der Söhne Megaprazons," in id., *Sämtliche Werke: Briefe, Tagebücher und Gespräche*, part 1, vol. 8, *Die Leiden des jungen Werthers; Die Wahlverwandtschaften; Kleine Prosa; Epen,* ed. Waltraud Wiethölter, 578–94 (Frankfurt a/M: Deutscher Klassiker Verlag, 1994)

SE   Freud, *The Standard Edition of the Complete Psychological Works of Sigmund Freud* (London: Hogarth Press and Institute of Psychoanalysis, 1953–74)

SF   Kant, *Der Streit der Fakultäten*, ed. Klaus Reich (Hamburg: Meiner, 1959)

SS   Goethe, *Scientific Studies,* trans. and ed. Douglas Miller (New York: Suhrkamp, 1988)

TA   Kierkegaard, *Two Ages,* trans. and ed. Howard V. Hong and Edna Hong, in *Kierkegaard's Writings*, vol. 14 (Princeton: Princeton University Press, 1978)

TP   Kant, "On the Common Saying: 'This may be true in theory, but it does not apply in practice,'" in *Kant's Political Writings*, trans. H. B. Nisbet, ed. Hans Reiss, 61–92 (Cambridge: Cambridge University Press, 1970)

UA   Goethe, *Unterhaltungen deutscher Ausgewanderten,* in id., *Sämtliche Werke: Briefe, Tagebücher und Gespräche*, part 1, vol. 9: *Wilhelm Meisters theatralische Sendung; Wilhelm Meisters Lehrjahre; Unterhaltungen deutscher Ausgewanderten,* ed. Wilhelm Voßkamp and Herbert Jaumann, 993–1114 (Frankfurt a/M: Deutscher Klassiker Verlag, 1992)

Preface

Duty! Thou sublime and mighty name that dost embrace
nothing charming or insinuating but requirest submission
and yet seekest not to move the will by threatening aught that
would arouse natural aversion or terror, but only holdest forth
a law which of itself finds entrance into the mind and yet
gains reluctant reverence (though not always obedience)—a
law before which all inclinations are mute even though they
secretly work against it: what origin is worthy of thee, and
where is the root of thy novel descent which proudly rejects
all kinship with the inclination. . . .

　　This root cannot be less than something that elevates man
above himself as part of the world of sense, something which
connects him with an order of things which only the understanding can think . . . It is nothing else than personality, i.e.,
the freedom and independence from the mechanism of nature.

　　　　Kant, *Critique of Practical Reason*, trans. Lewis White Beck

This panegyric to duty marks out in concise form the terrain of paradox that
is the focus of this study. The human subject, Kant is saying, is fundamentally
divided as a result of leading a double life as a natural being on the one hand
and a moral agent on the other. Moral activity demands the setting aside of
what we commonly take to be the defining features of our individuality: our
passions, desires, and habits—indeed, our sensuous experience as such. Hence
Kant's counterintuitive identification of "personality" with those aspects that
seem most removed from our human existence. Personality is the subjective
voice of moral law and is properly personal only where humans speak in the
idiom of the universal. This *impersonal personality* is the paradoxical goal of
moral life, which is therefore inherently conflictual: to be fully human is to in-

terrupt our immersion in the flow of ordinary life and to follow a universal law whose origin is both unknown and ineluctable.

But the division between passion and the law of freedom is not as absolute as might at first appear. The law incites a passionate devotion that surpasses not only the pull of ordinary inclinations but also the bounds of ordinary reason. The exalted rhetoric of the passage bears witness to this very dynamic. In the sober and arid landscape of Kant's *Critique of Practical Reason,* the panegyric to duty registers as a rare outburst of feeling, whose hymnic cadence interrupts the rational progress of argument and deduction. This rhetorical interruption reflects a fundamental theoretical diffculty. For while rational adherence to the law is the foundation of morality, the law itself transcends the resources of rational calculation. It is, as Kant famously says, "the sole fact of pure reason" (CPrR 31), whose truth is experienced, rather than understood, in the feeling of commitment imposed by the law itself. If the voice of reason fractures the subject, the dialect of feeling splits the discourse of reason.

In the chapters that follow, I argue that this notion of *impersonal passion*—of a passion that is beyond the bounds of both individual personality and reason—was important to how the French Revolution was received in Germany. In each of the texts I examine, the Revolution is read as the historical manifestation of a new form of subjectivity whose divided and unstable nature reverberates within the foundations of symbolic life. However, whereas Kant, at least in his first two *Critiques,* locates this extrapersonal dimension in the transcendence of pure reason, the texts under discussion show the subject to be driven by impersonal energies within language.

From the perspective of these texts, then, to speak and act is to open oneself to an impersonal energy that threatens the integrity of language and subjectivity. Another way of putting this is to say that such a threat—or what I shall call "crisis"—is understood as a vital condition of human activity or, more precisely, as the dynamic manifestation of a structural infirmity in the foundations of meaning. Meaning is infirm because its medium—the energetic sign—is constitutively heterogeneous, divided between sense and force, the semantic and the countersemantic. My claim is that Kant, Goethe, and Kleist discovered in the French Revolution the configuration of this heteroclite semiotic, and with it a new, and indeed revolutionary, model of history, language, and subjectivity.

It is hardly surprising that this attunement to questions of force and meaning emerges in texts written in the wake of, and in response to, the French Revolution, which patently focused attention on the basis of political authority and the tension between law and violence. Out of the vivid historicity of the Revolution, Kant, Goethe, and Kleist draw an extended problematic of sovereignty that moves beyond the explicit domain of politics to that of speech and subjectivity. In this sense, the present text may be said to provide a similar extension, both historical and conceptual, of the "paradox of sovereignty" famously articulated by Carl Schmitt in the 1920s and recently reworked in the writings of Giorgio Agamben.

Talk of paradox leads directly to talk of limits, and indeed limits, boundaries, and borders feature prominently in the following pages. The texts that form the focus of my study represent a marginal strand in the literary and philosophical discourse around 1800, but marginality here has an unusual and multifaceted sense. In the first instance, the discursive marginality is repeated in the relation of each text to the oeuvre of its respective author. Secondly, boundaries—geographical, bodily, textual—are an explicit thematic focus of all these texts. And finally, this thematization of boundaries is the narrative expression of a more general exploration of the liminal character of foundation. Working on the margins in a multiplicity of ways, then, the texts bring into sharp relief tensions and problems at the heart of the dominant discourses of their time. Kant's *Contest of the Faculties* raises questions about the foundations of moral life as laid out in his *Critique of Practical Reason*. Goethe's novella cycle *Conversations of German Refugees* raises questions about the narrative grounding of subjectivity and sociability delineated in his famous bildungsroman *Wilhelm Meister's Apprenticeship*. If things are more complicated with respect to Kleist's *Michael Kohlhaas,* his most celebrated text, this is because Kleist's entire oeuvre, and this text in particular, inhabits the domain of liminality and foundational crisis. This is the reason for Kleist's unique cultural position, what might be called his eccentric canonicity; and it is the reason why the following study both begins and ends with Kleist.

This book was written over a period of ten years, and it bears the stamp of many encounters with individuals and institutions. I am deeply grateful to Dorothea von Mücke, who has accompanied this project from its inception through its many detours with enthusiasm, intelligence, and gentle insistence. Her belief in it—and me—has kept me going. Franco Moretti showed me what it means to be passionate about truth; his unique blend of merciless criticism and exuberant praise continues to inspire me. I also wish to thank Andreas Huyssen, my chair at Columbia University, and my colleagues at the University of Minnesota, who have given me a new intellectual home.

Preface

A fellowship year at the Getty Institute in Los Angeles allowed me to test my ideas in a truly interdisciplinary setting. I am thankful to Michael Roth, the former associate director of the Research Institute, and to John Forrester, Deborah Silverman, David Summers, and Bill Viola for many eye-opening comments. A number of colleagues and friends have read selected chapters of this book and gave me helpful advice: James Chandler, Mladen Dolar, Charles Larmore, Sandra Macpherson, Robert Pippen, Eric Santer, Joshua Scodel, and Katie Trumpener. David Wellbery read the entire manuscript with meticulous care and offered me his mentor- and friendship at a crucial time. I am indebted to Michael Lonegro, my editor at the Johns Hopkins Press, for his patience with my impatience and his willingness to let the present book title stand. Many thanks also to Peter Dreyer for his attentive and thoughtful copyediting, and to an anonymous reader for the Press, who helped me understand myself better. Lisa Disch's love and optimism were a constant source of encouragement in the later stages of writing.

Above all, this book owes it existence and shape to the generosity and lucidity of two friends. Russell Newstadt, my toughest critic and most exacting reader, forced me time and again to clarify my ideas and refine my argument. Without his philosophical acumen, this book would be both longer and more nebulous. Christine Sterkel, while not reading a single word of it, helped me discover why I wanted to write this book in the first place. As a reflection on the indissoluble bond between language and passion, this book continues a conversation we began many years ago.

Parts of the introduction appeared in German in *Kleist-Jahrbuch* 2000, and in Slovenian in *Problemi* 3/4 (2004). An earlier version of chapter two appeared in *Modern Philology* 100 (2003).

Passions of the Sign

Energetic Signs

Autonomy and Novelty in the
Age of Revolution

Somewhere around 1805–6, while composing the first version of his novella "Michael Kohlhaas," Heinrich von Kleist began writing a short essay entitled "Über die allmähliche Verfertigung der Gedanken beim Reden" (On the Gradual Production of Thoughts Whilst Speaking). Published only in 1878, more than sixty years after his death, the essay was slow to gain critical attention and is still overshadowed by Kleist's famous and much commented upon essay "Über das Marionettentheater" (On the Marionette Theater).[1] Yet, like the latter, which makes no bones about its broad philosophical ambitions, the "Allmähliche Verfertigung" raises questions about the foundations of contemporary culture. If "Über das Marionettentheater" undermines the presuppositions of idealist aesthetics,[2] the "Allmähliche Verfertigung" takes aim at the progressivist model of history that dominates late eighteenth-century German thought. According to this model, what is new is always incorporated into an already articulated narrative; in Kleist's essay, on the contrary, it is articulation *itself* that generates the new. "Allmähliche Verfertigung" is concerned with the eventfulness of speech, of speech as a productive cause of both novel thought and novel historical events to which such thought gives rise. It is concerned, in other words, with the revolutionary character of language.

Kleist's essay is itself an instance of the event of speech it talks about.[3] The "Allmähliche Verfertigung" consists of a series of anecdotes that have the ostensible function of illustrating, by way of examples, the text's thesis. But rather than instantiating an already determined idea, each anecdote—indeed, almost each sentence—recasts the theoretical model it is meant to illustrate.

The essay's initial thesis is drawn into and altered by the particular examples cited, just as, *within* the examples, the initial thoughts of the speakers are transformed in the act of articulation. To read Kleist's "Allmähliche Verfertigung," then, is also to read the text's *own* slow production of thought.

Kleist's essay begins on relatively familiar ground. The setting is domestic and German, the characters are Kleist and his sister, and the problem concerns the proper method of acquiring knowledge. The first anecdote thus starts out in a paradigmatically Cartesian frame, that is, with the self's examination of an at first only dimly perceived interior concept. "Often I have sat at my desk over the papers of a difficult case and sought the point of view from which it might be grasped. My habit then, in this striving of my innermost being after enlightenment, is to gaze into the lamplight, as into the brightest point. Or a problem in algebra occurs to me and I need a starting point, I need the equation which expresses the given relationships and from which by simple calculation the solution may be found" (GP 405).[4]

But this Enlightenment image of thought—of thinking as a silent retreat to the interiority of reason—fails immediately upon presentation. For thought to succeed, the text suggests, one must go beyond the Cartesian frame of interiority and enter the Hegelian world of exteriority, the world of time, history, and intersubjectivity: "The French say 'l'appétit vient en mangeant' and this maxim is just as true if we parody it and say 'l'idée vient en parlant'. . . . And lo and behold! If I speak about it to my sister sitting behind me at her work, I learn more than I should have arrived at by perhaps hours of brooding (GP 405).[5]

Provocative as this sounds, we are still on philosophical terrain. The claim that knowledge depends on articulation, dialogue, and the efficacy of encounter underlies the idea of dialectic, both in Plato and, closer to Kleist, in Hegel, whose *Phenomenology of Spirit* appeared in 1807, one year before the completion of Kleist's essay. But precisely at this point, when the text has reached, as it were, the most advanced philosophical position of its time, the narrative takes a turn that eventually carries the argument beyond the epistemic realm:

> Not that she [the sister], in any real sense, *tells* me. . . . Nor is it that by skillful questioning she brings me to the crux of the matter, though that might often be the way to do it, I daresay. But because I do have some dim conception at the outset, one distantly related to what I am looking for, if I boldly make a start with that, my mind, even as my speech proceeds, under the necessity of finding an end for that beginning, will shape my first confused idea into complete clarity, so that, to my amazement, understanding

is arrived at as the sentence ends. I put in a few unarticulated sounds, dwell lengthily on the conjunctions, perhaps make use of apposition where it is not necessary, and have recourse to other tricks which will spin out my speech, all to gain time for the fabrication of my idea in the workshop of the mind. And in this process nothing helps me more than if my sister makes a move suggesting she wishes to interrupt; for such an attempt from outside to wrest speech from its grasp still further excites my already hard-worked mind and, like a general when the circumstances press, its powers are raised a further degree. (GP 405–6)[6]

Dialectic is necessary, but not for the reasons one might have thought. Thinking depends on the presence of the other, not because the other collaborates in the production of thought, but, on the contrary, because his role as a potential collaborator poses a *threat* to the completion of thought. Kleist's dialectic is a perverse one: the other enters the dialectical stage only as a mute obstacle, as an impediment on the speaker's path to knowledge; but in order to play this subordinate role, the other must first be recognized as an equal, as a speaker in his own right.[7] This peculiar logic surfaces most clearly in what might be called the anecdote's kairotic moment. Note that the sister becomes productive precisely at the moment when her movement suggests the possibility of her speaking, for it is this movement, read as a sign of impatience and impending interruption, that enlists the speaker's combative energies and propels him toward the completion of his thought. For Kleist, thought completes its circuit, achieves fulfillment, through the agency of an external irritant against which it must assert itself. But, and I shall come back to this, it needs to be stressed that what appears, from one standpoint, to be merely the discovery of an already established solution is, from another perspective, a creative act, the invention of a new thought.

With this turn of events, however, we have already moved beyond a purely epistemic model. For what began as a rational pursuit of a mathematical formula ends in a combative encounter cast in military metaphor: the mathematician as general on the battlefield of thought.[8] The question of knowledge is thus overtaken by the problem of survival, and with this, the cognitive is displaced by the affective. This is so—and here we have arrived at the theoretical kernel of the essay—because in shifting from the silent world of internal thought to the noisy world of utterance and communication, one has entered the domain of temporality. Thought as such operates in the framework of timeless possibility. Once the barrier into articulation is crossed, however, the vast field of possibilities yields to the linear progress of actualized speech.

Kleist's text emphatically underscores the significance of this crossing by describing the shift from thought to articulation as a passage from the logical tension of problem and solution to the temporal dynamic of beginning and end: in speaking, one operates under the constraints of narrative exigency, or as the text puts it, in "der Notwendigkeit, dem Anfang nun auch ein Ende zu finden" (under the necessity of finding an end for that beginning).

Now this "der Notwendigkeit, dem Anfang nun auch ein Ende zu finden," while a constitutive feature of utterance as such, is intensified by the presence of an interlocutor. For the other, as we have already seen, is not just an obstacle to the speaker, but his enemy. The reason for this is that the other is himself a speaker, and he is hence capable of commandeering speech and thereby exhausting the time of my utterance. More than anything else, it is therefore imperative to prevent the other from usurping speech. This is exactly the function served by Kleist's meaningless interjections, which gain time and thus keep it, so to speak, in the possession of the speaker: "I put in a few unarticulated sounds, dwell lengthily on the conjunctions, perhaps make use of apposition where it is not necessary, and have recourse to other tricks which will spin out my speech, all to gain time for the fabrication of my idea in the workshop of the mind."[9]

Let me interrupt *myself* at this point to make a more general observation. It would seem that the Kleistian model runs counter to our ordinary notion of speech. Are we not normally engaged in a much more communal and amicable form of interaction? In fact, there is a long tradition of conceiving of communication on the model of equitable exchange, as a reciprocal transaction that both binds and transcends the individual members of a linguistic community.[10] However, this is the model of *communication,* not of speech and utterance. And while communication derives from and serves the interest of the community, speech and utterance as such belong to the province of the individual. So viewed, there obtains a systematic tension between these two realms. And it is this tension that Kleist's manic egotism defies and brings into sharp relief. Kleist refuses to give his speech—and indeed, himself—over to communication.

But there is more to this tension than the mere opposition of individual to community. There is, once again, the question of time, for communication and utterance operate according to discrete temporalities. Whereas the driving principle of communication is to keep going, utterance is finite. In the final analysis, however, the finitude of utterance points to, and is encompassed by, a larger and more thoroughgoing finitude: that of life itself. And this is exactly what the figure of general brings out. Hence the urgency so evident in Kleist's anecdote, the sense of time running out and of speaking as a struggle, not simply against the possibility of interruption, but of the exhaustion of possibility *tout court*—that is, the exhaustion of life. Kleistian speech, in other words, operates under the permanent condition of crisis.[11]

The figure of the general on the battlefield that ends the first anecdote is thus more than a figure of speech. It reveals the literal truth of the anecdote. And yet, for this metaphor to arrive at its literal truth, another, *geographical* transfer, is required. With the second anecdote, the narrative moves from the domestic German setting of Kleist's home, where the eventfulness of speech is confined to parochial mathematical and bureaucratic problems, to the world-historical stage of the French Revolution, in which a turn in communication changes the fate of an entire nation.

> I believe many a great speaker to have been ignorant when he opened his mouth of what he was going to say. But the conviction that he would be able to draw all the ideas he needed from the circumstances themselves and from the mental excitement they generated made him bold enough to trust to luck and make a start. I think of the "thunderbolt" [*Donnerkeil*] with which Mirabeau dismissed the Master of Ceremonies who, after the meeting of the 23 June, the last under the *ancien régime*, when the King had ordered the estates to disperse, returned to the hall in which they were still assembled and asked them had they heard the King's command. "Yes," Mirabeau replied, "we have heard the King's command."—I am certain that beginning thus humanely he had not yet thought of the bayonets with which he would finish. "Yes, my dear sir," he repeated, "we have heard it."—As we see, he is not yet exactly sure what he intends. "But by what right . . . " he continues, and suddenly a source of colossal ideas is opened up to him, "do you give us orders here? We are the representatives of the nation."—That was what he needed!—"The nation does not take orders. It gives them. . . . And to make myself perfectly plain to you . . . "—And only now does he find words to express how fully his soul has armed itself and stands ready to resist—"tell your king we shall not move from here unless forced to by bayonets."—Whereupon, well content with himself, he sat down. (GP 406)[12]

Note how the second anecdote, while repeating the narrative structure of the first one—the opening act of *Setzung,* the stalling in the middle, the climactic end—begins in the arena of historical efficacy only gestured at by the latter. To begin with, the text has clearly moved beyond the cognitive. What matters is less the truth of the utterance than its vital effectiveness, its ability to strike down the other. Thus the combative, aggressive character of speech, held in check by the familial setting of the first anecdote and its ostensible concern with mathematical and bureaucratic problems, is fully brought out in the political context of the second anecdote. The intimation of civil and congenial dialectic is displaced by the manifest reality of political crisis, in which speech impinges directly on matters of life and death.

This politicization goes hand in hand with an intensification of the eventfulness of speech, in terms of novel occurrence both within speech and in the extralinguistic reality such speech generates. True, even the discovery of a solution to a mathematical problem is an event, but it is, so to speak, an uneventful event. The discovery of a solution is, logically understood, the discovery of something already inherent in the problem and not the invention of something new. The solution is immanent in the problem, which is to say, the time required for its articulation is inessential. In the Mirabeau anecdote, by contrast, time is of the essence. The Master of Ceremonies and the state he represents will not wait for Mirabeau to formulate the answer that will topple them. In fact, the effectiveness of Mirabeau's answer depends crucially on its timeliness: a minute, or even a few seconds later, the same answer is at best the occasion for impotent regret. Mirabeau does seize the moment, however, and his speech is eventful, and in both senses indicated above. First, because what he says has never been said before; and second, because what he says dramatically transforms the political landscape.

Recall the climactic moment of Mirabeau's speech, the *Donnerkeil* that strikes down the Master of Ceremonies: "'We are the representatives of the nation.'—That was what he needed!—'the nation does not take orders. It gives them.'"[13] This is not merely the invocation of a received idea; rather, it is the performative creation of an as yet unheard-of concept: that of the nation as sovereign. The text stages a historic shift in political semantics, the moment at which the people cease to be the passive subject of the law and instead become, under the rubric of "the nation," its source and foundation. (I say "stage" both because the formulation granted Mirabeau is Kleist's dramatic invention and is nowhere to be found in the sources he relies on, and because it captures in a single phrase what is arguably the decisive discursive shift of the French Revolution.)[14] Now this event of speech, in opening up a new conceptual space, exceeds the confines of utterance and breaks into and alters the fabric of the political and social context in which it occurs. When Mirabeau resumes his speech, he is no longer in the same world. The revolutionary event has occurred, and what follows now is the calm—almost bureaucratic, one might say—spelling out of the principles of the new political order: "We read that Mirabeau as soon as the Master of Ceremonies had withdrawn stood up and proposed (i) that they constitute themselves a national assembly at once, and (ii) declare themselves inviolable" (GP 407).[15] This is the new postrevolutionary form of political representation, a form that radically departs from the ritualized hierarchies of the ancien régime overseen by the Master of Ceremonies.

In discussing the anecdote so far, I have not said anything about the curious energetic metaphor of electrical discharge that Kleist employs to describe the confrontation between Mirabeau and the Master of Ceremonies. After Mirabeau has delivered his linguistic "thunderbolt," the text resumes as follows:

> Whereupon, well content with himself, he sat down.—As to the Master of Ceremonies, we must imagine him bankrupted by this encounter of all ideas. For a law applies rather similar to the law which says that if a body having no electricity of its own enters the zone of a body which has been electrified at once the latter's electricity will be produced in it. And just as in the electrified body, by a reciprocal effect, a strengthening of the innate electricity then occurs, so our speaker's confidence, as he annihilated his opponent, was converted into an inspired and extraordinary boldness. (GP 406–7)[16]

We have already seen in the first anecdote that Kleist's perverse dialectic operates on the principle, not of reciprocal exchange, but of exclusive exhaustion: given the linearity of speech, the other's interruption exhausts my reservoir of time and possibilities, and thus, in the final analysis, exhausts my life. The electrical metaphor both recasts and radicalizes this economy of speech. The speakers are no longer represented as human subjects, but rather as mere conduits for the circulation of an impersonal energy. In the first anecdote, interaction is understood in terms of the speakers' *experience* of time; now, it is a question of the passage of an extrapersonal force between two poles embodied momentarily and inessentially by the speakers in question. The bipolarism already present in the first anecdote achieves the almost pure formalism of a binary code, the plus and minus of electrical charge.

In the context of this formal machinery, what matters is not the speakers' subjectivity but their ability to open themselves up to the circulation of energy. In fact, Kleist suggests that Mirabeau's role in the ensuing revolution is due to his receptiveness to the accidental play of circumstance: "In this way it was perhaps the twitching of an upper lip or an equivocal tugging at the cuffs that brought about the overthrow of the order of things in France" (GP 407).[17] This sentence follows directly the above cited presentation of the electrical model, which it extends to another realm. Once again, the text emphasizes the crucial function of exteriority in the production of eventful speech. Yet bodily motions, the trigger of novel events, are not purely exterior, they are indeed accidental and intrinsically meaningless. To this extent, the text suggests that the meaningfulness of history derives from what is meaningless and contingent.

If Mirabeau's France is the productive site of historical novelty, the France of the third anecdote—a rewriting of a fable by La Fontaine—is a place of abiding conservatism. And yet eventful speech occurs even here, except that it now functions not to overthrow the existing political and social order but to reassert its dominance at a moment of crisis.

> The fable is well known. Plague is raging among the animals, the lion summons the grandees of the kingdom and informs them that heaven, if it is to be propitiated, must have a sacrifice. There are many sinners among the people, the death of the greatest must save the rest from destruction. Accordingly, he bids them make him a candid confession of all their crimes. He, for his part, admits that, driven by hunger, he has cut short the lives of many a sheep; dogs likewise, when they came too near; indeed, in delicious moments he has even been known to eat the shepherd. If no one is guilty of worse weaknesses than these then he, the lion, will gladly be the one to die. "Sire," says the fox, wishing to ward the lightning off himself, "in your zeal and generosity you have gone too far. What if you have done a sheep or two to death? Or a dog, a vile creature? And: quant au berger," he continues, for this is the chief point, "on peut dire," though he still does not know what, "qu'il méritoit tout mal," trusting to luck, and with that he has embroiled himself, "étant," a poor word but which buys him time, "de ces gens là," and only now does he hit upon the thought that gets him out of his difficulty, "qui sur les animaux se font un chimérique empire."—And he goes on to prove the donkey, the bloodthirsty donkey (devourer of grass and plants) is the most fitting sacrifice. And with that they fall on him and tear him to pieces. (GP 407–8)[18]

Coming as it does on the heels of the Mirabeau anecdote, the fable assumes a decidedly counterrevolutionary air. It shows how communal agitation, the incipient ferment of revolution, is contained through the creation of a scapegoat whose sacrifice enables society to purge itself of an internal irritant, to reestablish the sovereign order. The irony is of course that this irritant is self-made, a constitutive feature of the very system that seeks to eliminate it. The external plague is only a historical screen for a much more dangerous structural plague, and it is this malaise at the heart of the status quo that the sacrifice is meant to cover up. Kleist's fable, in other words, is about the intertwining of law and violence, and thus about the plague of sovereignty.[19] This is highlighted by the subtle yet significant change he makes in La Fontaine's fable. In the latter, the donkey is singled out for sacrifice owing to his marginal status. A herbivore among carnivores, he is a hybrid figure inhabiting the gray zone between the animal kingdom and human domesticity, between wild prey and cultivated grass. In Kleist's rewriting, this marginality of the donkey is intensified through his association with the surpassing sovereignty of the human world, represented by the shepherd. And it is this new link, the text unambiguously states, that is the decisive event in the fox's speech: "'de ces gens là,' *and only now does he hit upon the thought that gets him out of his difficulty,* 'qui sur les animaux se font un chimérique empire'" ("de ces gens là", *und nun erst findet er den Gedanken, der ihn aus der Not reißt:* "qui sur les animaux se font un chimérique empire").

The passage presents, in highly compressed form, the perverse dialectic of political sacrifice that recurs throughout Kleist's work. First, there is a moment of logical tension. Insofar as the donkey, the traditional figure of servility, is identified with the order of sovereignty, his almost arbitrary marginality is made to reveal an ambiguity in the functioning of political power. Kleist's version suggests that the master (sovereignty) cannot be differentiated from the slave (servility), and for good reason: the master is himself a slave to the slaves on whom he depends. However, for this recognition of ambiguity to turn into violence, ambiguity must be converted into polarity and the logical tension internal to the system externalized into a separable object. The fox's association of the donkey with the rival order of man, which fixes the former as a traitor and political foe, accomplishes precisely this act of semantic *disambiguation,* thus paving the ground for the third and final moment: the cathartic moment of sacrifice, in which society's anxiety over its ambiguous foundation erupts into murderous violence.

What is at stake here, in other words, is the legality of law and the legitimacy of the state. The sacrificial murder of the donkey is an echo of the inaugural transgression that establishes the order of society and the rule of sovereign law. Precisely because this transgression lies at the foundation of a given political order, addressing it is intrinsically revolutionary, and thus unmaneagable within the context of this order. It is this revolutionary threat that the sacrificial murder is meant to counteract. The effectiveness of the fox's rhetoric consists in the sublimation of the unmanageable foundational violence, in redirecting it toward a ritual murder that reunites, through the identification of an external foe, a community on the brink of disintegration.

In all three anecdotes so far, transgression and violence are not treated as occasions for critique but are instead promoted as necessary features of historically effective speech. The example of the fox shows that what is at issue is not the production of novelty itself but the innovative ability to channel and master the amorphous energies at the heart of crisis. While Mirabeau's rhetorical discovery directs the production of a new political order, the fox's merely serves to reestablish the status quo. It is the curtailment of such discovery, as the fourth anecdote makes clear, that is the true focus of Kleist's critique.

With the fourth anecdote, which returns the narrative to Germany, it becomes clear that Kleist's essay is intended as a meditation on a peculiar German—or more precisely, Prussian—misery, namely the petrification of discourse, and hence of thought. After the world-historical efficacy of Mirabeau's speech, where a turn of phrase transforms an entire political and social order, here social and bureaucratic ritual are revealed as the machinery of inhibition and repression. The first example is that of a young man at a party who, overcome by shyness and the immensity of his thoughts, breaks out into a stutter; the second is an examination scene, presumably for a civil servant, in which the candidate is asked to answer questions concerning, for example, the nature of the state. In both instances, speech misfires in the absence of a productive communicative framework. Both the artificial sociability and the bureaucratic state provide the moribund counterpoint to the vital public sphere of French society. The nation, the text suggests, is a linguistically efficacious political community; the state is not. Thus, while in France, there is a fluid movement from energetic utterance to an energetic body politic, in Germany, the state apparatus extracts all vital energies and circulates and recirculates it within the idiotic machinery of bureaucratic rule. Much of Kleist's work aims at generating a German analog to Mirabeau and the fox, creating a genre of speech that instantiates and produces novelty in the distinct domains of literature and historical eventuality.

Language, Force, Passion

Kleist reads the French Revolution as a sign that discloses the dynamic character of symbolic life. The historicity of the Revolution reveals the revolutionary character of historicity itself, at whose core lies the agonistic play between language and desire. True speech is eventful in that it produces changes outside itself, but it produces these changes only to the extent that it opens itself up to its *internal* outside, the extraverbal force of passion. Yet since passion draws its intensity from the encounter with an other and thus transcends the boundaries of the self, to give oneself over to it is to deliver oneself to a collective energy that threatens the integrity of language and subjectivity. I argue that this dialectic of self and other, speech and event, which is given unique prominence in the texts of Kant, Goethe, and Kleist on which this study focuses, is paradigmatic of a specific strand in the German reception of the French Revolution. In each of these texts, the French Revolution is read as a historical manifestation of the fundamental mechanism of political, conceptual, and aesthetic innovation. Implicit in this reading is a conception of history as crisis: history is crisis because it articulates itself through energetic signs, in symbols driven by an extrasymbolic force.

Hence the centrality of questions of foundation in my argument. Beyond the Rhine, the Revolution was received as a symptom of Enlightenment pathology marked not only by the malaise of rational self-determination but by a constitutional fragility—a paradoxical infirmity—in the foundations of meaning. My claim is that the paradox of the energetic sign is the linguistic manifestation of a more general *paradox of exteriority* that unsettles all symbolically orchestrated systems, whether political, social, psychological, or otherwise.[20] According to this paradox, the foundations of any system occupy a position both logically and topographically exterior to that system. Logically, because the foundation is not held in place by any of the operations and processes that define the system it legitimates; and topographically, because the foundation stands outside the structure it supports (hence, as we shall see, the extraordinary importance of borders and geographical location in these texts). I argue that Kant, Goethe and Kleist discovered in the French Revolution the configuration of this paradox of foundation and with it a new, and indeed revolutionary, model of history, language, and subjectivity. Unfolding in the medium of energetic signs, each of these domains is subject, at any instance of its articulation, to the countersymbolic force that lies within and beyond it. History is subject to contingency and thus understood not as a progressive narrative but as an expanse of revolutionary possibilities; language is subject to the extralinguistic context of utterance and hence primarily conceived not in semantic but in pragmatic terms; and the individual is subject to impersonal affect and is figured not as the locus of self-determination but as the site of passions that exceed the self and its pleasure principle.

Talk of energetic signs places my project in close relation to recent discussions of performativity in language. In the original conception articulated by J. L. Austin, performativity refers to the nonsemantic function of language, that is, to its extralinguistic effectiveness. A performative utterance "indicates that the issuing of an utterance is the performing of an action." Such utterances "do not 'describe' or 'report' or constate anything at all, are not 'true or false'; the uttering of the sentence is, or is a part of, the doing of an action, which again would not *normally* be described as, or as 'just', saying something." The force of the performative depends on the preexistence and functioning of a network of rituals and conventions, and is thus itself strongly formulaic. In Austin's famous example, the priest's utterance at the close of a marriage ceremony, "I now pronounce you husband and wife," is not a statement of fact but rather its enactment; yet its so functioning depends both on the conventional character of the utterance and on the ritually sanctioned authority of the utterer.[21]

In Derrida's radically expanded revision of Austin's theory, the performative recurs as a constitutive feature of every speech act, indeed, of every symbolic or linguistic presentation. Derrida treats the requisite invocation of convention as an instance of the more general requirement of the citation of context in linguistic utterance. Moreover, iterability now becomes a requirement not just of speech acts but of every sign, insofar as it derives its present meaning against the background of previous usage and the accumulated contexts of utterance. The open-endedness of context provides for an essential indeterminacy of meaning and establishes an eternal fissure within the structure of the sign: "a written sign carries with it a force that breaks with its context, that is, with the collectivity of presences organizing the moment of its inscription. This breaking force is not an accidental predicate but the very structure of the written text."[22]

While in Derrida the question of subjectivity remains peripheral, it moves to center stage in Judith Butler's expansion of the notion of performativity. The Derridian fissure within the sign recurs in Butler as a constitutive wounding in the linguistic constitution of the subject. Drawing on Althusser's notion of interpellation, Butler argues that identity is the result of the continuous chorus, in the drama of social address, of explicit and implicit invocation. In this citation of names and phrases, the full weight of historically sedimented norms and conventions is brought to bear on the production of the subject. Language, so understood, is inherently injurious: "The utterances of hate speech are part of the continuous and uninterrupted process to which we are subjected, an on-going subjection (*assujetissement*) that is the very operation of interpellation, that continually repeated action of discourse by which subjects are formed in subjugation."[23] And yet there is, Butler insists, a space for movement and agency. Since no context is fully closed, the subject can draw on conventionalized words and commandeer their future trajectory: "The appropriation of such norms to oppose their historically sedimented effect constitutes the insurrectionary moment of that history, the moment that founds a future through a break with the past."[24]

The problem with Butler's model is that this insurrectionary moment is difficult to account for within the bounds of her restricted notion of context. For while agency is said to depend upon the indeterminacy of context, Butler fails to include as part of this context the subjective dimension of speech, including its bodily instantiation in articulation. It is ironical, given her psychoanalytical "improvement" of Derridean deconstruction, that on this point Butler falls back behind Derrida, who in his reading of Austin had already drawn attention to the subjective and bodily dimension of context: "This breaking force is not an accidental predicate but the very structure of the written text. In the case of a so-called 'real' context, what I have just asserted is all too evident. This allegedly real context includes a certain 'present' of the inscription, the presence of the writer to what he has written, the entire environment and the horizon of his experience, and above all the intention, the wanting-to-say-what he means, which animates his inscription at a given moment."[25]

This richer notion of context and its intertwinement with the bodily is taken up by Shoshana Felman in *The Scandal of the Speaking Body:* "The act, an enigmatic and problematic production of the *speaking body,* destroys from its inception the metaphysical dichotomy between the domain of the 'mental' and the domain of the 'physical,' breaks down the opposition between body and spirit, between matter and language."[26] The speech act is scandalous, according to Felman, because its intertwinement with the body means that it necessarily exceeds the conscious intentions of the speaker and thus "cannot know what it is doing."[27] The body is present in speech in two ways: first, as the vehicle and medium of verbalization (think of the stutterer in the "Allmäh-liche Verfertigung," or of Kleist's emphasis on gestures—for example, the touch of the nose—and his tendency to transform "discursive scenes into dramatically physical theaters");[28] second, as sexuality, "understood not as an 'intentional' disposition, but as unconscious fantasy structuring desire"[29] Both as vehicle of verbalization and as sexuality, the body is the site of a force that transcends the consciousness of the speaking "I," and in that sense, it is extrapersonal.

My notion of "energetic sign" builds on Felman's "speaking body" and privileges the energetic, indeed libidinal, dimension of the performative, locating it in the singularity of the speaking body in its confrontation with an other of equivalent bodily singularity. The dynamic of Mirabeau's speech is shaped both by the interplay of bodily gestures and by the circulation of energy and incitement of passions that drive the communicative exchange. Moreover, this energetic dimension inheres not just in the utterance but also in the sign, which carries within itself, as Derrida reminds us, the history of its inscriptions. The sign "sovereignty" in Mirabeau's speech, for example, condenses in itself the cycle of passionate exchange which gives rise to it. My claim is that Kleist's anecdote lays open a constitutive feature of language. Every sign incorporates in its structure the energetic cycle of its own production. Every sign is performative with respect both to its past and its future: it is the residue of its own performative history; and it carries a charge—a "breaking force"—that, under felicitous circumstances, alters the landscape in which it is deployed.[30] Language, so understood, has aims of its own, and an individual utterance becomes performative—modifies reality—when it succeeds, as Mirabeau does, in aligning the extra-individual passions generated by the communicative exchange with the impersonal force sedimented in the sign. One sees here in paradigmatic form the performativity of the energetic sign, a performativity that lies at the center of Kant's, Goethe's, and Kleist's engagement with the French Revolution.

The Bounds of Bildung

My emphasis on the prominence—indeed, uniqueness—of Kant's, Goethe's, and Kleist's response to the French Revolution stands in contrast to more familiar characterizations of this period. To be sure, recognition of the world-historical significance of the Revolution is hardly unique to these writers, and its profound impact on German cultural life in the 1790s has been thoroughly studied. This impact is obvious in explicit responses to the events in France, from travel reports and letters, to philosophical debates about the right to resistance and the political experiments of German Jacobins.[31] But it can also be seen in a variety of literary and philosophical responses that seek to retain the rational kernel of the Revolution (the idea of self-legislation) while avoiding its violent historical shell (political unrest, the Terror). Schiller's model of *aesthetic education*, for instance, which is designed to "reunite the politically divided world under the banner of truth and beauty,"[32] is hardly conceivable without the French Revolution, and something similar could be said about the general "aesthetic turn" that characterizes postrevolutionary German thought.[33] Moreover, that this turn was inaugurated by a text that is contemporaneous with the Revolution—Kant's *Critique of Judgment* appeared in 1790—points to another, more conceptual, link between French politics and German culture. To many German intellectuals, Kant's philosophy achieved in the domain of thought what the Revolution accomplished in the political order, the dismantling of traditional structures and the establishment of a new order based on the principle of freedom and self-legislation. Friedrich Schlegel expressed the conceptual affinity between political (France) and cultural (Germany) revolution most pointedly: "The French Revolution, Fichte's *Science*, and Goethe's *Wilhelm Meister* are the greatest tendencies of the age."[34]

What is striking about Schlegel's aphorism is its omission of Kant. Yet Kant is absent precisely because he is omnipresent. Indeed, it was through the framework of Kantian philosophy that German intellectuals like Schlegel analyzed and assessed the French Revolution.[35] From this perspective, while the Revolution marks the entrance into the arena of history of autonomous man, its Terror signals the failure of abstract reason. In the reading that would be most explicitly formulated in Hegel's *Phenomenology*, the Terror is the symptom of the implasticity of Reason, its inadequacy to the rich particularity of human and historical life.[36] In short, it is a symptom of the fractured—impersonally personal—nature of the Kantian subject.

Now it is against this background that the specificity of the dominant idealist program can be outlined, and the cultural context can be established against which the countercurrent runs. Put most generally, idealism replaces the Kantian opposition between reason and experience, impersonal and personal, with a developmental model centered on the gradual integration of the universal and the particular.[37] Hence the centrality of the metaphor of the *organic* in idealist thought: in man, as the utopian template of a reconstituted unity; in history, as the inevitable unfolding of human freedom; and in theory, as the "self-movement "of a consciousness whose "inner life" is "Herausgehen, Sichauseinanderlegen und zugleich Zusichkommen" (going out, self-unfolding and at the same time returning to itself).[38]

Schiller's response is programmatic in this respect. Schiller views the Terror as the historical manifestation of a double fracture: between philosophical thought and historical development; and, within man, between reason and sensual life. The Revolution, while not disproving Kantian ethics, shows it to be in need of theoretical supplementation. On the one hand, the Terror reveals the anachronism of history. Humanity is not yet ready for the concept of freedom, whose historical articulation thus takes the form of a violent eruption that lacerates and disfigures, rather than uniting, the political body. Moreover, this collective fracture reflects an underlying anthropological rift. If the disjunction between history and concept tears apart the body politic, the split between reason and the senses dislocates the human organism from within. Schiller's response to this problematic is the conception of the aesthetic as a supplement to history and ethics. Engaging man in a contemplative play that momentarily suspends both the imperative of duty and the demands of the body, aesthetic education closes the gap between history and concept and restores humanity to its organic wholeness.[39]

Schiller responds to the Kantian dualism between reason and sensibility, nature and freedom, by "embedding the aesthetic sphere in a teleologically structured philosophy of history, that is, through the narrativization of theory itself."[40] But it is in Hegel's work that this trajectory finds its consummate articulation. Hegel's fundamental move consists in relocating the fracture that Kant and Schiller situated between concept and history within the concept itself. From this perspective, the task is not to enlighten history but to historicize the Enlightenment, not to educate man in order to make him receptive to the concept of freedom but to transform the concept and align it with history.[41] Hegel thus attempts to overcome the fracture by dissolving the rational distance separating thought from its object. "Scientific knowledge," he writes in the introduction to the *Phenomenology*, "requires that thought surrender itself to the life of its object [*sich dem Leben des Gegenstandes zu übergeben*]."[42] The concept, that is, must be animated with life; it must move and evolve—develop—like the life that it seeks to grasp. Hegel conceives of reason on the model of an organism, as a self-evolving process that unfolds through and from the concept as its seed. Moreover, this unfolding follows a double trajectory: through the material particularity of history, and through its reflective articulation in philosophy. The Hegelian dialect, in other words, attempts to resolve the Kantian dualism between concept and history, law and desire, and with this, the Kantian paradox of the impersonal personality.

Whether or not this resolution succeeds, the Kantian paradox remains central. According to Robert Pippen, one of Hegel's strongest contemporary defenders, Hegel's entire philosophy is an attempt to overcome the Kantian paradox of a self-legislating—free—subject. If the paradoxical character of this notion shows up most clearly in Kant's abandoning, in the *Critique of Practical Reason,* the deduction of the law of freedom in favor of its brute assertion (Kant's famous "fact of reason"), "Hegel's procedures in all his books and lectures are developmental, not deductive. . . . In this way [Kant's] self-legislating moral subject is reconceived as much more than a practically necessary idea and is instead animated with historical life."[43] The historical reconstruction of the emergence of freedom thus dissolves the latter's incomprehensive and coercive character: "For all the reasons we have discussed, in Hegel as in Kant, I am subject only to laws that I in some sense author and subject myself to. But the legislation of such a law does not consist in some paradoxical single moment of election, whereby a noumenal individual elects as a supreme governing principle, either obedience to the moral law as a life policy, or the priority of self-love and its satisfactions. The formation of and self-subjection to such normative constraints is gradual, collective, and actually historical."[44]

It is not clear, however, that this historicist reading does justice to the formal structure of Hegel's thought. Hegelian temporality is not merely one of accident; it is conceptually orchestrated and teleologically structured. On this reading, an initial articulation of the accidental and contingent features of the historical world is subsequently taken up in a second-order narrative that recasts these features in the modality of the necessary. In the *Phenomenology,* for instance, temporality is extracted from the historical world on two levels: first, in the formalization of change through the logical mechanism of thesis, antithesis, and synthesis; and second, in the epistemological unification of these disparate moments under the single concept of absolute spirit. And it is only from the perspective of this unified knowledge—that is, from the perspective of the end of the text—that our "self-subjection to normative constraints" can be viewed as the outcome of a "gradual, collective, and actually historical" process. In this sense, Hegel's system depends on the availability of an extrahistorical logical standpoint, what Thomas Nagel has called "the view from nowhere."[45]

The organicism implicit in Schiller's and Hegel's responses to Kant finds explicit and programmatic expression in Goethe's botanical studies in the

1790s.[46] Taking his cue from Kant's discussion of the antinomies of teleological understanding in the *Critique of Judgment,* Goethe develops a method of scientific observation that dissolves the opposition between concept and object, thought and intuition. To understand living beings, he writes, it is important "that my thinking is not separate from objects; that the elements of the object, the perceptions [*Anschaungen*] of the object, flow into my thinking and are fully permeated by it; that my perception is itself a thinking, and my thinking a perception" (SS 39 / M 306). Thought therefore must surrender itself to the mutability of its object and develop along with it. That is, it must become "as flexible and formative" as the life it observes: "When something has acquired a form it metamorphoses immediately to a new one. If we wish to arrive at some living perception of nature we ourselves must remain as flexible and formative [*beweglich und bildsam*] as nature and follow the example she gives" (SS 64 (trans. modified) / M 13). This gradual interweaving of observation and object constitutes an "intellectual ladder [*geistige Leiter*]" (M 30), which culminates, in Eckart Förster's words, in the "comprehension of the complete series of forms as an organic whole."[47] Goethe, Förster concludes, takes Kant's merely problematic notion of an "intellectual intuition" as an

> invitation to develop an extended, not only discursive, but at the same time intuitive thinking, one that leads from the general to the particular, from the particular to the general, and that becomes, in the intuition of the whole, an experience of a higher order, namely, of that which Goethe alternately called "type," "concept," or "idea," which is objectively realized in the organism. This has nothing to do with conceptual abstraction in the Kantian sense, and even less with Locke's "abstract idea." Quite the contrary: it is the concrete idea of that universal, which manifests in countless spatiotemporal variations and forms, which each represent the idea empirically and therefore in a limited and incomplete form.[48]

Leaving aside the plausibility of such a program, it is clear that Goethe's notion of "intuitive understanding" would resolve what for Kant is the irreducible opposition between reason and sensibility. (Accordingly, in the decisive paragraph in the *Critique of Judgment,* Kant adduces as a *refutation* of such a project the fact of duty as a fundamental feature of moral life [CJ 286–87].) Yet whether Goethe himself regarded this program as ultimately tenable beyond the realm of botanical life is a question raised by a text that, by generic program and title, addresses itself to the formation and growth of human subjectivity: Goethe's bildungsroman *Wilhelm Meisters Lehrjahre.* On the one hand, as David Wellbery has underscored, the bildungsroman provides a narrative and fictional solution to the same problem that Kant and, after him, Schiller had placed at the center of aesthetic theory: that of providing, in Kant's words, a "transition" capable of closing the "immense gulf" between theoretical and practical reason, nature and freedom, reason and sensibility (CJ 14–15). The bildungsroman, Wellbery writes, "represents the 'human being' with respect to that faculty which in aesthetic theory achieves the transition between the contradictory semantic realms; and it structures this transition in such a way as to make it recognizable as a purposeful development. Thus the thesis which I want to argue is that in the Bildungsroman, the *imagination* constitutes the main capacity of the protagonist, while *teleology* organizes the text's narrative trajectory."[49]

Indeed, the bildungsroman is homologous in problem and solution not only to Schiller's aesthetic education but also to Hegel's dialectic. If the *Phenomenology* narrates the history of Spirit's self-realization, the bildungsroman emplots the life of the individual as a developmental story that culminates in the protagonist's understanding of the unconscious forces and self-deceptions that have shaped his life from the beginning. *Bildung* thus takes the form of a progression from first- to second-order observation, from the implicit rationality of doing to the explicit rationality of understanding one's doing. The bildungsroman itself ends at the moment when this process has run its course and the protagonist is capable of reflecting, in the form of a coherent developmental narrative, on how he came to be the person he now is. As in Hegel, the contingent and accidental are integrated into a narrative that recasts them in the modality of the necessary: what looked, from the protagonist's initial perspective of lived experience, like a string of contingent events and random choices, appears, in the intelligible pattern of a resumptive narrative, as inevitable steps toward full self-realization. Moreover, as in Hegel, the teleological structure of this arrangement depends on the existence of an extrahistorical standpoint. This becomes clear toward the end of Goethe's novel with the unveiling of the uncanny concept of Wilhelm Meister, which is delivered to him in the form of his completed biography by the Tower Society, whose members are therein revealed to have arranged his life from its beginning. In this sense, Wilhelm's life, with all its detours and seeming contingencies, is shown to be the unfolding in time of a concept that stands outside time. The view from the tower, one might say, is the narrative representation of the "view from nowhere."

But things are more complicated. Whereas Hegel, as Förster has shown, draws on Goethe's botanical studies to develop an organic conception of human life, Goethe himself seems to have been more skeptical about the possibility of such an undertaking. For if, on the teleological reading sketched above, Goethe's novel narrates the organic growth of a human being in the laboratory of the Tower, it must be added that the laboratory of the Tower is not identical to that of the novel, and that Wilhelm's *Bildung* does not end with the reading of the *text* of his biography but instead is further elaborated. Added on to the teleological story, these *supplements,* as Wellbery has called them, reveal the limits of idealism's organic project; that is, they reveal the impossibility of fully inscribing the subject into the concept. "The operation of ending that characterizes *Wilhelm Meister,*" Wellbery writes, "thus depends on a double transgression of reason and its legislation. Just as the fool Friedrich provides a comic complement to the operations of the Tower society in order to bestow justice to the unsublatable structural fracture within human existence, so does his sister Natalie provide a complement in the dimension of the sacral. . . . *Wilhelm Meister* does not end with the hermeneutic restitution of the lost origin but with a reference to an ethical transcendence that supplements the defective anthropological structure [*anthropologische Fehlstruktur*]."[50] Natalie thus becomes, in Wellbery's reading, the true heroine of the novel and the purest embodiment of Goethe's aesthetic-ethical program: "What Goethe seeks to think in the figure of Natalie is the emergence of an ethical transcendence, which freely gives itself to the defective, lacerated, and impoverished anthropological state. The pure image beholds the human being in his immemorial wounding and takes to heart—*misericordia*—his misery. Thus the pure image has the exact logical status which the text ascribes to Natalie's actions: It is *substitute, pure supplement, purity* (this key word Goethe's) *as supplement.*"[51]

While Wellbery is right in pointing out the acknowledgement of fissure in Goethe's text, I disagree with his characterization of the supplementarity of ethical transcendence. Goethe's solution remains an instrument of devitalization, albeit one that differs significantly from that of idealism. Wellbery's description of Natalie as a "holy figure" is telling in this respect.[52] If Natalie accomplishes the task of supplementing the human fracture, this is because she herself has overcome its fundamental manifestation: desire. "Natalie, the pure one," writes Wellbery," whose name cites the event of Christ's birth, is the return of the virgin Mary."[53] Ethical transcendence is freedom from desire, and Natalie's function, as the embodiment of this transcendence, is to cure Wilhelm from his attachment to the intensely erotic female figures in his life

(Mariane, Philine, and Mignon) and thus to heal the human fracture through the removal of its vital source. This suggests another reason why the novel does not end with Wilhelm's reading of his biography, namely, the recognition, on Goethe's part, that writing cannot alone undo the intensity of erotic attachment and, instead, must be complemented by the seductive image of pure femininity. On this reading, Natalie supplements not only the "defective anthropological structure" but also, and perhaps more importantly, the Tower's machinery of socialization.[54]

"A History That Does Not Belong to History"

Conceptual and narrative models that privilege continuity, inclusiveness, and devitalization dominate postrevolutionary German culture: classicist aesthetics (Schiller), idealist philosophy (Hegel), and the modern novel (Goethe). What follows is an attempt to bring out in detail a significant, if overlooked, countercurrent to this dominant discourse, a marginal strand in the reception of the French Revolution that paradoxically brings into sharp relief the tension and problems that reside at the core of the dominant discourse. The texts that form the focus of this study reject the possibility of a developmental solution to embrace groundlessness instead as the engine of human life. Thus the significance in all of these texts of foundational crisis, of moments when the sovereignty of political, psychological, and linguistic orders is shattered by the intrusion of a succession of uncanny undersides: of violence into the domain of law; of the body into speech; and of the extrasubjective—impersonal—into the subject. In each case, the internal fracture of the energetic sign radiates within the economy of the relevant system, generating a foundational crisis. Implicit in this conception is a model of culture as intrinsically conflictual and irresolvably fractured. Unfolding in the medium of the energetic sign, cultural life is subject, at each point of its articulation, to an irrepressible excess of force over meaning. It is the site of the constant undoing of established forms.

As mentioned earlier, the topography of the border manifests itself in a variety of ways. First, the border features as a *geographic* locus, as the site furthest removed from the center of power, and thus most susceptible to instability and crisis. The action of Goethe's *Unterhaltungen deutscher Ausgewanderten* (*Conversations of German Refugees*), for instance, is located on the Franco-German border, and the crisis the text narrates is triggered by an explicit transgression of borders, "when the Frankish army burst into our fatherland through an ill-protected gap." A similar logic is at work in Kleist's *Michael Kohlhaas,* where the protagonist's rebellion is precipitated by a border incident and ultimately decided by the intertwinement of law and political territory. In contrast, Kant's construction of historical progress in *Der Streit der Fakultäten (The Conflict of the Faculties)* depends on the maintenance of aesthetic distance and on the existence of a political border separating the French Revolution from its German spectators. Second, the border features a *historical threshold.* Each text treats events located on the boundary of traditions, on moments of crisis when a received culture gives way to the emergence of a new and as yet unarticulated form of life. History is thus conceived of not in developmental terms but as an event or, better, as eventfulness. That is, it is conceived of as a moment of becoming that exceeds the bounds of conceptual and narrative articulation. Finally, there is an issue of *biographical* boundaries. Not only do these texts form a marginal countercurrent with respect to the dominant discourse of the time, they are also marginal, in Kant's and Goethe's case, within the authors' oeuvres. Kant's *Conflict of the Faculties* is either dismissed as the product of a senile mind or simply ignored in favor of his more canonical texts, while Goethe's novella cycle has been completely overshadowed by his simultaneously written bildungsroman *Wilhelm Meister.* If Kleist's *Michael Kohlhaas,* his most celebrated story, runs counter to this argument, this is because Kleist's entire work inhabits the topography of the boundary.

The following chapters explore in detail this topography of the boundary and its relation both to the dominant discourse of the time and the canonical writings of these authors. At this point, I want to sketch briefly a generic embodiment of this topography. In Chapter 2, I argue that the emphasis on boundaries and residues generates a new literary genre, that of the modern novella, which emerged in the last decade of the eighteenth century. The novella intensifies the feeling of transitoriness already expressed in the developmental bent of the dominant discourse by focusing on events that resist narrative integration. In so doing, it throws into relief precisely that aspect of change that the semantics of progress was designed to neutralize: the contingency and meaninglessness of the new.[55]

How does the boundary figure into the turn toward developmental models in Schiller, Hegel, and Goethe? It does so as part of a more general process of temporalization during the last quarter of the eighteenth century that affected all areas of knowledge, as thinkers as diverse as Michel Foucault, Niklas Luhmann, and Reinhart Koselleck have shown. Koselleck in particular has argued that the late eighteenth century was a historical threshold during which a new and somewhat paradoxical concept of "history" took shape.[56] On the one hand, writers begin to stress the unity of history: one begins to speak of history with a capital *H*, of world history, emphatically understood as a global process that comprises all local events and histories. On the other hand, the structure of this world history is grounded in a notion of time as a medium of acceleration and differentiation: "history" becomes a dynamic concept in the sense that it strings together a past, a present, and a future otherwise conceived of as radically different from one another. The decisive point is that these two sides of the new concept of history—unity and change—stand in a problematic tension. Taken by itself, the stress on change tends toward the destabilization of the present: "Our time," Wilhelm von Humboldt writes, "seems to us to turn from one period, which is just passing, into a new one which is not less different."[57] Koselleck aptly speaks in this context of the growing difference between the space of experience and the horizon of expectation. The rapid pace of change devalues experiences and makes the future appear undetermined and open. Hence the self-perception of the period as a moment of transition and point of reversal, so obvious in Humboldt's remark. This perception infuses the present with the sublime aura of a new and absolute beginning; but it also makes it appear unstable, strange, and threatening. It is this threat that is warded off by the secondary modeling of change as "progress." By providing a narrative link between past and future, the concept of progress integrates, and thus grounds, the fleeting present in an intelligible whole consisting of a beginning, middle, and end. Cast as the telos of past events or, in Kant's words, as a sign of a tendency toward the better, the new is thus narratively and symbolically domesticated. "In an age of profound and pervasive change," writes Christian Meier, "this concept [progress] provided orientation for vast numbers of people. It gave meaning to their lives: the oppressive sense of impermanence, instability, and contingency was transformed into a sense of progress."[58]

We have seen this accommodation of the new at work in classicist aesthetics (Schiller), idealist philosophy (Hegel), and the modern novel (Goethe), which all relied on teleologically structured, and thus progressivist, models. The novella, in contrast, is an anti-developmental narrative form that focuses its formal operations on the unmetabolizable residue of organicist thought. Significantly, the first poetological reflections on the genre of the novella emphasize precisely its opposition to progressivist world histories. Thus Friedrich Schlegel writes in 1801: "The novella is an anecdote, an as yet unknown history . . . that must be in itself interesting, regardless of the connection of nations, or times, or the progress of humanity and its relation to *Bildung*. Thus it is a history that, strictly speaking, does not belong to history."[59]

On the one hand, then, there is an emphasis on singularity in novelistic narrative; on the other, a drive toward inclusiveness and development in official histories. Friedrich Schlegel was not the only critic to define the genre in these terms. His brother August Wilhelm describes the novella as "a history outside of history" (eine Geschichte außerhalb der Geschichte).[60] And a few years later, Friedrich Schleiermacher speaks of "a torn-out historical event" (ein herausgerissenes historisches Ereignis).[61] Read against the above discussed formation of the modern concept of history, of history with a capital *H*, this repeated stress on singularity and discontinuity points to a crucial polemical dimension within the genre. The novella, I argue, emerges in critical response to the semantic domestication of the new within progressivist thought.

Read in this context, Goethe's famous "definition" of the genre "as an unheard-of event that has actually occurred" acquires a new and heightened significance.[62] "This formulation," Wellbery comments, "merely accentuates what had been the salient feature of the genre since its beginning with Boccaccio and Cervantes. As its name indicates, the novella has always been directed toward the new, that is: the case (*casus*) without precedent which is therefore not yet subsumed by law or canonical narrative; the 'unheard-of' case."[63] Much as I agree with the thrust of Wellbery's definition, the genre's traditional emphasis on the unheard-of event acquires, one might say, an unheard-of significance when understood in the context of the simultaneous changes in the semantics of "history." Singular, real, intractable: the novelistic case challenges the mechanisms of the progressivist models of history through which temporality is extracted from the historical world.

We have just seen how this extraction works: first, by inscribing the real—that which is the case—into the intelligible whole of a framing narrative; and second, by the teleological unification of this narrative development under a single concept, be it that of absolute spirit, *Bildung*, or humanity. The novella brings out the other side of this symbolic machinery, that which it must expel in order to close in upon itself. The unheard-of event throws into relief the limits of symbolic, narrative, and systemic integration. As we have seen, structurally speaking, the new is first of all a difference, that is, a deviation from, and irritation to, existing structures. Like all systems, however, progressivist models can tolerate deviation only to the extent that it is compatible with existing structures. The irritant must be selected by and drawn into the system, leading to the system's structural reorganization, not to its destruction. Put simply, progressivist models articulate the new only in the domesticated form of an *innovation*. Novellas, conversely, represent the new as an inassimilable surd. This is the significance of the unheard-of event. The genre poses the paradox of a symbolic form that focuses on *the limits of symbolic integration.* Novellas are borderline narratives in the precise sense that they center their formal operations on an event that resists integration within a framing narrative and in so doing marks the threshold of narrativity.

And this is not all, for the novella's emphasis on the unheard-of case does more than simply point to the limits of symbolic representation. The new is not an inert center of indecipherability; rather, it effects an inversion of the normalized relationship between the meaningful and the meaningless. In a manner not unlike Mirabeau's electrical deanimation of the Master of Ceremonies, the novelistic narrative sets into motion a process whereby semantic energy is evacuated from the everyday and condensed into the enigmatic event, which thus becomes an energetic sign par excellence. Similarly, the temporality of the ordinary is drawn into the compressed temporality of the enigmatic. The time of the novella, in other words, is a time of crisis, a time in which the hermeneutic decision, the solution to the enigma, must assert itself against the horizon of fleeting time. To the open-endedness of time offered by the progressivist model, the novella opposes a model of immanent finitude.

The rise of the novella is only *one* response to a congeries of political and social dilemmas besetting German culture at the turn of the nineteenth century. The countercurrent found a variety of philosophical and literary expressions, each of which addressed itself to the inadequacy of the idealist domestication of disruption and discontinuity.

I begin with Kant's last published reflection on history—the second essay of *Der Streit der Fakultäten* (1798)—because it represents the most heroic attempt to integrate the fact of revolution into a progressivist idealist conception of history. In this essay, Kant attempts to locate a historical event that points to "the disposition and capacity of the human race to be the cause of its own advance toward the better" (CF 151). He finds this sign of progress, not in the French Revolution as such, but in the distinctive emotional response that the Revolution elicits from those who observe it from afar. Indeed, it is the *enthusiasm* of the German spectators for the revolutionary events in France that reveals the principle and fact of progress, and with this the possibility of a true philosophical history.

Kant envisions philosophical history, not as a chronicle of historical occurrence, but as an intervention into history itself. From this perspective, it is the unique role of philosophy to discern and uncover the emotional attachment to the principle of freedom in the murderous violence of revolution. Yet the lawlike nature of this principle is in fact established by its irresistibility, which is itself demonstrated by the excessive and violent character of enthusiasm. In this shift from action to reception, from political to affective violence, Kant sees the sole possibility of avoiding the illegality of revolutionary foundation and inaugurating the gradual and reasoned reform of political order. Thus for all his stress on reason and continuity, Kant grounds the possibility of progress in a moment of rational transgression, in an instance of ecstatic enthusiasm.

Chapter 2 is concerned with Goethe's response to the French Revolution and, in particular, with his invention of a new literary genre, the modern novella. In his *Unterhaltungen deutscher Ausgewanderten*, published two years before Kant's essay, Goethe draws on and radicalizes traditional novella cycles—most notably, Boccaccio's *Decameron*—to depict the catastrophic impact of the French Revolution on received social and communicative life. The external plague from which the storytellers in the *Decameron* retreat now reaches beyond the frame and recurs as a pathology in the midst of the narrative community. Goethe emplots the Revolution as a traumatic event that exceeds the grasp of reason and generates emotional response of such intensity as to dissolve the circumscribed structures of aristocratic sociability. Far from embracing the Revolution as the harbinger of a coming community organized around the principle of freedom, as Kant does, Goethe sees in it only the plague of unfettered subjectivity and the disintegration of all social bonds.

Yet for Goethe, it is also of principal importance to convert the unmanageability of revolution into an assimilable form. This, it turns out, is precisely the function of the novellas. By encapsulating in homeopathic measure the otherwise toxic force of revolution, the novellas allow the group to work through their initial shock and to restore, through the ritual of storytelling, the shaken bonds of culture and community. The lesson of the Revolution, for Goethe, is the requirement of the aesthetic—and ultimately, of an autonomous aesthetic sphere—as the necessary counterweight to the disastrous seduction of politics and the loss of culture to fetishized ideology.

The relationship between politics and art receives a rather different and unexpected treatment in Kleist's novella *Michael Kohlhaas* (1810), the focus of my final chapter. Written against the background of the threat of Napoleonic invasion, Kleist's work in general, and *Michael Kohlhaas* in particular, is concerned with generating a German analog to Mirabeau's rhetoric, that is, with creating a genre of speech that instantiates and produces novelty in the distinct domains of literature and history. In other words, Kleist, through Kohlhaas, imagines himself as a German Mirabeau who, with the energy of his eventful prose, will rouse the public from its moribund slumber and stimulate its enthusiasm for the national cause. Thus, under the sign of the horse trader Kohlhaas, one of the "most righteous men of his time," Kleist launches a narrative insurrection against the stultifying machinery of political bureaucracy and intrigue we have already encountered in the last part of "Allmähliche Verfertigung." Drawing their charge from an agonistic encounter with an other whose petrified semiotic they seek to explode, Michael Kohlhaas and *Michael Kohlhaas,* the protagonist and the text, both operate as energetic signs. *Michael Kohlhaas* is Kleist's *Donnerkeil,* his attempt at truly revolutionary writing.

Kleist's novella might be thought of as a perverse rewriting of Kant's Enlightenment project under the conditions of emergent nationalism. Whereas Kant deciphers enthusiasm as a sign of the will to freedom that betokens a world society built on universal law, Kleist's interest lies in revitalizing the political order and harnessing the force of principled commitment against the French invasion. The intent here is perverse, inasmuch it is nationalistic not cosmopolitan, partisan not impartial, and bellicose rather than pacific; it is nonetheless a rewriting of Kant, because Kleist's energetic signs are fueled by precisely the *impersonal passion* that lies at the core of the Kantian conception of morality.

The Conclusion identifies the novella as a border genre and then proceeds to analyze a lesser-known review by Kierkegaard of a novella about the French Revolution, which becomes for Kierkegaard the occasion for a critique of mid-nineteenth-century culture as suffering from the devitalization of signs. Finally, I look briefly at the emergence of foundational questions in early twentieth-century philosophy, connecting these issues to the simultaneous discussions in the works of Carl Schmitt and Walter Benjamin of the status of the exception in history, politics, and law.

1

Revealing Freedom

Crisis and Enthusiasm in Kant's Philosophy of History

Kant's *Der Streit der Fakultäten (The Conflict of the Faculties)* (1798) more or less explicitly addresses all the issues of principal concern to us here. In his attempt to establish a foundation for a philosophical history, an enterprise he considers the intrinsic political responsibility of philosophy, Kant raises fundamental questions about foundations as such. In particular, he uncovers what I earlier called the paradox of exteriority, the fact that foundations stand outside the systems they support. It is the peculiar genius of Kant's little essay that it embraces such paradox and discovers the foundation of moral and political law in anomic passion. Hence Kant's uncanny argument: a moment of crisis reveals the permanence of progress; the suspension of established rules announces the inevitability of the future rule of law; and a sudden outburst of intense feelings proves the existence of moral principle.

The focus of Kant's essay is an interpretation of the French Revolution in terms of its reception in Germany. Kant reads the emotional response to the Revolution as an apodictic sign both of the determinative role of moral principle in human history and of the possibility of a true philosophical history. While the occurrence of revolutionary enthusiasm notwithstanding strict political prohibition establishes its extraordinary intensity, this intensity, construed by Kant as the irresistible drive of moral conviction, in turn demonstrates the sovereignty of the principle of progress in the life of man and the possibility, on its basis, of a teleological history. Kant thus places at the core of his account of reason in history not reason but the passion for reason, a passion that, while singularly trained upon moral law, nonetheless belongs irreducibly to the province of affect. Moreover, he conceives of this affect as the instantiation of freedom as such, of freedom unfettered by psychological, moral, and political rule; on the other hand, it is precisely its unconstrained character that moves Kant to insist on the rationalization of passion through the legislative machinery of the state.

A Conflict of the Faculties

Kant's last essay on philosophical history, the "Erneuerte Frage: Ob das menschliche Geschlecht im beständigen Fortschreiten zum Besseren sei" (Renewed Question: Is the Human Race Constantly Progressing?) appeared in 1798. The essay forms the second part of the short book entitled *Der Streit der Fakultäten,* which discusses the inner organization of the university and the relation of knowledge to power. The book's central controversy, explored across three fairly independent essays, concerns the right of the lower faculty (philosophy) to pass critical judgment on issues that ostensibly fall within the jurisdiction of the higher faculties (theology, law, medicine). In his introduction, however, Kant situates this intra-academic altercation within the larger context of a debate on the presumed right of government to rule over the affairs of the university. Written in a climate of political unrest and amidst a wave of repressive counterrevolutionary measures (Kant's own text was a casualty of tightened censorship laws for two years),[1] the *Conflict of the Faculties* is both a defense of the principle of Enlightenment critique and an attempt to expand philosophy's academic and political sphere of influence.

Kant launches his attack by exposing the interdependence of academic and political hierarchies. The higher faculties, he claims, owe their elevated status in the university not to their intellectual worth but to their usefulness for the authorities. Charged with the vocational training of "clergymen, magistrates, and physicians," who as "tools of the government" (CF 25/18)[2] oversee and enforce public norms, the professors of theology, law, and medicine are essentially academic handmaidens of the state. Since the higher faculties stand under the "command of an external legislator" (CF 33/22) to which they have ceded the right to "sanction" (CF 27/19) their teachings, their doctrines are ultimately grounded in "statutes"; that is, they "proceed from an act of choice on the part of an authority" and "demand obedience" (CF 33/22) rather than understanding. This dependence is reflected in an uncritical scholarly attitude, which restricts thought to the explanation of existing norms, whose legitimacy remains unquestioned. The jurist, for instance, "as an authority of the text, does not look to his reason for the laws that secure the *Mine* and *Thine,* but to the code of laws that has been publicly promulgated and sanctioned by the highest authority (if, as he should, he acts as a civil servant). To require him to prove the truth of these laws and their conformity with right, or to define them against reason's objections, would be unfair. For these decrees first determine what is right, and the jurist must straightaway dismiss as nonsense the further question of whether the decrees themselves are right" (CF 37–39/ 24–25).

The juridical scholar—and something similar could be said about the theologian and the doctor—secures the application of written laws. And since these laws, like all statutes, in turn secure the preservation of a regular and continuous order, the task of the higher faculties is none other than to uphold the status quo. More precisely, the university is politically significant, Kant suggests, because it complements the coercive and negative exercise of state power with the persuasive force of a knowledge that appeals, under the guise of disinterested truth, to the citizens' vital interests. For insofar as the higher faculties claim knowledge on issues that are dear to the people—eternal well-being, civil well-being, physical well-being—the government can use them to anchor its regulatory interests in the people's own desire for happiness; that is, to ground power in "incentives" (CF 31/21):

> The following order exists among the incentives that the government can use to achieve its end (of influencing the people): first comes the *eternal* well-being of each, then his *civil* well-being as a member of society, and finally his *physical* well-being (a long life and health). By public teachings about the *first* of these, the government can exercise very great influence to uncover their inmost thoughts and guide the most secret intentions of its subjects. By teachings regarding the *second*, it helps to keep their external conduct under the reins of public laws, and by its teachings regarding the *third*, to make sure that it will have a strong and numerous people to serve its purposes. (CF 31–33/21–22)

In his 1793 essay "On the Common Saying: 'This may be true in theory, but it does not apply in practice,'" Kant had maintained that the paternal form of government, in which the ruler, under the pretense of benevolence, dictates to the people how to be happy, is the most despotic of all regimes, because it suspends "the entire freedom of its citizens" (TP 74). The "Renewed Question" describes a more refined form of despotism, one in which paternal legislation takes the form, not of commands issued by politicians, but of teachings professed by academics. While in both cases the restriction of freedom is dressed up as concern for the welfare of the people, it is only in the latter case that the appeal to happiness and "enjoyment" (CF 49/30), couched in the quasi-religious language of the people's *Heil* (welfare, salvation) and invested with the symbolic trappings of academic offices, acquires an almost transcendent and magical force: "But now the people are approaching these scholars as if they were soothsayers and magicians, with knowledge of supernatural things, for if an ignorant man expects something from a scholar, he readily forms exaggerated notions of him. So we can naturally expect that if someone has the effrontery to give himself out as such a miracle-worker, the people will flock to him and contemptuously desert the philosophy faculty" (CF 49–51/30–31).

On one level, the *Conflict of the Faculties* aims to dismantle, by means of philosophical critique, the "magic power that the public superstitiously attributes to these teachings" (CF 51/31). But Kant's effort goes beyond critical destruction. The text's polemical downsizing of the higher faculties is part of a larger strategy aimed at expanding the academic and political clout of philosophy. Thus, step by step Kant articulates the significance of philosophy by defining it in *opposition* to the higher faculties. The philosophical faculty "is the rank in the university that occupies itself with teachings which are *not* adopted as directives by order" (CF 43/27; emphasis added); it "must be conceived as free and subject only to laws given by reason, *not* by the government" (ibid.); and it promises *nothing*, least of all happiness and welfare, but instead formulates the principles by which people ought to live in order to be free. Hence the conflict to which the text owes its name. Whereas the teachings of the higher faculties promote the commands and interests of the state in the name of happiness, the philosophical faculty judges the conformity of these teachings to the principle of freedom in the name of reason.

Not surprisingly, this critical judgment has a double target. While ostensibly aimed at academic doctrines, the critique cannot but touch on the extra-academic "statutes" upon which these doctrines are based. Which is to say, the conflict of the faculties raises the question of the legitimacy of the laws and must inevitably address the relationship between violence and law, as I shall show. For Kant, it is philosophy's insistence on the intrinsically rational character of laws—its demand that laws derive their force not from violence or coercion but from their internal reasonableness—that is the source of its political force. Philosophy is political because it reminds politics to pursue, not just power, but *just* power. Hence its role as a critical "left hand of power," which Kant describes in a passage that introduces a political-symbolic topography that is still with us today: "The rank of the higher faculties (as the right side of parliament of learning) supports the government's statutes; but in as free a system of government as must exist when it is a question of truth, there must also be an opposition party (the left side), and this is the philosophy faculty's bench. For without its rigorous examinations and operations, the government would not be adequately informed about what could be to its own advantage or detriment" (CF 59/35).

All's well that ends well, and Kant's introduction concludes on the best of all notes, that of a fairy tale. Ultimately, philosophy is rewarded for remaining faithful to its plain-spoken lover truth, and this Cinderella among her more glamorous stepsister faculties enters the palace and comes to sit next to her prince. "In this way, it could well happen that the last would some day be the first (the lower faculty would be the higher)—not, indeed, in the exercise of power, but in counseling the powerful (the government). For the government may find the freedom of the philosophy faculty, and the increased insight gained from this freedom, a better means for achieving its end than its own absolute authority" (ibid.; trans. modified).

A power fantasy of powerless intellectuals (Kant as the Don Carlos of Königsberg)? Tempting though such mockery might be, it misses the strategic accomplishment of Kant's introduction: to launch a philosophical critique of political authority that establishes the political authority of philosophical critique. For Kant's text cuts two ways: it defends critical thought against state regulation, and it bestows a monopoly of critique on a particular institution and its members—professional philosophy and philosophers. We have already seen how Kant discredits the higher faculties both academically and politically by reducing them to "civil servants [*Beamter der Regierung*]" (CF 37/24). Compared to their more prestigious colleagues, philosophers are not only better political critics but also better scholars—and they are the one *because* they are the other. But Kant does not stop there. The philosophical faculty also holds a critical monopoly with respect to the "people," which is said to be constitutionally incapable of pursuing the higher interests of reason.

The people, says Kant in no uncertain terms, consists of *Idioten* (CF/18) who have nothing on their mind but their own "enjoyment" (CF 49/30). Pleasure-driven and unreceptive to the austere language of truth, the masses are ready prey for seduction. "The people want to be *led,* that is (as demagogues say), they want to be *duped*" (CF 51/31). Philosophy draws its consequences from this sorry state of affairs by canceling the people from its list of possible addressees. For while the "faculties engage in public conflict in order to influence the people," (CF 47/29) this debate must never be brought "before the judgment seat of the people (who are not competent to judge in scholarly matters)" (CF 57n/34n). Instead, it is fought out within the circumscribed space of "a different kind of public—a *learned* community", that is, the university (ibid.), from where it exerts indirect pressure on the government in the form of philosophical criticism of state-sanctioned teachings.

In identifying the university as the *only* site of critique and legitimate political dissent, then, Kant upholds the right to critical speech at the price of excluding all but a group of professional truth-seekers from it. As a consequence, the people are reduced to passive recipients of laws resulting from the dispute between higher and lower faculties, government and professional intellectuals. The people's "voice," deprived of respectable channels of expression, turns into formless noise, associable only with the *disarticulation* of all discursive and political orders: "But those who introduce a completely different form of government, or rather a lack of any government (anarchy), by handing over scholarly questions to the decision of the people really deserve to be branded neologists; for they can steer the judgment of the people in whatever direction they please, by working on their habits, feelings, and inclinations, and so win them away from the influence of a legitimate [*gesetzmäßigen*] government" (CF 57–59n/34–35n).

Philosophical critique, the introduction suggests, maneuvers between two extremes: despotism and anarchy. Kant thus advocates a model of gradual reform achieved through the alliance between philosophical critique and political power. In the "Renewed Question," he will ground philosophy's demand for reform in the enthusiasm of the German spectators for the events in France, claiming that this enthusiasm, while inspired by revolutionary ideas of justice and freedom, never yields to outright revolution and violence. But the very structure of Kant's argument raises the question of whether it is possible to separate enthusiasm—as a moral sign—from political anarchy, the desire for a transcendent law from the illegal attempts to establish it, and the meaningfulness of a progressive *sign* of history from the inchoate *noise* that permeates all popular articulations? In short, how is it possible to cleanse the will to revolution—that is, to freedom—from all traces of violence?

Philosophical Soothsaying

Kant discusses the notion of progress in the second essay of his book, which is devoted to the conflict between the faculties of philosophy and law. In contrast to the legal scholar, who contents himself with explaining (and hence upholding) the constitutional status quo, the philosopher operates with an ideal notion of a just constitution and interprets history in view of the progressive unfolding of this ideal. This teleological perspective was already present in Kant's earlier essays on history, but in the "Renewed Question," Kant raises the argumentative stakes considerably. For he now claims (a) that progress is not only desirable but inevitable, (b) that it can be known, and (c) that this knowledge applies necessarily to the future.

1. WHAT DO WE WANT TO KNOW IN THIS MATTER?

We desire a fragment of human history and one, indeed, that is drawn not from past but future time, therefore a *predictive* [*vorhersagende*] history; if it is not based on known laws (like eclipses of the sun and the moon), this history is designated as *divinatory* [*wahrsagende*], and yet natural; but if it can be acquired in no other way than through a supernatural communication and widening of one's view of future time, this history is called *premonitory* [*weissagend*] (prophetic). (CF 141/79)

But how is it possible to foretell the future without recourse to the supernatural? Does predictability not refute the very reality it is supposed to establish, namely, human freedom? As we shall see, Kant's notion of a *Geschichtszeichen* (historical sign, but also sign of history), which limits the scope of prophecy to the unveiling of a historical tendency, provides a curious answer to this paradox. And yet, before he introduces the notion of the historical sign, Kant addresses the problem of prediction head-on, in a stunning passage that outlines the relationship of philosophical writing to historical reality.

2. HOW CAN WE KNOW IT?

As a divinatory [*wahrsagende*] historical narrative of things imminent in future time, consequently as a possible representation a priori of events which are supposed to happen. But how is a history a priori possible? Answer: if the diviner [*Wahrsager*] himself *creates* and contrives [*macht und veranstaltet*] the events which he announces in advance. (ibid.)

Philosophical-historical prediction, the passage suggests, does not merely describe the future but somehow brings it about. This conception brings philosophy into dangerous proximity to the kinds of magical speech from which Kant, in the introduction to the *Conflict,* so eagerly sought to distinguish it. What exactly is the difference between philosophical soothsaying and the demagogic contrivances by which the "soothsayers and magicians" (CF 49/30) of the higher faculties spellbind the people? And what about those other fortune-tellers, women no less, who like the philosopher claim to be able to interpret predictive clues? Is the deciphering of history in terms of progressive signs substantially different from certain oracular practices associated with wandering gypsies and palm reading? Kant is clearly aware of these difficulties, for as soon as he has distinguished (good) natural divination from (bad) prophetic speech based on supernatural communication, he adds a footnote that draws yet another distinction, this time between good and bad types of divination: "From Pythia to the gypsy girl, whoever dabbles in divination (doing it without knowledge or honest) is said to be a soothsayer [*Wer ins Wahrsagen pfuschert (es ohne Kenntnis oder Ehrlichkeit thut), von dem heißt es: er wahrsagert, von der Pythia bis zur Zigeunerin*]" (AA 80n). Just one letter distinguishes between philosophical truth saying (*Wahrsagen*) and gypsy soothsaying (*Wahrsage<u>r</u>n*), a rather frail barrier, and even then, in order to make the distinction, Kant was obliged to join the ranks of the much-maligned "neologists" (CF 57/34) and invent the verb *Wahrsagern*.[3]

So what, precisely, is at stake for Kant giving his willingness to tread such dangerous ground? What does it mean to say that the philosopher "macht und versanstaltet"—creates and contrives—the events he predicts? Kant's insistence on the a priori character of his prediction points to its resolutely philosophical character. Philosophy, generally speaking, is concerned not with the actual but with the necessary or possible, not with specific events or objects but with the character of laws governing them. This is the reason why for most of the tradition, philosophical *history* is a contradiction in terms. Though Kant shared some of the traditional objections, he believed that a specifically philosophical account of history was not only possible but desirable. Philosophy, however, approaches history not as a series of events or actions, as empirical historians do, but in terms of the unfolding of its principles. And since what is at stake here is *human* history, to write a philosophical and thus a priori account of this history is to draw out the necessary analytical consequences of the principle or concept of man. Hence the peculiar character of philosophical prediction and its difference from prophetic (premonitory) speech. If the latter gives a description of actual events yet to come, and thus depends on a supernatural standpoint from which the future can be seen, philosophical prediction starts out from the concept of man, which is available through the merely mortal instrument of reflection, and derives from this the general direction of human history, a "tendency and faculty in human nature for improvement" (CF 159/88).

Despite its limited scope, philosophical prediction has a decisively pragmatic value, that of counteracting a moral paralysis that can befall even the most reasonable man. A realistic look at human nature seems to suggest that good and bad are combined in it in such a way as to neutralize one other, producing a history not of sublime progress but of lowly farce: "Bustling folly is the character of our species: . . . an empty business [*leere Geschäftigkeit*] that alternates good with evil in a see-saw motion, such that the whole play of traffic [*Spiel des Verkehrs*] of our species with itself on this globe would have to be considered a mere farcical comedy [*Possenspiel*], which can endow our species with no greater value in the eyes of reason than that which other animal species possess, species which carry on this game with fewer costs and without expenditure of thought" (CF147/82). Seesawing between progressive and regressive undertakings, human history seems conceivable only in terms of a circle, as the "eternal rotation in orbit around the same point" (145/81). Despite its apparent commonsensical factuality, this image of a circular, repetitive past threatens to foreclose even the future. Since moral action, like all human action, is necessarily oriented toward certain ends, a conception of history that abandons the good as an attainable goal threatens moral action with paralysis and pointlessness.[4] Why act morally if the results of our interventions add up to a zero-sum game?

Philosophical history counteracts this feeling of resignation by showing that our belief in freedom is not a mere *Hirngespinst* (chimera).[5] In other words, we need some overall assurance that our moral vocation is not Sisyphean, and the logical possibility of historical progress (in which the empirical conditions relevant to our being able to exercise our moral capacity becomes more and more favorable) serves that role. Moreover, the recognition of the true law of humanity is itself a necessary component of progress, because only if we understand these laws can we act accordingly. Critical philosophy thus provides the learned public with a historical narrative that enables it both to understand what is happening and to help bring about what should happen. In this sense, philosophical prediction can be said to "macht und veranstaltet" the progress it foretells:

Ninth Thesis: A philosophical attempt to work out a universal history according to a natural plan directed to achieving the civic union of the human race must be regarded as possible and, indeed, as contributing to this end of Nature. (IUH 23)

Everyone can see that philosophy can have her belief in a millennium, but her milleniarism is not Utopian, since the Idea can help, though only from afar, to bring the millennium to pass. (IUH, 21–22)

However, this pragmatic conception of philosophical history as inspiring, and thus helping to realize, our moral vocation was already present in Kant's earlier essay, his "Idea for a Universal History from a Pragmatic Point of View" (1783), from which the above quotations are taken. The "Renewed Question" marks a clear radicalization of the earlier essay, in that Kant now claims that progress is not just possible or probable but necessary and inevitable. Thus, whereas in 1783, Kant suggested that a hypothetical model of teleological history would strengthen our belief in progress, in 1798, he claims to have found a real event that enables him to predict progress with certainty. Hence the absolutely new, and indeed unheard-of, character of Kant's philosophical prediction, which brings into contact two seemingly distinct conceptual planes. On the one hand, and in keeping with the traditional character of philosophical inquiry, Kant proceeds analytically rather than empirically, starting from an a priori concept and predicting, on its basis, not actual events but the general direction of human history. On the other, the possibility of this a priori prediction is said to rest on the existence of a historical event. Necessity thus seems to depend on actuality, a priori concepts on empirical events, and moral law on the expression of a feeling (enthusiasm).[6]

As we shall see in more detail shortly, the structure of Kant's argument here is very similar to his discussion of respect in the *Critique of Practical Reason*, where he likewise claims that the existence of a feeling (respect, enthusiasm) proves the existence of moral law as a motivational force in the world and assumes apodictic status for his argument. The feeling of enthusiasm, like that of respect, proves that human beings bear an emotional relation to impersonal principle. But does it really *prove* this? In other words, is the connection between feeling and its supposed cause as tight and certain as Kant believes it to be? Are we not dealing here, rather, with an act of reading, or more precisely: with an interpretation of manifest phenomena as clues indicating absent causes? And is it possible to claim apodictic certainty for the reading of signs, as Kant clearly does when he announces the necessary character of his prediction?

It is precisely this problem, I suggest, that prompts Kant to distinguish his type of prophecy (*Wahrsagung*) not only from magical speech (*weissagen*) but also, what is more important, from the predictions of the gypsy soothsayer (*wahrsagern*). For unlike the former, which claims access to supernatural communication, the gypsy's prophetic art is based on the reading of the future through signs of the present, and it is thus conspicuously close to philosophical prediction. The question is therefore whether Kant can outline a mode of reading that overcomes the specious character of prediction and establish a philosophically plausible link between the present and the future.

A Sign of the Present

Kant argues that in order to predict progress with certainty, one must discover an actual historical event that, as a phenomenon, points to "the disposition and capacity of the human race to be the cause of its own advance toward the better" (CF 151/84). He finds this *Geschichtszeichen*, not in the French Revolution as such, but in a singular emotional response that the Revolution elicits from those who observe it from afar. For Kant, the harbinger of progress is the *enthusiasm* of the German spectators, who, exhilarated by the "game of great revolutions" in France, publicly proclaim their "sympathy for the players on one side against those on the others, even at the risk that this partiality could become very disadvantageous for them" (CF 153/85).

This sign of history is first of all a sign of the present. For while enthusiasm points to a permanent moral "disposition [*Anlage*]" (AA 85), the actual manifestation of this feeling has a much more fleeting temporal existence. Before enthusiasm can signify anything, it is simply the momentary expression of a feeling, a transient phenomenon that occurs at a particular moment in time. And it is this highly ephemeral affect (enthusiasm, Kant writes in the *Critique of Judgment,* is a "passing accident" (CJ 135) a temporary excess of feeling), which Kant invests with the meaning of signifying the present. This becomes clearer when we look at the various ways in which he circumscribes the expression of enthusiasm: it occurs "now" (CF 159/88), at the time he is writing his essay; it is new, in that it makes visible something that was "never seen before to this degree" (AA 22: 622); and in its fusion of now-ness and newness, it exerts an "epoch-making influence" (CF 157/87). Together, these three aspects suggest that enthusiasm, as the outstanding "[e]vent of our time" (CF 153/85), crystallizes the meaning of "our time" as a new epoch. "The signs of *this* time," Kant writes in a preparatory note, "disclose publicly . . . a moral disposition in the human race that was *never seen before* to this degree" (AA 22: 622; emphasis added).

This line of argument finds support in a telling semantic innovation. Kant's discussion of enthusiasm's "epoch-making" character is itself epochal. Until then, "epoch" had been used to designate a point in time that marked the beginning of a historical period, not the period itself.[7] In Kant's interpretation, the word retains this meaning as a punctual event but is simultaneously expanded to characterize the entire historical constellation it opens up. Enthusiasm is thus not simply a momentary rupture but a veritable turning point, a "punctum flexus contrarii" (CF 149/83). The public occurrence of enthusiasm transforms history in two interrelated ways. First, as the historical manifestation of a moral disposition that, while "never seen before," points to an enduring causal force, enthusiasm transforms our understanding of *all* of human history. As Kant puts it, the semiotic scope of enthusiasm extends to all three historical dimensions; it is a "signum rememorativum, demonstrativum, prognostikon" (CF 151/84). But, and here the second epochal transformation comes in, for enthusiasm to exert this force, it is first of all necessary to strip it of its mere contingency as event and instead to attend to it as a sign. And since this type of hermeneutic abstraction requires a distinctively philosophical approach, enthusiasm's significance as a historical turning point is intimately connected with a transformation of philosophy's role in history. For insofar as enthusiasm's character as a *Geschichtszeichen* depends on its philosophical interpretation, the epochal "event of our time" marks the moment at which both freedom and philosophical consciousness enter history. Philosophy enters history—becomes a historical force—as philosophical history.

The philosophical interpretation of history in terms of progress itself becomes an "actor" within that history both in providing a regulative framework for action and in making transparent the dependence of historical change on moral development. Hence Kant's claim that the soothsayer "macht und veranstaltet" the events he describes.

As Foucault has suggested in a reading of Kant's essay "What Is Enlightenment," Kant's emphasis on a discontinuous present is bound up with a new philosophical attitude toward his time.

> The question which, I believe, for the first time appears in this text by Kant is the question of today, the question about the present, about what is our actuality: what is happening today? What is happening right now? And what is this right now we all are in which defines the moment at which I am writing? . . . It is not simply: what in the present situation can determine this or that philosophical decision? The question is about the present and is, at first, concerned with the determination of a certain element of the present that needs to be recognized, distinguished, deciphered among all others. What is it in the present that now makes sense for philosophical reflection?[8]

With Kant, then, philosophy is no longer conceived in terms of the uninvolved contemplation of timeless truths, but rather as thought's self-reflective engagement with the Now of its own becoming (Deleuze). The present is no longer an object of historical knowledge but a particular historical constellation whose meaning and singularity philosophy is called upon to express, and in which it "has to find both its reason for being and the foundation of what it says."[9] Implicit in this conception is that in understanding the present, thought is both receptive and active: receptive, in that it opens itself to the reign of principle in history; and active, in that it intervenes in history so as to promote the political articulation of the principle of freedom.[10]

Passion and Event

As Foucault put it, enthusiasm points to a "will to Revolution . . . which is something other than the revolutionary enterprise itself."[11] Read as a sign, the revolution discloses a "permanent virtuality" that exceeds its empirical manifestation.[12] Kant arrives at his thesis by twice splitting the Revolution, and each of these splits is designed to extract the virtual from the factual, the will to revolution from the particular empirical formation to which this will gives rise. First, Kant shifts the historical focus from production to reception, from the Revolution as a political event to the emotional response it inspires in those that observe it from afar. Second, he splits the occurrence of enthusiasm, distinguishing between its actual expression as a feeling, which is a phenomenon occurring in historical time and geographical space, and the moral disposition to which this feeling points as its cause, which inheres in the phenomenal event but is not reducible to it. Both displacements are also forms of distanciation that turn the Revolution from a transparent event into a sign to be read: the enthusiastic spectators are removed enough from the Revolution to describe it as a "game" and "spectacle," while the philosopher is further removed from the enthusiasts to describe their action in terms of a *Geschichtszeichen*.

This double move implies a complex process of abstraction, as we have seen. Kant's philosophical history does not aim to report preexisting events but rather to delineate them through the prism of a conceptual framework that simultaneously unearths and facilitates the progress of moral teleology: philosophy "eventualizes" and in this sense actualizes history. This is not just a matter of seeing the past in a different light but of seeing a different past. Note that Kant does not simply propose a different interpretation of the Revolution but in fact identifies a different revolution. The truly revolutionary "event of our Time," he says at the beginning of section six, "consists neither

40

in momentous deeds nor crimes committed by men whereby what was great among men is made small or what was small is made great, nor in ancient splendid political structures which vanish as if by magic while others come forth in their place as if from the depths of the earth. No, nothing of the sort. It is simply the mode of thinking of the spectators which reveals itself publicly in this game of great revolutions" (CF 153/85). The Revolution is not located where received wisdom would place it, on the level of political event-history. Instead, what is important for Kant is the ethical revelation, a revolution that unfolds not in the play of events but in the medium of affect and emotion. This shift from event to affect goes hand in hand with a shift from action to reception. Enthusiasm, Kant writes in a footnote, will not result in immediate political action, especially when it occurs "in a country more than a hundred miles removed from the scene of the revolution" (CF 155/86). The spatial distance limits participation to an imaginary act (*Teilnehmung dem Wunsche nach* [AA 85]) whose moral value is unimpaired by the "misery and atrocities" that accompany the political events in France. Accordingly, the German spectators remain in the position of an "uninvolved public" that "sympathizes with the exaltation" of the French revolutionaries "without the least intention of assisting" (mit welcher Exaltation das äußere, zuschauende Publicum dann ohne die mindeste Absicht der Mitwirkung sympathisirt) (AA 85ff.).

Moreover, this spatial displacement creates an interpretative distance. Viewed from afar, the revolution is no longer merely a physical *Begebenheit* (event) but an *Eräugnis* (happening),[13] that is, a sense-event whose meaning and nature is intimately connected to its being witnessed and represented. This essentially mediated quality of the revolution qua *Eräugnis,* while arguably already part of its nature as an empirically perceived event,[14] is even more obvious when we take into account that the spectators are "more than hundred miles away from the scene of the Revolution" and do not actually see the events but only hear and read about them. As Kant writes in an earlier draft, the spectators' thirst for participation expresses itself in an "impatient and hot desire for newspapers [*Zeitungen*]" (AA 19: 604). No matter how "hot" this desire is—and I shall address the question of enthusiasm's affective intensity shortly—it is clear that the newspaper, while inflaming its readers, also secures a certain reflective distance between event and subject. The linguistic mediation opens up a space for the subject, a space that, among other things, enables the spectators to attend to the meaning and sense of the observed events. In short, before the philosopher deciphers the "signs of the time" (AA 22: 622) in the Revolution, the Revolution itself has already acquired a representational status in the eyes of those who observe it from afar.

Kant's claim that the truly important historical event of the time consists in a mode of feeling shifts the historico-political focus from action to affect. This shift cannot be understood in terms of the ancient opposition between action and contemplation, for the spectators' behavior is not just a form of mental viewing but involves desire ("a wishful participation") and even an excess of affect ("enthusiasm"). Establishing the meaning of history, for Kant, is not just a matter of reflection but involves the subject's emotional involvement in events. In interpreting enthusiasm as the sign of progress, Kant poses the question of the entanglement of passion and principle in the production of history.

Yet Kant's emphasis on passion is also an emphatic retreat from the Revolution and the link between violence and law the Revolution exposes. This link is operative on two levels. First, the Revolution draws attention to the violence intrinsic in the act of instituting a new law; it shows that the rule of law is built on the extralegal foundation of violence. Second, this violence is not limited to the foundation of a legal order but sustains and undergirds the regular functioning of this order, taking the form (a) of the coercive force backing it, and (b) of what I shall call procedural violence. Both foundational and procedural violence intersect in what for Kant was the "horrible crime" of the trial and execution of the king, a trial in which revolutionary action disavowed its foundational violence by cloaking it in juridical procedure.

Foundational Violence

According to Kant, there cannot be such a thing as a "lawful revolution" for the simple reason that a right to overthrow the existing system of rights is paradoxical.[15] A constitution that includes, as a clause, the condition under which it can be suspended, is "self-contradictory" (MM 463). Whereas contemporaries like Johann August Eberhard seek to carve out a juridical space for a *Widerstandsrecht* (right of resistance), Kant insists that the concepts of *Widerstand* and *Recht* are mutually exclusive, because revolutions are acts of disrupting the chain of legality that not only infringe the law but suspend it altogether: "but insurrection in a constitution that already exists overthrows all civil rightful relations and therefore all rights" (MM 480).

This destruction is tantamount to a relapse into the *status naturalis*. Revolutions undermine all lawful constitutions and "produce a state of complete lawlessness (*status naturalis*) where all rights cease at least to be effectual" (TP

82). "The *status naturalis,*" Kant specifies in an unpublished reflection, "is the state of freedom without legal coercion" (AA 20: 477, refl. 7649). It follows, for Kant, that even the worst law is better than no law at all, and that

> all resistance against the supreme legislative power, all incitement of the sub-
> ject to violent expressions of discontent, all defiance which breaks out into
> rebellion is the greatest and most punishable crime in a commonwealth, for
> it destroys its very foundation. This prohibition is absolute. And even if the
> power of the state or its agent, the head of state, has violated the original
> contract by authorizing the government to act tyrannically, and has thereby,
> in the eyes of the subject forfeited the right to legislate, the subject is still
> not entitled to offer counter-resistance. (TP 81)

Revolution and law must not be mixed together, and yet Kant acknowledges that it is also impossible to separate them entirely. For the revolutionary re-lapse into the *status naturalis* is the obverse of the very passage from which the rule of law emerged. If the extralegal violence of the revolutionaries destroys the unity of the commonwealth, another kind of extralegal violence created this unity in the first place. Unlike Rousseau, Kant makes no bones about the fact that the social contract is not a historical fact but a theoretical fiction, or "an idea of reason" (ibid.).

> It is perfectly true that the will of all *individual* men to live in accordance
> with principles of freedom within a lawful constitution (i.e. the *distributive*
> unity of the will of all) is not sufficient for this purpose. Before so difficult a
> problem can be solved, all men together (i.e. the *collective* unity of the com-
> bined will) must desire to attain this goal; only then can civil society exist as
> a single whole. Since an additional unifying cause must therefore overrule
> the different particular wills before a common will can arise, and since no
> single individual will can create it, the only conceivable way of executing the
> original idea in *practice*, and hence of inaugurating a state of right, is by
> *violence* [*Gewalt*]. On its coercive authority, public right will subsequently
> be based. (PP 117; trans. modified)

Law and legitimacy owe their existence to a groundless act of force. The act is groundless in the sense that, while foundational of the rule of law, it is itself without foundation in an established law. Neither legal nor illegal, this groundless decision opens up the semantic space structured by the distinction between legality or illegality, a space that coincides with a juridico-political or-der that claims to bind members of a society through the normative force of general and impartial rules, rather than coercing them through the exercise of brute violence.[16] Since these rules derive a good deal of their binding force from their presumed impartiality, any investigation into their violent origin weakens the rule of law and carries a threat to the juridico-political order.

> A people should not inquire with any practical aim in view into the origin of the supreme authority to which it is subject, that is, a subject ought not to reason subtly for the sake of action about the origin of this authority, as a right that can still be called into question (*ius controversum*). . . . Whether a state began with an actual contract or submission (*pactum subjectionis civilis*) as a fact, or whether power came first and law arrived only afterwards, or even whether they should have followed this order: for a people already subject to civil law these subtle reasonings are altogether pointless and, moreover, threaten a state with danger. (MM 461–62)
>
> It is futile to inquire into the *historical documentation* of the mechanism of government, that is, one cannot reach back to the time at which civil society began. . . . But it is culpable to undertake this inquiry with a view to possibly changing by force the constitution that now exists. (MM 480)

But this violent and extralegal dimension is not limited to the moment of emergence of law. Read again the end of the passage from "Perpetual Peace" where Kant discusses the emergence of the state: "the only conceivable way of executing the original idea in *practice,* and hence of inaugurating a state of right, is by *violence* [*Gewalt*]. *On its coercive authority, public right will subsequently be based*" (PP 117; trans. modified, emphasis added). The normative force of law rests on, and is bound up with, the state's right to enforce legal decisions by means of physical violence. This is what Walter Benjamin famously called law-preserving violence (*rechtserhaltende Gewalt*), as opposed to law-making violence (*rechtssetzende Gewalt*), and saw most clearly constituted by the police.[17] What Benjamin only intimated, however, is that this law-preserving violence is intrinsic in legal decisions, whose normative force derives not from their adequacy to an intrinsic or substantial notion of justice but from the procedures that articulate them. Like the act of force that establishes the rule of law, these procedures function as the source of norms without being themselves derivable from other norms. As Christine Korsgaard has argued: "We may try to design our procedures to secure the substantively right, best, or just outcome. But—and here is the important point—the normativity of these procedures nevertheless does not spring from the efficiency, goodness, *or even the substantive justice* of the outcomes they produce. The reverse is true: it is the procedures themselves that confer normativity on those results."[18] Kant essentially acknowledges the same logic when he states that once a revolution has succeeded, the newly established government is as legitimate as the one it replaced (MM 465–66). *All* governments are legitimate, for the simple reason that governments comprise the institutions and procedures that confer legitimacy in the first place. As for these procedures, there simply is no point from which *their* legitimacy can be (legitimately) questioned. The logic here is similar to that which Wittgenstein pinpointed in noting: "There is *one* thing of which one can say neither that it is one metre long, nor that it is not one metre long, and that is the standard metre in Paris."[19] And just as every actual measurement rests on the purely arbitrary character of this paradigmatic meter, so every legal decision, in following the procedures that invest it with legitimacy, rests on and iterates the extralegal violence of the foundational act that instituted these procedures. In the final analysis, then, the rule of law rests on a performative *Setzung* that carries coercive authority and imperative force: The Law is the law! Or as Kant puts it: "the presently existing legislative authority ought to be obeyed, whatever its origin" (MM 462).

It is partly Kant's fear of this senseless dimension of legal procedures that underlies the much-discussed long footnote in the *Metaphysics of Morals* in which he expresses his "horror" at the trial and execution of Louis XVI.[20] The murder of the monarch is an abominable crime, but it is

> itself not the worst, for we can still think of the people as doing it from fear that if he remained alive he could marshal his forces and inflict on them the punishment they deserve, so that their killing him would not be an enactment of punitive justice but merely a dictate of self-preservation. It is the formal *execution* of a monarch that strikes horror in a soul filled with the idea of human rights, a horror that one feels repeatedly as soon and as often as one thinks of such scenes as the fate of Charles I or Louis XVI. . . .
>
> The reason for horror at the thought of the formal execution of a monarch *by his people* is therefore this: that while his murder is regarded as only an exception to the rule that the people makes its maxim, his *execution* must be regarded as a complete *overturning* of the principles of the relation between a sovereign and his people (in which the people, which owes its existence only to the sovereign's legislation, makes itself its master), so that violence is elevated above the most sacred rights brazenly and in accordance with principle. Like an abyss that irretrievably swallows everything, the execution of a monarch seems to be a crime from which the people cannot be absolved, for it is as if the state commits suicide. There is, accordingly, reason for assuming that the agreement to execute the monarch actually originates not from what is supposed to be a rightful principle but from fear of the state's vengeance upon the people if it revives at some future time, and that these formalities are undertaken only to give that deed the appearance

of punishment, and so of a *rightful procedure* (such as murder would not be). But this disguising of the deed miscarries; such a presumption on the people's part is still worse than murder, since it involves a principle that would have to make it impossible to generate again a state that has been overthrown. (MM 464–65n; trans. modified)

In putting the king on trial, the revolutionaries invest their actions with the aura of legitimacy. As they follow formal procedures, employ the rhetoric of legal language, and draw on juridical symbols and rituals, they present their actions, not as a revolutionary suspension of the chain of legality, but as the application of an already established law. According to Kant, in so doing they not only disavow responsibility for their deeds but also mock and pervert the language of rights they evoke. In cloaking the disruption of the rule of law in the very procedures that confer normativity on this rule, they divest them once and for all of their legal and moral value, thereby destroying the foundation of law, justice, and government.[21]

Kant goes even further and equates this crime with a particular form of evil. In *Religion Within the Limits of Reason Alone,* he distinguishes radical evil, described as a "natural propensity, *inextirpable* by human powers" (RLR 32), from diabolic evil, in which an agent wills evil for its own sake. Radical evil is rooted in self-love and consists in making oneself an exception to the law in order to satisfy one's egotistical interests; diabolic evil is free of pathological motivation, originating instead in a will that raises the infraction of the law to the level of a categorical imperative that must be obeyed regardless of the costs to the subject. The truly terrifying nature of such diabolic will is that it shares the categorical and nonpathological aspect of moral acts, a parallel that threatens to collapse the entire edifice of Kant's moral theory, which centers on the claim that the morality of an act depends entirely on its accommodation of and adequacy to formal principle. Hence Kant's implicit invocation of the trial of the king as an act of diabolic evil: just as the existence of diabolic evil would explode the possibility of morality, so the trial of Louis VXI, if motivated by no other maxim than that of transgressing the law, would destroy the possibility of justice and political order. No wonder then that Kant evokes the hypothesis of diabolic evil in *Religion Within the Limits of Reason Alone,* only immediately to deny its existence: "As far as we can see, it is impossible for a human being to commit a crime of this kind, a formally evil (wholly pointless) crime; and yet it is not to be ignored in a system of morals (although it is only the idea of a most extreme evil [*Äußerst-bösen*])" (MM 464n). Something very similar happens in Kant's discussion of the trial of Louis VXI, where the hypothesis of diabolic evil is introduced and immediately rejected. What motivated the revolutionaries, Kant concludes his footnote, was not "a rightful principle" (MM 465n) but "the fear of the state's vengeance upon the people" (ibid.). The feeling of being drawn into an "abyss that irretrievably swallows everything" (MM 464n; trans. modified) is thus overcome. It was just a moment of dizziness, an imaginative contraction of fear on the part, in fact, of the revolutionaries.

Decision

As Peter Fenves has pointed out, the diabolically evil action of the French revolutionaries has the same structure as that of sublime response: both occur without regard for personal gain, both mark a kind of historical caesura, and both involve an extreme and unforgettable affect (the crime, Kant says, "remains eternally," and the horror associated with it returns time and again.)[22] The execution of the king, then, would seem to be a kind of inverted or perverted *Geschichtszeichen,* one that threatens to haunt and undermine all hope of progress. All of this might seem to suggest that in claiming that the king's execution was motivated by fear, and thus was not diabolically evil, Kant is projecting onto the French actors his own fear of "being swallowed up in an abyss from which there is no return." There would be, then, two radically incompatible historical signs, a "bad" one associated with the political revolution in France and a "good" one linked to the moral enthusiasm in Germany.

But if this is so, how can it be that the Revolution, which is so thoroughly despicable from a legal standpoint, elicits such almost maddeningly joyful enthusiasm? What is it that makes the Revolution thrilling despite its extralegal character? It is hardly enough to proclaim that the revolution is sublime because it is a chaotic and formless event, an abyss like other sublime objects, as Lyotard does.[23] The sublimity of the revolutionary spectacle lies elsewhere:

> [G]enuine enthusiasm always moves only toward what is ideal and, indeed, to what is purely moral, such as the concept of right, and it cannot be grafted onto self-interest. Monetary rewards could not elevate the adversaries of the revolution to the zeal and grandeur of soul which the pure concept of *right* produced in them; and even the concept of honor among the old martial nobility (an analogue of enthusiasm) vanished before the weapons of those who kept in view the right of the nation to which they belonged and of which they considered themselves the guardians; with what

exaltation the uninvolved public looking on sympathized then without the least intention of assisting. (CF 155/86; trans. modified, emphasis added)

The enthusiasm of the German spectators is the product of a sympathetic identification with the enthusiasm of the French revolutionaries. Fueling the spectators' exalted response is their belief that the French revolutionaries act, not from self-interest or in view of worldly gains, but out of purely moral motives. They risk their lives because they believe in the dignity of rights they see trampled. What Kant does not say, but what can be inferred from the preceding discussion, is that this revolutionary "participation in the Good" is all the more astonishing in that it coincides with the transgression of written laws, which simply prohibit revolt. Paradoxically, then, revolutionary enthusiasm seems to be at once purely moral and thoroughly illegal; it is moral in its alignment with moral principle, and illegal in that its expression necessarily runs afoul of established law. Christine Korsgaard has emphasized the peculiar character of this paradox with respect to revolutionary action:

> [T]he universalization test cannot serve as a guide when we make it. The imperfections of the actual state of affairs are no excuse for revolution—if they were, revolution would always be in order. . . . There is no criterion for deciding when imperfection has become perversion [i.e., of justice], when things have gone too far. If we turn for help to the Universal Principle of Justice, all it says is: Do not revolt. The revolutionary cannot claim he has a justification, in the sense of an account of his action that other reasonable people must accept. That consolation is denied him. It is as if a kind of gap opens up in the moral world in which the moral agent must stand alone.[24]

Another name for this "gap in the moral world" is crisis. The decision to revolt occurs in a symbolic void, in a space in which rules and laws—social, legal, and moral—have lost their validity and hold. And it is because of this lack of support in preexisting rules that the decision to revolt assumes the force of a truly moral act. Standing alone in the interregnum between the old order and the new, deprived of the comfort of rational justification, faced with the paradoxical task of transgressing the law in order to preserve justice—the person who decides to revolt embodies what may be called the obligatory essence and ultimate core of every moral act: the fact that the subject must assume full responsibility for it. To put this in slightly different terms: the exceptional situation of the revolutionary highlights a feature that pertains to all ethical acts: namely, that the application of a general rule to a particular case is never just that but instead always involves a contingent and unformalizable moment of decision on the part of the subject. This is especially clear in the case of Kant's highly abstract ethics, which tells me what *form* my actions must assume to be moral but not what exactly I should do in a given concrete situation. Which means, in Slavoj Žižek's words, that "the subject himself has to assume the responsibility of 'translating' the abstract injunction of the moral Law into a series of concrete obligations."[25] And it means that this translation is literally an *Über-setzung,* that is, a crossing from one realm (abstract principle, or law) to another (particular situation) that is itself without a ground in existing rules but is sustained only by the subject's finite and singular decision to act right now.

So while revolutionary action is morally unacceptable for Kant, it nonetheless contains a sublime moral dimension that makes it thrilling to the spectator. Viewed in this light, the problem with the king's trial is perhaps not that it reflects the working of a diabolically evil will strong enough to brush aside all pathological desires. Just the opposite: When the revolutionaries put Louis XVI on trial, they disavow the dimension of responsibility and decision that forms the sublime kernel of revolutionary action—deny their own will, so to speak. It is as if in clothing their regicide in the language, symbols, and ceremonies of a legal process, they are saying, "It is not really we who are doing this as individuals—we are the agents of another will; we are merely applying the law" (i.e., rather than abrogating it). Speaking on behalf of the other, acting in the name of law, they abjure responsibility for their deeds and thus destroy the sublime ethical and political dimension of revolutionary action.

Not so the German spectators, whose gesture manifests the features of a moral act without any contamination by either violence or cowardice. Like the "good" (pretrial) revolutionaries, the enthusiasts put their lives on the line: "[T]his revolution, I say, nonetheless finds in the hearts of all spectators (who are not engaged in this game themselves) a wishful participation that borders closely on enthusiasm, *the very expression of which is fraught with danger;* this sympathy, therefore, can have no other cause than a moral predisposition in the human race" (CF 153/85; emphasis added). The expression of revolutionary fervor occurs in a political order that is hostile to the Revolution. Kant is clearly thinking here of Germany, where the governments of most states sided with the ancien régime in France and punished sympathetic responses to the Revolution with harsh repressive measures. Now, his argument is that since the spectators, in expressing their "wishful participation," endanger their own lives, they must act from a motive other than self-love. And since all sensuous desires are motivated by self-love, the spectators' enthusiasm must be free from empirical motives altogether. No pathological need or desire occasions the outbreak of enthusiasm, and no gain or advantage is connected to it: it is entirely unselfish.

Moreover, like the decision to revolt, the expression of enthusiasm is free in the sense of being undetermined by any rule. There is no obligation to exalt, no categorical imperative that demands the sympathetic identification with the French actors as a duty. All there is, in fact, is a prohibition against the public display of revolutionary sympathy, and a political order that severely punishes such outbreaks of feelings. Finally, the enthusiastic communication is not only not dictated by laws; it is also free from any demand for the implementation of new laws. Unlike the revolutionaries who transgress the law in order to establish a new one, the spectators do not even desire to act on their feelings: "the uninvolved public looking on," we are told, sympathizes with the revolutionaries "without the least intention of assisting" (CF 157/87). Kant's choice of verb in another passage further underscores this aspect: "Es ist bloß die Denkungsart der Zuschauer, welche sich bei diesem Spiele großer Umwandlungen *öffentlich verräth* [it is simply the mode of thinking of the spectators that *betrays itself publicly* in the game of great revolutions]" (AA 85; emphasis added). The spectators speak up without any purpose in mind: they want neither to convince nor to provoke or instigate action. If they express their feelings and risk their lives, they do so solely out of the desire to communicate their exaltation. Enthusiasm betrays itself, in sum, in a public speech that is at once pleasurable and dangerous, purposeless and unselfish.

Constituting Power

Enthusiasm, then, is an unmediated moral expression, a countenancing of the principle of freedom, neither compromised by "misery and atrocities" nor confined to a specific practical purpose. But what is the political significance of this seemingly apolitical expression of freedom? In what way can the expression of a feeling that is entirely divorced from action be said to be of any relevance to the progress of society? My claim is that enthusiasm, as pure energetic attachment to principle, is the fundamental drive behind liberation and hence political progress. It is the engine of human history properly understood, that is, of history as the realization of freedom. Kant defines freedom, or what he calls transcendental freedom, negatively as the power "to pass beyond any and every specified limit" (CPR A317/B374), and positively as the "power of beginning a state spontaneously" (CPR A533/B561).[26] I am especially interested in freedom's dynamic and inexhaustible character, in its nature as a force driving human actions but not reducible to them. Freedom, so conceived, is the extrahistorical source of historical actions, or, to paraphrase Lacan, it is something in history that is more than history. And it is this ahistorical abyss or hole, which is at the same time a kind of inexhaustible reservoir and "pure reserve" (Deleuze),[27] that lies at the core of Kant's conception of History. Taking a short detour through the work of Hannah Arendt, I want now to argue that the experience of such a creative, inexhaustible, and extrahistorical force emerged during the French Revolution and became codified in the juridical notion of the constituting power of the people, which lies at the heart of all democratic thought.

For Arendt, as is well known, the modern concept of revolution is inextricably bound up with the idea of freedom and the experience of a new beginning.[28] Revolutions must be distinguished from mere rebellions: whereas the aim of the latter is the liberation from oppression, the former are positive acts of self-determination comprising the destruction of the old order *and* the creation of a new one. It is this creative and productive dimension of revolutions—"the task of foundation, the setting of a new beginning" and the formation of a new body politic[29]—that is at the center of Arendt's interest and that feeds the ontological undercurrent of her study. Revolutions, for Arendt, are historical embodiments of an extrahistorical quality: of "man's faculty to begin something new," of his freedom from historical determination.[30]

I want to take my cue from Arendt but redirect her argument slightly. True, revolutions manifest the capacity to begin a new state, but they do so by immediately resolving this capacity, which is an open and limitless potential, into a determinate and circumscribed reality. As Arendt herself emphasizes, it is the measure of a successful revolution that it transforms the undefined power of constituting into a circumscribed legal-political constitution. My claim is that the exaltation of the German spectators assumes the value of a historical sign evincing progress precisely because it is an expression of freedom that does *not* resolve itself into a distinct political reality. Hence also enthusiasm's two faces: insofar as it is public, it manifests the *actuality* of a disposition for freedom; insofar as it is not attached to a specific goal, it signifies the *potentiality* for freedom tout court. From this perspective, Kant's aim in shifting the focus from France to Germany is to capture and magnify the force that expresses itself in the Revolution but is not reducible to it—that is, the creative power of human freedom. And enthusiasm can signify this power better than the Revolution itself, because it embodies, due to its purposelessness on the one hand and its mobilization of moral principle on the other, an unqualified commitment to freedom as such.

The idea of such a creative and inexhaustible force was already expressed, on the eve of the French Revolution, in the juridical concept of the *pouvoir constituant,* or constituting power. In theories of constitutional law, the term refers to the productive ground of the legal-political order, or the place from which this order receives its legitimacy. In the words of Antonio Negri, who devoted an entire book to the subject:

> For juridical science, what is constituting power? It is the source of the pro-
> duction of constitutional norms, or the power to make a constitution and
> therefore to dictate the fundamental norms that organize the forces of the
> state; in other words, it is the power to establish a new juridical order and
> thus to regulate the juridical relations at the heart of a new community.
> "Constituting power is an imperative act of the nation that emerges out of
> nothing and organizes the hierarchy of powers."[31]

A recent description of constituting power as a juridical "border-concept" seems to hit the mark.[32] Constituting power is prior to all constitutional forms, yet it shapes and sustains them; it emerges from nothing and organizes everything; and it is an absolute power distinct from, and productive of, all political powers.[33] The religious and metaphysical undertones of the concept are obvious and point to its genealogy: Sieyès, who borrowed the notion from Montesquieu but elaborated it decisively, drew on medieval theology (where constituting power belongs to God) and made, on occasion, analogies to Spinoza's distinction between generating and generated nature (*natura naturans* and *natura naturata*).[34] Sieyès's decisive move, of course, was to transfer the transcendent attributes associated with this concept onto the nation as its new subject, a move marking "an essential moment in the secularization of power and politics."[35] And yet, one only has to look at the essentially rhetorical and "performative" dimension of the concept of nation during the French Revolution—at the fact that the "nation" existed only in the words of those who succeeded in speaking on its behalf [36]—to realize that this secularization of constituting power, far from abolishing its transcendency, turned it into a dynamic principle that was now immanent in politics and history. Simply put, the problem was that the subject of constituting power (the nation) was at once the ultimate political reality and a pure abstraction. It was the ultimate political reality because the nation, conceived of as "a unitary body of citizens exercising an inalienable common will,"[37] was absolute sovereign, and thus, in Sieyès words, "the source of all legality."[38] And it was a pure abstraction because this unitary body of citizens existed nowhere in reality. The nation "was not a datum or a concept that reflected existing society";[39] it was a mythical and primordial entity, existing, for Sieyès, "independent of any rule or any constitutional form"—that is, outside history.[40]

This is not the place to discuss how the failure of the revolutionaries to translate the idea of popular sovereignty into political reality affected the course of the French Revolution, a failure leading, as some have argued, straight into the Terror.[41] Suffice it to note that the fusion of the old concept of sovereignty with the new idea of a constituent will of the people—the idea of popular sovereignty—posed a number of problems intrinsic to what Claude Lefort has called the "democratic invention": How to save the democratic promise inherent in the idea of national sovereignty without surrendering politics to the vagaries of popular mood swings and the rhetorical skills of party demagogues. How to channel the amorphous will of the people into institutional venues without depriving it of its creative and productive dimension. And how, finally, to cleanse this new sovereign of its volatile nature and bestow on it permanence and absolute authority—the nation's will, said Sieyès, "is the law itself."[42]

Kant did not use the concept of constituting power, but the difficulties associated with it nonetheless surface in his political writings: firstly, in his half-hearted discussion of popular sovereignty, and secondly, in his wavering over the figure of the legislator. Popular sovereignty, in Kant, is an ideal with no political reality. On the one hand, all laws derive from the will of the people: "legislative authority can belong only to the united will of the people" (MM 457), so that the universal sovereign "can be none other than the united people itself" (MM 459).[43] But this is only how matters look "from the viewpoint of laws of freedom" (ibid.); in reality, things are less rosy. As we have seen, what makes a people unified "is that there are procedures under which they are unified, procedures that make collective decision and action possible, and give them a general will."[44] Which means that while ideally it is the people that constitute the laws, empirically it is the existing laws that constitute the people. Kant thus seeks to resolve the tension between constituting power and constituted order by reducing the former to a manifestation of the latter. For where every government by definition embodies the general will of the people, that will is degraded to the role of legitimizing the status quo and thus deprived of all political reality.[45]

While Kant's treatment of popular sovereignty is at least coherent, his discussions of the source of law are somewhat muddled. Kant's terminological vacillations take two forms: his wavering over the role of the sovereign legislator, and his occasional distinction between the sovereign and the absolute authority that bestows legitimacy on all legislative acts. The first equivocation is both easier and less consequential. Kant thought that the general will of the people (the supreme legislative authority) had to be represented in order to acquire political reality, and he believed that the unity of the general will was best represented in the person of a single ruler with supreme legislative authority. But he wavered over what precisely the status of this sovereign was with respect to both laws and state. He sometimes identifies the sovereign with the head of state (MM 479) or speaks of the "*sovereign authority* (sovereignty) in the person of the legislator" (MM 457), but elsewhere he distinguishes the head of state, described as a kind of chief executive of the government, from the sovereign, who is said to be "invisible" and "not an agent but the personified law itself" (TP 77n). And to make matters worse, in the same essay in which the sovereign is endowed with these contradictory attributes ("invisible" yet "personified law"), Kant also says of the head of the state that he "alone is not a member of the commonwealth, but its creator and preserver" (TP 75), a description that would seem to fit the sovereign if it fits anyone.[46]

This terminological vacillation points to a fundamental problem concerning the source and legitimacy of (republican) law. If the sovereign was merely an agent of the state, how could such a prosaic figure endow the law with unassailable authority? And if he was the "personified law itself," how could this law, identified with the will of an empirical person, be anything other than contingent and relative?[47] What Kant needed, in other words, was "an absolute principle capable of founding the legislative act of constituting power."[48] It is the same need, as Hannah Arendt has shown, that inspired Rousseau's and Sieyès's search for a "higher authority"—higher even then the general will—and that motivated Robespierre's cult of a "Supreme Being":

> What he [Robespierre] needed was by no means just a "Supreme Being"—a term which was not his—he needed rather what he himself called an "Immortal Legislator" and what, in a different context, he also named a "continuous appeal to Justice." In terms of the French Revolution, he needed an ever-present transcendent source of authority that could not be identified with the general will of either the nation or the Revolution itself, so that an absolute Sovereignty—Blackstone's "despotic power"—might bestow sovereignty upon the nation, that an absolute Immortality might guarantee, if

not immortality, then at least some permanence and stability to the republic, and finally, that some absolute Authority might function as the fountainhead of justice from which the laws of the new body politic could derive their legitimacy.[49]

In fact, Kant at times resorts to a language similar to Robespierre's. For the law to carry unconditional force and demand absolute obedience, it has to be thought to come from a transcendent source and assume a sacred character:

> A law that is so holy (inviolable) that it is already a crime even to call it in doubt *in a practical way*, and so to suspend its effect for a moment, is thought as if it must have arisen not from human beings but from some highest, flawless lawgiver; and that is what the saying "All authority is from God" means. This saying is not an assertion about the *historical basis* of the civil constitution; it instead sets forth an idea as a practical principle of reason: the principle that the presently existing legislative authority ought to be obeyed, whatever its origin. (MM 462)[50]

So we are left with a number of problems. First, while constituting power belongs to the general will of the people, this will has no voice of its own; rather, it is always already expressed in the existing procedures that embody it—the existing government. (To paraphrase Schiller: "Wo aber das Volk spricht / Ach, da spricht das Volk schon nicht mehr.") Second, this amounts to a failure of representing, not only the people, but also the free activity whereby a people, in an act of self-determination, gives itself a civil constitution.[51] Third, entrusted to the empirical figure of the sovereign, the law threatens to lose its transcendent character and coincide with the expression of a contingent will. This poses the problems of legitimacy and of a potential weakening of the laws' authoritative force. But the identification of laws with a contingent will also raises another danger, first disclosed in the experience of the Terror: the danger of an absolutely autonomous and omnipotent subject, unconstrained by any law, obeying only its own will, and conceiving of others as mere impediments to the realization of his absolute power.

It is against this backdrop of the theoretical (Kant) and practical (French Revolution) failure to articulate the idea of constituting power that enthusiasm acquires its utopian dimension as a (pre-political) harbinger of democratic community. The expression of enthusiasm on the part of the German spectators is a free and spontaneous gesture, uncoerced by public law or moral imperatives; it is voiced publicly, forming a community of people freely joined together by their shared love for freedom; and it is bound up with the subject's respect for the other, be it the absolute Other of a transcendent law, or the relative other who is the fellow-enthusiast. In other words, what Kant believes he has found in the German spectators is both a prefiguration of an ideal democratic society, and a historical embodiment of the creative, extrahistorical, and inexhaustible force driving progress—that is, the constituting power of moral passion. The example of the enthusiasts thus provides Kant with another scene of foundation, one that avoids the troubling identification of law and violence and enables him to hold on to an idea of justice as distinct from the more or less coercive nature of laws.

Enthusiasm

Yet what is the nature of this peculiar passion, trained as it is on the singular object of freedom? Freedom, according to Kant, has two aspects: it is the absence of dependency on external force or internal needs and desires—freedom *from*; and it is "the property that the will has of being a law to itself"—freedom *to* (GMM 114). We are free, that is to say, if we are moved to action by a law we impose on ourselves. We have already seen how Kant tackles the negative aspect of his argument—the proof that the spectators are free from self-interested motives—by reference to their willingness to risk their lives. A passion so powerful as to elevate the subject beyond petty concerns for its well-being, Kant maintains, must point to a motivational independence from our needs as sentient beings. Indeed, the frame of mind in which the spectators greet the events in France is extraordinary and exceptional. The revolutionary fervor burns away the elaborate web of quotidian attachments, replacing the peripheral vision of everyday life, full of distractions and dispersions, with the sharp focus on a single object. Negatively, then, enthusiasm implies the disruption of ordinary feelings and loss of interest in worldly affairs. But this renunciation of the empirical world is accompanied by the projection of all feelings onto a nonempirical, unworldly object. At the heart of revolutionary enthusiasm lies the exclusive attachment to an idea: "[G]enuine enthusiasm always moves only toward what is ideal and, indeed, to what is purely moral, such as the concept of right, and it cannot be grafted onto self-interest. Monetary rewards will not elevate the adversaries of the revolution to the zeal and grandeur of soul which the pure concept of right produced in them; and even the concept of honor among the old martial nobility (an analogue of enthusiasm) vanished before the weapons of those who kept in view the right of the nation" (CF 155/86).

Aristocratic honor deserves the title of an analogue of enthusiasm because it "coaxes" (as Kant had written thirty years earlier in his *Beobachtungen über das Gefühl des Schönen und Erhabenen (Observations on the Feeling of the Beautiful and Sublime)* (Königsberg, 1764) "many a sacrifice out of us" (OBS 61). Honor may cause people to do rather unpleasant things, such as dying in a duel. As a motivation, it is capable of defying the eudemonistic concerns of self-interest—the pursuit of happiness—and of inciting the self to incur pain deliberately. But for all its ability to override pathological determinations, aristocratic honor is still tied up (or rather tied down) with worldly considerations: the judgment of others and the desire for social distinction. Not so enthusiasm. Their eyes fixed on "the right of the nation"—that is, on an invisible idea—both the French revolutionaries and their German supporters remain completely unaffected by worldly allure. And yet they do feel. What sets them afire is a wholly nonempirical motive:

> This moral cause inserting itself is twofold: first, that of the right, that a nation must not be hindered in providing itself with a civil constitution, which appears good to the people themselves; and second, that of the end (which is, at the same time, a duty), that that same national constitution alone be just and morally good in itself, created in such a way as to avoid, by its very nature, principles permitting war. It can be no other than a republican constitution . . . it thus establishes the condition whereby war (the source of all evil and corruption of morals) is deterred; and, at least negatively, progress toward the better is assured humanity in spite of all its infirmity, for it is at least left undisturbed in its advance. (CF 153–55/85–86)

This, then, is the dual claim around which Kant's essay revolves: "genuine enthusiasm always moves only toward what is ideal, and indeed, to what is purely moral" (CF 155/86)—it is a passion for autonomy, for the right to have rights; and the French Revolution has proven that this nonegotistical passion has the power to override all particular interests and shape historical reality. The exaltation of the spectators attests to humankind's receptiveness to the idea of right. It proves that the republican constitution—the form of government consistent with the principle of freedom—is more than a moral imperative, an idea reason dictates to us; rather, this imperative finds actual support in man's moral disposition, in his capacity to be affected by moral law. What makes enthusiasm so exceptionally important for Kant, then, is what might be called its affective transcendence: as a passion for principle—that is, a transcendent feeling moved by, and itself sustaining, moral law—enthusiasm brings together for the shortest of moments the categorical and the emotional, law and body, the impersonal and the subjective.

Unlike Marx, who sixty years later would fault the French Revolution for having produced, not a proper "revolutionary principle of its own, but only an 'idea', and hence only an object of momentary enthusiasm and only seeming uplift,"[52] Kant believed that this feeling of elation effected more than a temporary release of hot air. Enthusiasm "is sublime aesthetically," he writes in the *Critique of Judgment,* "because it is a straining of our forces by ideas that impart to the mind a momentum whose effects are mightier and more permanent than are those of an impulse produced by presentations of sense" (CJ 129). Kant makes no bones about the political significance of this link between abstraction and motivation, body and pure thought:

> Perhaps the most sublime passage in the Jewish Law is the commandment: Thou shalt not make unto thee any graven image, or any likeness of any thing that is in heaven or on earth, or under the earth, etc. This commandment alone can explain the enthusiasm that the Jewish people in its civilized era felt for its religion when it compared itself with other peoples, or can explain the pride that Islam inspires. The same holds also for our presentation of the moral law, and for the predisposition within us for morality. It is indeed a mistake to worry that depriving this presentation of whatever could commend it to the senses will result in its carrying with it no more than a cold and lifeless approval without any moving force or emotion. It is exactly the other way round. For once the senses no longer see anything before them, while yet the unmistakable and indelible idea of morality remains, one would sooner need to temper the momentum of an unbounded imagination so as to keep it from rising to the level of enthusiasm, than to seek to support these ideas with images and childish devices for fear that they would otherwise be powerless. (CJ 135)

The passage is from the *Critique of Judgment,* and in all probability was written before the events of the summer of 1789. Eight years later in the "Renewed Question," Kant no longer needs to appeal to the history of religion to explain the foundational force of imageless presentations and the feelings they inspire. Like the enthusiasm of the Jewish people for an unrepresentable God, the enthusiasm of the revolutionaries for the invisible idea of right founds a community by grounding social bonds—the ties between individuals—in the attachment each individual forms to an absolutely transcendent Other. In both cases, the transcendent idea furnishes a kind of collective *focus desiderii,* a unified object of desire for the members of a group. The unusual strength of this object derives from its invisible and unimaginable quality: that is, from the subject's inability to assimilate this object to its own modes of imagining the world (imagination is always *my* imagination, my way as a subject of integrating the world into my experience). The unrepresentability of the object thus becomes the index of a force that is beyond my control, a transcendent Other in comparison to which I, as an empirical subject, am as nothing.

Although Kant's discussion of enthusiasm in the *Critique of Judgment* occurs in the context of his analysis of sublimity, it is his first discussion of moral feeling—that of "respect" in the *Critique of Practical Reason*—that provides the proper point of orientation for understanding the role and dynamic of enthusiasm. Kant defines respect as a bivalent passion that manifests the divided nature of the human subject. On the one hand, insofar as moral activity demands the setting aside of personal motives and natural inclinations, the subject experiences the law as a constraint and counterforce: the law "strikes self-conceit down" (CPrR 76); it "humiliates us in our self-consciousness" (CPrR 78), producing "pain" (CPrR 76) and "displeasure" (CPrR 82). On the other, through this humiliation, the subject gains awareness of another—extrapersonal—side of his being which, "as striking down, i.e. humiliating, self-conceit, . . . is an object of the greatest respect and thus the ground of a positive feeling which is not of empirical origin" (CPrR 77). Standing between two worlds, the bivalence of respect is an expression of the circumstance of the divided self, of man's double life as both a natural being and a moral agent.

If we now turn to enthusiasm, what is striking is the *absence* of bivalence and internal conflict. Enthusiasm, it seems, is an entirely joyful passion, devoid of pain and humiliation and even, as we shall see in a moment, of the sacrificial logic prevalent in Kant's other descriptions of moral experience. It is not, of course, that the divided self has been overcome. What has happened, rather, is an externalization of the psychological split made possible through the aesthetic splitting of the action. Instead of a moral subject divided by opposing emotions, we are confronted with a scene divided between revolutionary action and enthusiastic observation. Hence Kant's persistent use of theatrical metaphors: the revolution is "a game of transformations [*Spiele großer Umwandlungen*]," the revolutionaries are "players [*Spielenden*]," and the enthusiasts are "spectators [*Zuschauer*]." Kant's conception here bears some resemblance to Aristotle's understanding of the ethical role of theater. According to Aristotle, theater affords an engagement at a distance with moral activity. Placed at a spatial and ritual remove, the audience witnesses the contours of tragic action and imaginatively engages with the emotions it evokes. The theatrical barrier makes possible the experience of passion abstracted from its pragmatic context and thus furnishes an encounter with emotion as possibility of action. Kant's interpretative divide between revolution and enthusiasm functions similarly, though in the service of moral induction rather than psychological purification, for here too the spectatorial remove serves to isolate passion as the seed of action, as sheer motivational force.[53] In enthusiasm, then, the subject comes to witness the defining condition of his humanity—his own moral disposition for freedom—as both an interior commitment to autonomy and an embrace of its public enactment. This preconceptual grasping of "truth," while dependent on reflective awareness, nonetheless occurs outside of discursive understanding, in the modality of feeling. Kant thus places at the core of his account of reason in history not reason but passion, and moreover a passion that is inextricably bound up with an aesthetic attitude toward historical reality.

This intertwinement of aesthetics and morality returns us to Kant's *Critique of Judgment,* and in particular to his treatment of the sublime. The feeling of the sublime, it will be recalled, emerges when the subject is confronted, from a safe distance, with an overwhelming and thus anxiety-producing object or event. Kant distinguishes two modes of the sublime, and hence two sources of sublime anxiety: the dynamic sublime, in which the subject is placed in imaginative relation to a terrifying object whose might "makes us, considered as natural beings, recognize our physical impotence" (CJ 120); and the mathematical sublime, which turns on the failure of the imagination to comprehend the form of an object, a failure in which the "point of excess for the imagination (towards which it is driven in the apprehension of the intuition) is like an abyss in which it fears to lose itself."[54] The first act of the drama of the sublime thus stages a scene of terror and humiliation in which the observer, placed in relation to external forces out of scale to his physical existence or his mental powers of presentation, experiences his own inadequacy as a natural being. But at least in the Kantian version of the drama, there is a peripeteia in the shape of a second act in which the subject's painful experience of impotence qua sensuous being turns into the joyous realization that, considered as an intelligent being, he commands powers of reason in comparison to which every object of nature, regardless of its size and might, is small and insignificant (CJ, § 27). The fear and trembling associated with the first stage gives way to the pleasurable "arousal [*Erweckung*] of the feeling of a supersensible power with us" (KU 94), and the observer's heightened experience of physical impotence resolves itself into the recognition of his power to violate the natural dictate of self-preservation: "In the same way, though the irresistibility of nature's might makes us, considered as natural beings, recognize our physical impotence, it reveals in us at the same time an ability to judge ourselves independent of nature, and reveals in us a superiority over nature that is the basis of a self-preservation quite different from the one that can be assailed and endangered by nature outside us" (CJ 120–21).

Standing between two worlds, the subject of the sublime experiences both the triumph of rational mastery and the anxiety of sensory inadequacy. The sublime is therefore a complex feeling, mixing pleasure with pain; or in Kant's amazing phrase, it is a "negative pleasure" (CJ 98). "Hence the feeling of the sublime is a feeling of displeasure that arises from the imagination's inadequacy, in an aesthetic estimation of magnitude . . . but is at the same time also a pleasure, aroused by the fact that this very judgment, namely, that even the greatest power of sensibility is inadequate, is [itself] in harmony with rational ideas, insofar as striving toward them is still a law for us" (CJ 114–15).

Like respect, the sublime is a bivalent moral passion that manifests the divided nature of the human subject; and like enthusiasm, it depends on the subject's remove from, and imaginative engagement with, a distant object. But why does enthusiasm not share the bivalency of sublime passion? Recall that the sublime results from an inadequation of mental powers, from a conflict of faculties brought about through the impossibility of apprehending an object of the senses. In enthusiasm, on the other hand, there is no strife of the faculties, because there is no defining encounter with an object to be grasped. Put differently, the sublime turns on and reveals the limits of categorical understanding, whereas enthusiasm involves not the faculties of conception (reason, understanding) but the noncategorical faculty of will. Kant's description of enthusiasm as a "wishful participation [*Teilnehmung dem Wunsche nach*]" (CF 85/153) pinpoints the unique character of this relation: enthusiasm is a drive to action—and thus an engagement with an object in terms of will—that remains suspended at the level of wish owing to its spectatorial character. Now a pure drive to action that does not, in fact, resolve itself into action avoids the dissonance of the divided self in aesthetic (sublime) and moral (respect) experience: in the first place, because it sidesteps the conflict of faculties related to the inadequacy of conceptual understanding; and in the second, because it does not descend into the pragmatic realm where its lack of conceptual mediation almost necessarily breeds violence.

This last point is of utmost importance. In fact, I think it is the main reason for Kant's belief that the enthusiasm of the spectators provides a solution to the political problems raised by the Terror. Recall Kant's difficulty with the concept of popular sovereignty and his, as well as Robespierre's, search for a "higher authority" capable of grounding and containing the legislative power of the people. Essentially, the problem was that of articulating a democratic concept of sovereignty, one that would accommodate the idea of popular self-legislation, without, however, turning the people or the figure embodying it into an absolute and omnipotent Master. As Friedrich Balke puts in a fine book on Carl Schmitt, whose work constitutes perhaps the most elaborate refusal to conceptualize such an idea of democratic sovereignty: "How can a society act upon itself without assuming a fantasmatic agency that 'alone is in full control of all action'?"[55]

The crucial difficulty here concerns the status of the lawgiver, and more precisely, Kant's refusal to personify this lawgiver, and thus to reduce the source of law to the phantasmagoric image of a sovereign master. This is at once a political and a moral problem. According to Friedrich Delekat, Kant's moral theory rests on the distinction between the concepts of *auctor legis* and legislator: "The reference to the *auctor legis* indicates the agency from which the law receives its legitimacy; the reference to the *legislator* indicates by whom the law is promulgated."[56] As a rather dense passage from the *Metaphysics of Morals* makes clear, this means that the moral subject must conceive of himself as promulgating laws that proceed from the will of some "supreme lawgiver."[57] That is, the subject must somehow realize that the source of his capacity for self-determination—his freedom—resides not in his subjective self but instead in what I have called his impersonal personality. Hence Kant's emphasis on the inassimilable exteriority of the law. Freedom is a "fact of reason" whose origin remains entirely mysterious, yet which exerts on us an emotional pull "in comparison to which every object of nature, regardless of its size and might, is small and insignificant" (CJ, § 27).

The Terror reveals what happens when this emotional force is wedded to a distorted conception of sovereignty. In beheading the king, the revolutionaries lay claim to a legality founded upon the general will of the people. Yet "the will of the People," for them, is neither a regulative idea nor an abstract principle; rather, it is a primordial reality that preexists all legal mediation and inheres "in the body of the nation as a whole."[58] The revolutionaries thus reverse the relation between laws and general will that Kant, and before him Rousseau, had insisted upon:[59] instead of conceiving of the general will as *resulting* from laws, they followed Sieyès and *identified* law and will (the nation's will, said Sieyès, "is the law itself").[60] This amounts, at least from a Kantian perspective, to a perversion of the criterion of universalization, for it mistakes the collective and the abstract (i.e., "the people") for the universal and the impersonal (the law). The revolutionaries, in other words, substantialize the locus of sovereignty by creating a "fantasmatic agency that alone is in full control of all action"—the collective self of the people. And since "the will of the people" is constrained neither by reality nor by law, far from providing any obstacle to the expression of revolutionary enthusiasm, it in fact imparts legitimacy and political force to it. Seen in this light, the Terror results from an absence of rational and legal mediation. Enthusiasm, Kant writes in the *Critique of Judgment,* is an "unbridled" passion (CJ 136) that makes the mind "unable to engage in free deliberation about principle with the aim of determining itself according to them" (CJ 132). On the one hand, the revolutionaries are driven by a passionate will to freedom devoid of any conceptual regulation. On the other, this unmediated passion, which in its intensity is "comparable to madness" (CJ 136), is allowed unfettered political expression through a conception of sovereignty that short-circuits the law. The Revolution, in sum, provides the terrible drama of a moral will run amok, of the undoing of respect and legality.

If the German enthusiasts avoid the fall from psychological madness (enthusiasm) into political criminality (Terror) that occurs in France, it is not because of any difference in feeling, but because of their spectatorial distance from events, which allows them to observe the sublime drama of revolutionary action without subjecting themselves to it.

From afar, they can witness the law of freedom that governs human beings and vicariously experience the intensity of moral passion without having to resolve their feeling into action. The enthusiasm of the German spectators thus provides Kant both with evidence of man's receptiveness to moral law and with a counterimage to the Terror. As the passionate registering of moral law, it proves the existence of a link between idea and body, personal and impersonal self; and as a drive to action suspended at the level of wish, it displays the motivational force behind all moral acts, the will as potentiality, unspoiled by the spectacular enactment of violence.[61]

Communication

Yet enthusiasm lives a double life: it belongs to the interior world of private feeling but operates in the public world of communicability. As such, it provides a bridge between psychic and social life. The passionate grasp of freedom gives rise to a public gathering, and it is this intrinsically sociable dimension of enthusiasm that underlies its utopian value as the sign of a community to come: "It is simply the mode of thinking of the spectators which betrays itself *publicly* in this game of great revolutions, and manifests such a universal yet disinterested participation of the players on one side against those on the other, even at the risk that this partiality could become very disadvantageous for them if discovered. Owing to its universality, this mode of thinking demonstrates a character of the human race at large and all at once; owing to its disinterestedness, a moral character of humanity" (CF 153/85).

Given the backdrop of a highly repressive political system, one that denies its citizens the right to free speech, enthusiasm does not simply manifest itself publicly but rather forms a community of free agents. In going public with their feelings, the diverse spectators create a public sphere. An earlier draft suggests the concrete historical experience that informs Kant's reflections on this point: "This *factum* is undoubtedly true and, in the midst of the crisis of the French Revolution and despite its horrible miseries and atrocities, it can be perceived unmistakably in the behavior, not of the pub politicians, but of the well-informed, enlightened and reasonable man, [who shows an] impatient and hot desire for news/papers [*Zeitungen*] as the stuff for the (most interesting) social conversations [*gesellschaftlichen Unterhaltungen*] (which nonetheless are not political clubs)" (AA 19: 604). These "gesellschaftlichen Unterhaltungen" are, in specific empirical terms, the phenomenon of universal participation that grounds Kant's prognostic history. Progress is possible, in fact, necessary, because a unique type of conversation has taken place.

I have already touched on the free character of this conversation, which proceeds on the basis, not of rational consideration, but of the pure passionate embrace of the idea of freedom. The spectators, in communicating their exultation, are free not only of pathological desires but of moral obligation. They speak neither out of pragmatic considerations nor duty.[62] In fact, reason and intention play subordinate roles at best in the expression of enthusiasm. In Freud's words, the "thinking of the spectators" "*betrays* itself publicly [*verrät sich öffentlich*]," that is, independent of, even against, their will, like lapses of the tongue that "betray opinions [*Verrat von Meinungen*] which the speaker sought to keep secret" (SE 13: 168 / GW 8: 394) or neurotic symptoms that "betray [*verraten*] what they seek to conceal" (SE 13: 61 / GW 9: 78). In each case, the unintentional character of the communication follows from the intensity of emotion elicited on this occasion. Enthusiasm—the passionate apprehension of freedom—transcends the strictures of reason and individual will and materializes publicly in speech that spreads from person to person, thus forming a community of free human beings.

It is worth considering the spontaneous character of this gathering. According to the *Critique of Pure Reason*, spontaneity is understanding's free ordering of the sensuous world into its own concepts and categories. Unlike this theoretical synthesis, the social gathering accomplished through enthusiastic communication is free without conceptual mediation. What joins the diverse spectators into one community is the shared pull of a passion that, while trained upon the idea of freedom, nonetheless belongs to the province of affect. In brief, the conversation of the enthusiasts is a spontaneous association of free individuals in their particularity. The spectators give themselves a law—not a codified, institutional law but the law that grounds all specific laws as a condition of their possibility: the law of self-legislation, namely, freedom. And this virtual community—virtual because it rests on the mere potential for lawgiving—is the prognostic sign that illuminates the progressive teleology of human history: "This moral cause inserting itself is . . . second, that of the *end* (which is, at the same time, a duty) that that same national constitution alone be just and morally good in itself, framed in such a way as to avoid, by its very principles, offensive war" (CF 153/85; trans. modified). The communication of enthusiasm augurs a future world community, because it testifies to a universal interest of humanity that overrides all unsociable egoistic desires and founds communality among all people and states. "It thus establishes the condition whereby war (the source of all evil and corruption of morals) is deterred; and, at least negatively, progress toward the better is assured humanity in spite of all its infirmity, for it is at least left undisturbed in its advance" (CF 155/86). A communication that makes no demand, a speech that relinquishes any claim to interfere with the order of things, a conversation that neither attacks nor overturns existing power structures becomes the fountainhead of a gradual, yet profound, transformation of history.

Kant's argument here must be placed in the context of his more general turn toward questions of communication beginning with the publication of the *Critique of Judgment,* where he writes: "It seems that for all fine art . . . the propaedeutic does not consist in following precepts but in cultivating our mental powers by exposing ourselves to what we call *humaniora*: presumably because *humanity* means, on the one hand, the universal feeling of *participation* [*universelle Teilnehmungsgefühl*] and on the other, the power to *communicate* oneself intimately and universally; which properties combined comprise the sociability of humanity, and distinguishes it from the limitations of animals" (CJ 231; trans. modified).

This passage testifies to Kant's attempt to supplement the austere universalism of his moral theory with a less rigorous intersubjective component, one that reintroduces difference as a basis for, rather than a threat to, the concept of community. For *humanity* names a whole that is brought about, not through universal adherence to laws, but rather through the ability of diverse individuals to take part passionately in this whole (to be affected by it) and to impart this passion, to communicate the pleasure of participation. As Samuel Weber puts it, the words <u>teil</u>*nehmen* (to participate) and *mit*<u>teilen</u> (to communicate, impart oneself) convey the nature of "a taking-part and of an imparting that never entirely overcomes its particularity."[63]

Yet Kant's take on communication in the "Renewed Question" differs in one crucial aspect from his earlier treatment. In the *Critique of Judgment,* aesthetic communication, the *sensus communis,* and sociability are connected to the experience of the beautiful, whereas the sublime is said to be bound up with the subject's feeling of isolation from both nature and other beings (CJ 136–37). The "Renewed Question," by contrast, combines the sublime orientation toward a supersensible law with the intersubjective dimension characteristic of the experience of the beautiful. Kant's text thus outlines a model of sociability that is no longer dependent on emotional harmony and the presumed fit between mind and nature, but instead rests on the irrepressible communicativity of an excessive passion. This, then, is the paradox on which Kant's model of history turns: a feeling whose intensity borders on madness proves the progress of reason, an uncontainable affect augurs the advent of a constitution based on rationalized freedom and law.

But what certainty is there that this uncontainable affect remains within the bounds of expression Kant delineates? Who says that enthusiasm's infectious communicativity will remain within the circumscribed sphere of the enlightened public and not give rise to a riotous crowd? What happens to Kant's ideal of communication—to the "(most interesting) social conversations (which nonetheless are not political clubs)"—when "the voice of the people" (CF 57–59n/34–35n) is beginning to make itself heard, the same voice that Kant describes in the introduction as incapable of reasoned articulation, and thus incapable of "conversation"? In short, what assurance is there that enthusiasm, this "blind" affect, will remain reasonable without reason to look after it? It is because of enthusiasm's anarchic nature, I suggest, that Kant insists on a top-down approach to the implementation of freedom:

10. IN WHAT ORDER ALONE CAN PROGRESS TOWARD
    THE BETTER BE EXPECTED?
The answer is: not by the movement of things *from bottom to top*, but *from top to bottom*. (CF 167/92)

Though enthusiasm's energetic force signifies progress, its emotional intensity and immediacy also disqualify it as a means of advancing this progress. Precisely because it is an emotive expression of freedom, enthusiasm must not be allowed free political articulation but instead must be mediated institutionally: progress is to be found exclusively in the development of legal institutions designed to articulate and oversee the universal principle of freedom. Kant's insistence on the authority of written law, while certainly informed by the experience of the Terror, is motivated above all by concern about enthusiasm's intrinsic excessiveness and by the requirements of rationalization, satisfied in this case by institutional rules of application. Enthusiasm's affective excess must be contained within a legal-political framework, its rapturous spontaneity converted into the slow pace of gradual reform. In short, the source of revolution must feed an evolutionary process.

Progress and Repetition

But even if enthusiastic communication remains within sociable bounds, how can we infer the continuity of progress from this momentary embrace of freedom? Recall Kant's definition of the historical sign: for an event to function as a *Geschichtszeichen,* it must point to the past (in this case, indicating that the human race has always been progressing—*signum rememorativum*), to the present (indicating that it is in progress right now—*signum demonstrativum*), and to the future (indicating that it will be progressing—*signum prognostikon*). The second of these criteria poses no problem. Enthusiasm, an event of "our time," demonstrates "a moral character of humanity . . . which not only permits people to hope for progress toward the better, but is already itself progress in so far as its capacity is sufficient for the present" (CF 153/85). But what about the other criteria? Is it possible to extend enthusiasm's indexical range to the past and the future, to read it as a *signum rememorativum* and *prognosticon*? In fact, Kant not only fails to prove that humanity "always has been in progress" (CF 151/84) but even suggests that it has not: "Now I claim to be able to predict to the human race—even without prophetic insight—according to the *aspects and omens of our day,* the attainment of this goal. That is, I predict its progress toward the better which, *from now on, turns out to be no longer completely retrogressive"* (CF 159/88; emphasis added).[64] Crucially, enthusiasm secures not just the existence of freedom but the constancy of its development. The view of history Kant calls "abderitic" allows for human freedom: human history, it holds, seesaws between progress and regress, alternating between acts of freedom and acts of evilness. Yet with the appearance of enthusiasm, the retrogressive cycle is curbed (though not eliminated) and the inconstancy of freedom is diminished. From now on, advancements made in institutionalizing freedom will never completely be canceled out by retrogressive acts, "nicht mehr gänzlich rück-gängig werdend." Instead of simply testifying to the continuity between past, present, and future, as Kant seems to suggest, the particular historicity of en-thusiasm attests simultaneously to their sudden attunement, their prerevolu-tionary discontinuity, and to the abyss that separates the "abderitic" past from the postrevolutionary present. In this sense, enthusiasm is clearly a "punctum flexus contrarii" (CF 149/83), a revolutionary turning point in human history, albeit one that, paradoxically, effects and grounds an evolutionary process.

And yet, enthusiasm will also be a *signum rememorativum,* a sign that reaches into the past. *But this past will be a future past.* More precisely, enthu-siasm will operate as a *signum rememorativum* when read and interpreted by future generations:

> That is, I predict its progress toward the better which, from now on, turns out to be no longer completely retrogressive. For such a phenomenon in human history *is not to be forgotten* [Kant's emphasis], because it has revealed a tendency and faculty in human nature for improvement such that no politician, affecting wisdom, might have conjured out of the things hitherto existing. . . .
>
> But even if the end viewed in connection with this event should not now be attained, even if the revolution or reform of a national constitution should finally miscarry, or, after some time had elapsed, should relapse into its for-mer rut . . . that philosophical prophecy still would lose nothing of its force. For that event is too *big, too much interwoven with the interest of humanity,* and its influence by the peoples which would then be *roused to a repetition* of new efforts of this kind; so that, in an affair so important for humanity, the intended constitution, at a certain time, must finally attain that constancy which *instruction by repeated experience* would not fail to establish in the minds of all men. (CF 159/88; trans. modified, emphases added)

Progress is necessary because the communication of enthusiasm will never cease to make itself heard: "the event of our time" will always be remem-bered.[65] The impossibility of forgetting thus conditions the possibility of progress; there is no future without memory, no step forward that is not also a step back—that is, a repetition. Repetition, for Kant, is not opposed to progress, but is its very modus operandi.

To understand this seemingly paradoxical claim, recall Mirabeau's 'thunderbolt' in Kleist's "Allmähliche Verfertigung." In defining the nation as sovereign ("We are the representatives of the nation"), I argued, Mirabeau's utterance breaks into and alters the political and social context in which it occurs. His speech is a performative creation that transforms the world by changing its horizon of possibilities. That is, once the idea of popular sovereignty is publicly expressed, the network of concepts defining the social and political world (authority, law, justice, etc.) loses its consistency and is reconfigured around the new term. For Kleist, true speech transforms its linguistic and extralinguistic context—it is an event that, ideally, induces a revolution. Kant's claim about enthusiasm's "epoch-making influence" (CF 157/87) implies a similar conception of the revelation of truth. The communication of enthusiasm is unforgettable, because it alters our view of both man and history. In manifesting the power of moral law to influence collective behavior, enthusiasm demonstrates not only the true law of humanity—man's disposition to freedom—but also this law's historical efficacy. "From now on," freedom and self-determination are actual, rather than merely theoretical, possibilities. That is, they are possibilities that future generations can take up and embrace as the goal of their actions, that is, as a historical project. Hence Kant's intertwining of all three historical times: the memory (past) of enthusiasm's unactualized potentiality (present) delineates the horizon of action (future) of coming generations. Moreover, note that for Kant future generations are, as it were, compelled to choose freedom as their historical project. Enthusiasm cannot be forgotten (literally, it no longer forgets itself—*es vergißt sich nicht mehr*). Uncontainable within its historical moment, the passionate embrace of freedom transmits itself across time and keeps insisting, making itself felt as an obligation to action. Like Mirabeau's "thunderbolt," the enthusiasts' utterances carry a charge that affects both symbols and bodies, linguistic and extralinguistic context.

Conclusion

At the heart of his account of reason in history, Kant places not reason but the passion for reason. More precisely, while progress itself is made to depend on institutional organization, as the legal-political implementation of the principle of freedom, the possibility of this institutional advancement depends on the existence, in human beings, of an extrarational commitment to law, of a drive to freedom. In testifying to the power of moral law to affect human beings, the enthusiasm of the German spectators reveals the energetic side of moral will, its dimension as a motivational force. As such, it reveals the extent to which Kant's paradoxical model of history is based on a paradoxical conception of moral subjectivity. The passion that lies at the core of Kant's model of history is the *impersonal* passion that belongs to the subject qua universal agent. It thus expresses itself in the register of the divided self, albeit in ways that undercut the neat opposition between nature and reason commonly associated with Kantian dualism. Enthusiasm exceeds *both* reason and individual personality: while its affective intensity defies rational control, its intellectual origin poses a threat to individual "life and its enjoyment." Casting the subject along a trajectory that transcends the boundaries of selfhood, enthusiasm thus carries with it the threat of violence directed both internally against the individual and externally against the community of individuals at large.

It is because of this transgressive dimension that Kant insists on the necessity of legislative *and* philosophical regulation. For the top-down model that Kant embraces at the end of his essay must be complemented by the left-right topology he establishes in the introduction to his book:

> The rank of the higher faculties (as the right side of parliament of learning) supports the government's statutes; but in as free a system of government as must exist when it is a question of truth, there must also be an opposition party (the left side), and this is the philosophy faculty's bench. For without its rigorous examinations and operations, the government would not be adequately informed about what could be to its own advantage or detriment. . . .
>
> In this way, it could well happen that the last would some day be the first (the lower faculty would be the higher)—not, indeed, in the exercise of power, but in counseling the powerful (the government). For the government may find the freedom of the philosophy faculty, and the increased insight gained from this freedom, a better means for achieving its end than its own absolute authority. (CF 57–59/35; trans. modified)

In interpreting the people's revolutionary sentiments as the sign of a moral disposition, philosophy reminds the government of its responsibility (which is "to its own advantage") to implement legislative structures that articulate, and hence regulate, the people's drive to freedom. Philosophy thus operates as society's higher faculty, as its conscience and consciousness. That is, it mediates between the conflicting forces of political, legal, and moral life, balancing between ruler and people, violence and law, passion and principle. Advanced to the rank of highest faculty, philosophy thus not only settles the conflict of the faculties waged within the university, but also helps to quell, through its rationalizing influence on society, that other and more encompassing conflict, which is the "greatest obstacle to morality":

> [B]ut for that which can be expected and exacted from *men* in this area toward the advancement of this aim, we can anticipate only a negative wisdom, namely, that they will see themselves compelled to render the greatest obstacle to morality—that is to say war, which constantly retards this advancement—firstly by degrees more humane and then rarer, and finally to renounce offensive war altogether, in order to enter upon a constitution which by its nature and without loss to power is founded on genuine principles of right, and which can persistently progress toward the better. (CF 169/93)

But is this more than a wishful fantasy? How tenable is Kant's reading of enthusiasm as a progressive sign, and of philosophy as society's political consciousness? Even assuming that the German spectators are as impartial and disinterested as Kant suggests (which is already quite unlikely), there remain a number of possible objections that cut to the core of Kant's argument. The first objection concerns the location of the spectators. What happens if the spectators are situated not in relative cultural and geographical proximity to the events but, say, in a French colony such as Haiti, where the revolutionary discourse of rights takes on a radically different meaning, a meaning that varies according to the spectators' position within the social field of reception (slave, landowner, etc.)?[66] Put more generally, to what extent can the enthusiasm of a few cultivated German spectators exemplify a moral disposition of *humanity as a whole*? Second, Kant insists on the mediated and aesthetic quality of what he calls the "game/spectacle [*Spiel*] of great revolutions" (CF 153/85), while clearly assuming that this is a spectacle of the real. This raises questions about the possible role of art in the production of sublime spectacles. Is enthusiasm less real, and less historically effective, when it occurs in response to a theatrical performance, or to a political spectacle created for propagandistic purposes? And what happens to the enthusiasm of the spectators if they discover that they have been had?[67] Third, Kant's reading of enthusiastic communication as a disinterested and educated "conversation" stresses its rational and socially circumscribed character. But this stands in clear tension with the impersonal, and in principle uncontainable, dynamic of communication. Consider the following remarks on humanity and communication from the *Metaphysics of Morals*:

> Now, humanity can be located either in the *capacity* and the *will* to com-
> municate [*mitzuteilen*] feelings (*humanitas practica*) or merely in the recep-
> tivity, given by nature itself, for a feeling of joy and sadness in common with
> others (*humanitas aesthetitica*). The first is free and is therefore called *par-
> ticipating* [*teilnehmend*] (*communio sentiendi liberalis*); it is based on practi-
> cal reason; the second is *unfree* (*communio sentiendi illiberalis, servilis*); it can
> be *communicative* [*mitteilend*] (like that communication of warmth or con-
> tagious diseases) and also compassionate, since it spreads naturally among
> human beings living near one another. (MM 575; trans. modified)

To be sure, Peter Fenves is right to say that Kant insists, "that under the reign
of reason [communicability] once again could be saved."[68] But, as Fenves himself powerfully asks, how absolute is this reign of reason, how free is enthusiastic communication? Is the communication of enthusiasm wholly unlike the
communication of disease or strong emotion, for example, which proceeds
without reflection or will? Is the mechanism that conditions the possibility of
a truly human world community absolutely different from the mechanism
that results, say, in the deadly communication of rumors, or the mass frenzy
triggered in moments of crisis?

Fourth, Kant's emphasis on communicative containment is intimately connected to his fear of the masses. As with so many German thinkers of his time,
Kant is wary of the uneducated classes—the pleasure-driven *Idioten* (AA 18)—
whose political immaturity, if allowed expression, is bound to result in anarchy. As Ferenc Fehér has argued, while Kant's position is informed by the experience of the French Revolution, his top-down approach seriously undercuts
his own reformist intentions: "The price Kant had to pay in political philosophy for his own extraordinary sensitivity toward the future dangers of modernity was blocking his own way to the much-longed-for realm of freedom, the
republic, by discounting popular action altogether."[69] In refusing to create a
conceptual space for popular actions, in other words, Kant fails to integrate
into his political thought the very agent of historical transformation that, for
better or worse, was ushered onto the scene with the French Revolution: the
masses.

This points to the fifth and final objection. As we have seen, Kant's model
of progress ultimately depends on his conception of philosophy as society's
supreme rational faculty. For humanity to progress, the transgressive forces unleashed by the Revolution must be channeled and contained—that is, institutionally regulated. But this regulation itself must be reflectively guided by a
proper understanding of the forces at play. Philosophy is uniquely equipped to

accomplish this task, because it alone is capable of converting anomic passions into progressive forces, through the mechanisms of conceptual purification: first, by interpreting revolutionary enthusiasm in moral terms, as a drive to freedom; and second, by overseeing, and thus conceptually regulating, the institutional implementation of this drive in legislative structures. But is it really plausible to assume that in postrevolutionary societies, philosophy can play such an elevated role? What happens when the "conflict of the faculties" is extended beyond the circumscribed space of the university to the domains of literature or mass media? Given the importance of aesthetics in mobilizing emotions, which Kant himself so powerfully stresses, can philosophy really compete with discourses that by their rhetorical nature seem to be much closer to the theatricality of the Revolution? Once representation and emotion are identified as powerful political forces, does philosophy's insistence on concept and argument not seem naive or anachronistic?

Kant's interpretation reveals the new type of transgression that was ushered onto the historical scene with the events in France. What Kant finds at the heart of the Revolution is the impersonal force of moral passion, that is, the force of a passion that casts the subject and his speech along a trajectory that transcends the confines of both reason and individuality. This is precisely the terrain of the modern novella as developed by Goethe in his *Unterhaltungen deutscher Ausgewanderten* (*Conversations of German Refugees*). That Goethe does so in ways that casts profound doubts on Kant's hope for a community of free individuals is the subject of the next chapter.

2 ■ *The Poetics of Containment*

Goethe's *Conversations of German Refugees*
and the Crisis of Communication

While working on his novel *Wilhelm Meisters Lehrjahre* (*Wilhelm Meister's Apprenticeship*) in the winter of 1794, Goethe also wrote the novella cycle *Unterhaltungen deutscher Ausgewanderten* (*Conversations of German Refugees*). In a curious exchange of provenance, the former, which builds on the specifically German form of the bildungsroman, became a model for the great French and English novels of the nineteenth century,[1] while the latter, which borrows from the neo-Latin literary tradition, initiated the dominance of the novella form in Germany.[2] Neither the simultaneity of the two works nor the crossings of tradition is mere accident. Both the novel and the novella thematize novelty, though in importantly different ways: while the novel accommodates novelty within a regulatory framework, the novella insists on novelty's intractability and resistance to symbolic integration.

Goethe's *Conversations,* though by title concerned with sociability and communication, begin with the French Revolution and the failure of traditional institutions. As the narrative unfolds, the threat to the order of the ancien régime is swiftly aligned with a more general challenge to the continuity of symbolic life. More specifically, the Revolution is identified with the unruly forces of desire and its catastrophic disruption of communication. Like Kant, Goethe reads the Revolution as the expression of a passion that is both within and outside history: within, because it mobilizes energies that transform the social and political landscape; and outside, because identified as a manifestation of a passion for freedom, it is independent of the contingency of historical events. So understood, this passion exemplifies an innate human capacity for lawlessness, transgression, and violence. While Kant recruits the resources of philosophy and the enlightened state to rationalize and subdue this uncivil passion, Goethe calls on the resources of art and aesthetic education to sublimate and rework it.

And there is another parallel: the centrality of communication. But whereas in Kant, revolutionary passion establishes community around the commitment to the universal right to political self-determination, in Goethe, it is fundamentally divisive. Drawing on Boccaccio's *Decameron,* the *Conversations* narrate the plague of desire in communication. This plague does not befall communication from outside; rather, it is a pathological development inherent in its functioning. More specifically, desire emerges as the force that drives communicative and symbolic life, while itself retaining an irreducibly extrasymbolic vitality and hence potentially disruptive quality. The problem, expressed in Goethe's novella cycle and fundamental to the genre it gives rise to, can be put briefly: how to respond within communication to that which exceeds the resources of communication?

Trauma

The plot of the *Conversations* is quickly told. The setting is the Franco-German border on the Rhine, around 1793. Threatened by revolutionary troops, a group of German aristocrats abandon their French properties and seek refuge on their country estate east of the Rhine. There, the group engage in political debates that soon erupt into open hostility. On the verge of disintegrating into irreconcilable factions, the refugees agree to ban all political talk and instead tell private stories. The strategy works: as they exchange and discuss tales of ghosts, love, and renunciation, the refugees forget their anxieties and political differences and resume a more sociable tone. The text closes with a longer and highly hermetic story, programmatically entitled *Märchen* (Fairy Tale), without returning to the frame narrative.

Put abstractly, the *Conversations* dramatize the disturbance of a system by a foreign body. The text raises the question of how a certain order of discourse and interaction will react to the intrusion of a radically different element. Will the system succeed in coping with the irritation, through defense, integration, or the reorganization of its own structures; or will the irritation instead overwhelm the system and dissolve its boundaries? Goethe's *Conversations,* that is, recount an existential crisis that threatens to destroy the organized whole in which it occurs.

The survival of the system depends on the making of boundaries, the demarcation of an internal form from an external environment: "An outside begins," writes Jean Starobinski, "where the expansion of a structuring force ends. Or, to put it another way: an inside is constituted when a form constitutes itself by defining its own boundaries."[3] Precisely this definition becomes problematic in the *Conversations*. The geographical setting on the border between France and Germany already suggests as much. But it is the opening sentence that establishes the central theme of boundary as foundation: "In those unhappy days, which for Germany, for Europe, indeed for the whole world had the saddest consequences, when the Frankish army burst into our fatherland through an ill-protected gap [*eine übelverwahrte Lücke*], a noble family abandoned their property in the region and fled across the Rhine" (CR 15).[4]

The sentence is to be read programmatically. In opening his novella cycle with an invasion—that is, with an event that reverses the form-constituting act of demarcation—Goethe explicitly centers his text on the problem of systemic self-preservation. The following events bear this out. As the story unfolds, the irruption of the new and strange (the Revolution) into the traditional and proper (the fatherland) extends from the military realm to the level of the attacked order itself, punctuating the interaction between group members and the relation of self to self. At stake in the *Conversations*, then, is less the violation of external boundaries than the dissolution of internal ones; not the threat posed by an outer enemy but the weakening of the "structuring force" that individuates and unifies the system. Goethe's novella cycle is concerned with systemic traumas, with moments in which the operations of a system turn against it and threaten to disrupt it from within.

Before analyzing these forces of auto-destruction in detail, let me clarify the theoretical models guiding my reading. As the phrase "systemic traumas" indicates, I want to draw on both system-theoretical and psychoanalytic models. The great advantage of systems theory, especially in the version developed by Niklas Luhmann over the past few decades,[5] lies in its enormously flexible notion of system. Systems are defined by, and depend for their existence on, their differentiation from an environment with which they nonetheless interact continuously. In every case the boundary that marks off the system from its environment is defined by the operations of the system itself. In psychic and social systems, however, this boundary is not a physical one (membrane, skin, wall, etc.) but is established in the domain of meaning. The survival of psychic and social systems, that is, depends on the continuous activity of sense-making, an activity that has to assert itself against an overcomplex and asemantic environment.[6] Crisis thus becomes in Luhmann's theory a constitutive feature of systemic functioning. However, this accommodation of crisis, while in itself theoretically fruitful, goes hand in hand with a trivialization of the forms of cultural and societal breakdown (revolution, states of emergency, war, etc.) to which the term "crisis" has traditionally applied.

Here the Freudian concept of trauma is of help. "Trauma" is Freud's name for the momentary breakdown of psychic systems, for the mind's inability to assimilate an (internal or external) irritation. Freud gives the fullest account of this breakdown in *Beyond the Pleasure Principle,* whose immediate historical reference is the widespread phenomenon of war neuroses after World War I. The traumatized soldiers tended to repeat in their dreams the scenes of horrors that had caused their disturbances. Since these repetitions were accompanied by intense anxiety attacks, they contradicted Freud's existing theory according to which dreams, like all other products of the unconscious, served the aim of wish fulfillment. So why did the patients repeat events that caused them such distress? Freud's answer reconsiders the pre-psychoanalytical notion of trauma as organic lesion, which is now grafted onto a new model of the mind.[7] The integrity of the mental apparatus, Freud writes in *Beyond the Pleasure Principle,* rests on the existence of a "special envelope or membrane" (SE 18: 27; GW 13: 26) that separates and protects the mind from its environment. The function of this "protective shield" (ibid.) is "to preserve the special modes of transformation of energy operating in it against the effects threatened by the enormous energies at work in the external world—effects which tend towards a leveling out of them and hence toward destruction" (SE 18: 27; GW 13: 27). A trauma occurs when the stimuli are so strong as to break through the protective shield: "There is no longer any possibility of preventing the mental apparatus from being flooded with large amounts of stimulus, and another problem arises instead—the problem of mastering the amounts of stimulus which have broken in and of binding them, in the psychical sense, so that they can then be disposed of" (SE 18: 29–30; GW 13: 29). The compulsion to repeat thus has to be understood as a persistent and retroactive attempt of the psychic apparatus to bind these stimuli.

Whatever its specific content, the trauma first of all effects an overflow of internal stimuli, an excess of affect that throws the mental apparatus off balance. But Freud's emphasis on economic description cannot be separated from a more narrowly psychological one. The mind assimilates stimuli by binding them to representations, and it is precisely the failure of symbolization—that is, the failure to invest the event with meaning—that triggers the trauma.

Moreover, this failure is not limited to a single moment. The genesis of the trauma does not end with the event that caused it but continues into the subject's retroactive attempts to symbolize, and thus bind, its asemantic kernel. Trauma, in other words, covers the entire complex of psychological elaborations designed to redress it, elaborations that may include somatic and neurophysiological symptoms, but also fantasies, theories, or stories the subject develops about "his" trauma and thus about himself.[8]

Like Luhmann, Freud thinks in systemic terms: the mental apparatus is an operational network whose integrity rests on the maintenance of system-specific meaning boundaries (in Luhmann, these boundaries are determined through so-called symbolically generalized and communicatively coded media; in Freud, they coincide with the subject's self- and world- understanding, which in turn is the product of his singular life history). Unlike Luhmann, however, Freud conceives the relationship between system and its other in dialectical and conflictual terms. Insofar as the concept of trauma covers both the momentary breakdown of the mind's integrity and its persistent attempts to redress this collapse retroactively, the structure of the (psychic) system is fundamentally shaped by that which exceeds and threaten it. Consequently, the breakdown of meaning boundaries, which for Luhmann simply coincides with the end of the system, becomes for Freud a historical and eventually structural dimension of the life of the system.[9] Freud's model is therefore capable of addressing a range of phenomena traditionally covered by the term "crisis" that drop out of Luhmann's theory: crisis as conflict, life-threatening danger, state of emergency, and moment of truth. Above all, Freud assigns crucial significance to the irreducible tension between drive and meaning, affect and language. Trauma is beyond the pleasure principle, because it implies an affective surplus that cannot be translated into representations, into the manageable world of the pleasurable and unpleasurable, and thus integrated into the self-reproduction of the psychic system. Unbound and unsymbolizable, affect floats as pure energy in the psyche, an internal foreign body whose enormous energetic charge overtaxes the mental apparatus, threatening to destroy the system from within.

This is exactly what happens in the frame narrative of the *Conversations*. In Goethe, just as in Freud, the traumatic impact of the event is intimately connected with its suddenness and its ability to circumvent the protective shields of expectation and anxious anticipation.[10] To recall the quasi-Freudian image of the opening sentence, the French troops break into the homeland by way of an "ill-protected gap" in the latter's defense lines. This dynamic of lapse and transgression structures all events in the frame narrative, though with an important difference. As the frame narrative evolves, the military invasion registers as an assault on boundaries of meaning, and the "ill-protected gap" becomes the figure of the frailty of social and psychic orders. Before exploring this dynamic in more detail, I shall briefly illustrate the breakdown of meaning boundaries using its first, and thus perhaps paradigmatic, narrated instance: that of Luise, the Baroness's daughter, who is caught unawares by the news of the invasion while daydreaming about her lover, and who, we are told, "completely lost her head at the first alarm, and in her confusion, indeed in a kind of trance, had in all seriousness gathered the most useless things to be packed and had even mistaken an old family servant for her fiancé" (CR 16; trans. modified).[11]

Goethe encodes the invasion as a gap in the system of codification. For the subject lost in the private theater of her daydreams, the military news is not a meaningful piece of information, but a senseless signifier that cannot be integrated into her mental universe. Hence the destabilizing effect of this event. Luise's inability to assimilate the news, to make sense of what is happening, provokes a surge of anxiety that floods "the mental apparatus with large amounts of stimulus" (SE 18: 29–30; GW 13: 29) and triggers a series of breakdowns: of the imaginary boundaries of the ego (Luise's loss of *Fassung*: self-control, or frame of mind), of the symbolic boundaries of social codes (private/public, master/servant), and, finally, of the rules of behavior structuring the social order.

Luise's case exemplifies what happens to the emigrants. Goethe emplots the French Revolution as both a psychological and socio-symbolic trauma. The Revolution marks the breakdown of traditional mental and communicative structures and the emergence of new models both of communication predicated on newness, and of subjectivity built around affective excess. This story also has a generic cultural-historical dimension. In drawing on the traditional frame-tale structure (most notably, Boccaccio's *Decameron*) to emplot this event, Goethe self-consciously radicalizes an older literary form and inaugurates a new genre, the *modern* novella. Put simply, with the *Conversations,* the novella becomes a traumatic narrative concerned with the catastrophic force of newness and the articulation of a subject that is beyond the pleasure principle, and thus beyond the resources of *Bildung*. It was this anti-developmental genre that dominated the German literary scene throughout the nineteenth century, and not the tradition of the bildungsroman launched by Goethe's *Wilhem Meisters Lehrjahre,* which flourished in France and England.[12]

The Fragility of Sense

The old world that collapses under the impact of the invasion assumes a double presence in the text: on the level of story, or represented action, it takes the form of eighteenth-century sociability, or politeness, and on the level of discourse, or mode of representation, it appears as epic narration. Sociability and the epic are conservative both in form and function: while sociability consists in, and derives its internal coherence from, the repetition of interactive and communicative ritual, epic "discourse is a discourse handed down by tradition"[13] and geared toward the memorialization of the past in the present. In both cases, the utterance's referential and emotive aspects are subordinated to its phatic and poetic ones: what is being said matters less than the way the act of speaking links speaker and listener through the citation and display of shared forms and traditions. Sociable and epic utterances thus (re)produce a stable and bounded symbolic universe—a closed universe of sense, *le monde,* as it is styled in sociability, and *tradition* in the case of epic.

The universe the characters inhabit prior to the narrated events is the "conversible world" of eighteenth-century polite culture.[14] Its fundamental law is articulated by its main representative, the Baroness: "But I can ask of the community in which I live, that like-minded people come together quietly to talk in a civilized manner in that one person says what the other is thinking" (CR 23; trans. modified).[15] I can be asked to say what the other person thinks because we are fundamentally the same, are *Gleichgesinnte* [like-minded people]. I see myself, I feel myself in the other, and there obtains between us a sympathy that enables me to experience the other's experience.[16] This ethos of empathy and equality determines a society grounded in reciprocity: "Everything is reciprocal," writes Friedrich Schleiermacher in a 1796 essay on sociability, "thus there can be no other goal than the free play of thoughts and feelings, through which all members excite and stimulate each other."[17] Every public gesture and utterance ideally enters into this network of reciprocal satisfaction, upholds and reinforces a communicative bond based on mutual pleasuring. Sociability entails a model of the social understood as a stable and equilibrated system of exchanges, as a closed yet living form: "For this is the proper character of society in view of its form, that it be a reciprocal action which runs through all of its participants while also determining and perfecting them."[18]

This form owes its stability to the persistent articulation of its own boundaries. Each sociable speech act newly divides the world into what can and cannot be said, establishes and defines the borders between the cultivated "inland" of *le monde* and its unspeakable "outland."[19] The organic unity of *le monde* thus depends on the speakers' readiness to internalize and reproduce a set of tacit rules and obligations. First, for polite conversation to flourish, it must avoid divisiveness and exclude categorical statements that close off discussion. Hence the ban on topics such as religion and politics: "Everyone used to be so careful in public not to touch on a subject that might distress others. In the company of a Catholic no Protestant would ridicule a religious ceremony; the most zealous Catholic would never let the Protestant suspect that the old religion was a more certain path to eternal bliss" (CR 23).[20]

Second, the danger of divisiveness is intimately connected to the threat of fixation. Since the "conversible world" depends for its existence on the continuity of communication, it requires from its practitioners the ability to move quickly from one topic to another and to subordinate improvisation and self-expression to the drift of public and communal speech. The law of manners, writes Friedrich Schleiermacher, demands "a certain *elasticity,* an ability to expand or contract the surface one presents to society on demand; one must have at one's inner grasp a multitude of topics, and be capable of running through many of them easily and swiftly if society is mobile; and then, easily forgetting everything else, modestly dwelling on a little topic, patiently developing it in many ways."[21] Third, this elasticity goes hand in hand with what might be called a will to ignorance. Tact, writes Georg Simmel in his early twentieth-century sociological account of sociability, "consists not only in respecting the other's secret, his direct will to conceal from us this or that; it even requires that one renounce the knowledge of all that which the other does not want to reveal explicitly."[22] My own pleasure is bound by the other's right to pleasure, which I must not violate. Polite conversation thus rests, fourth, on a "dynamic of self-giving";[23] it entails a sacrificial dimension, the willingness, in the words of the Baroness, "von unseren Eigenheiten auf(zu)opfern [to sacrifice our personal ways]" (UA 1007–8). It is for this reason that Simmel links the concept of tact to that of the gift, conceiving sociable speech as an act in which I give myself to the other. Polite conversation "is the gift of an individual to the community, but one behind which the one who gives remains as it were invisible."[24]

In sum, polite conversation is pure communication, speech whose purpose lies less in what it communicates than in the act of communication as such. Its primarily phatic function is sustained through ritual, which articulates and reproduces, through the iteration of received forms, a shared symbolic world that connects both self to other and present to past. It is, in other words, radically conservative, resistant to newness. Moreover, this formal conservatism is also a political one. Sociability is intimately connected to a hierarchical order, whose system of stratification it reproduces by narrowly circumscribing the class of its participants. Polite discourse is the modus operandi of the upper classes, and its historical heyday coincides with the high point of the status of the eighteenth-century French nobility within the ancien régime. "Nobility," writes François Furet, "had never been so brilliant; never had civilization been so 'aristocratic' as in the time of the Enlightenment, and specially marked at this point by the adaptation of fine court manners to the conversation of the salon."[25] In depicting the French Revolution in terms of its impact on sociability, Goethe thus focuses attention on its quality as a communicative event: the Revolution marks a radical transformation of the medium through which society reproduces itself.

Before analyzing this transformation in more detail, I want to draw attention to another kind of collapse. The crisis extends beyond the social into the realm of aesthetic communication, affecting the very language used to represent it. The *Conversations* depict the French Revolution's effects on literary form, suggesting that the radical transformation of political and social life requires an equally fundamental change on the level of poetic form: the (re)invention of a new genre. Goethe's text enacts its own generic emergence, the emergence of the novella form out of the crisis of narrative representation. As the opening paragraph of the text announces:

> In those unhappy days, which for Germany, for Europe, indeed for the whole world had the saddest consequences, when the Frankish army burst into our fatherland through an ill-protected gap, a noble family abandoned their property in the region and fled across the Rhine in order to escape the afflictions threatening all excellent people, who were accused of the crimes of remembering their fore-fathers with pleasure and respect, and enjoying advantages which any well-meaning father would be happy to provide for his children and descendants. (CR 15; trans. modified)[26]

Tone here runs counter to the reported events. The passage depicts a moment of crisis, but it does so in a mode of narration that downplays the disorder it reports, diffusing its intensity. Self-assured, judicious, and composed, the narrator's magisterial voice introduces a measure of stability that counteracts the disturbances of the represented content. It is the voice of paternal authority, of an all-knowing master who hovers above events, depicting and judging them from a seemingly metahistorical perspective. The rhetoric of mastery articulates itself in three semantic shifts, each designed to contain the sense of crisis and urgency unleashed by the invasion: (a) it relativizes the suddenness of the event by locating it in a closed-off past ("In those unhappy days"), (b) it minimizes its foreignness through the evocation of familiar moral categories (noble, excellent), and (c) it counters the challenge to authority with a triple evocation of the paternal trope and the emphasis on tradition (fatherland, forefathers, father). The opening paragraph, then, does more than just depict the intrusion of a foreign body into a protected system; it also stages a rhetorical attempt to contain the effects of this intrusion. The beginning of the *Conversations* is a piece of metanarrative testing the symbolic efficacy of a specific mode of narration in the face of the pressures exerted by the Revolution.

The mode in question is epic narrative. The passage evokes several hallmarks of epic discourse: the embrace of traditions; the emphasis on historical distance; the resistance to change; the contrast between the dramatic nature of the story and the tranquil demeanor of its presentation.[27] The list suggests a significant homology between sociable and epic discourse. Like the former, epic speech is fundamentally conservative in form and function. Its principal trajectory is the reconstitution of tradition and the evocation of a closed, completed, and bygone world of forms.[28] More precisely, newness enters the epic world not on the referential but on the poetic level, in the presentation of an already-known content. As James Redfield has written of Homer's *Iliad:* "The audience does not ask for news of the fall of Troy but for one of the songs about it. The song acquires a value of its own, and men ask for it, not because they want to know something, but in order to enjoy the pleasure of song. A reversal then takes place. It seems that the event took place in order that a song could be made of it."[29] As with sociability, then, there is a foregrounding of the "how" rather than the "what" of the utterance, and with it, an emphasis on the dual—vertical and horizontal—humanizing power of speech: vertical, in that speech asserts its autonomy over the presymbolic world of events; and horizontal, in that it establishes intersubjective bonds between speaker (bard) and listener (audience). Epic communication functions in Goethe's *Conversations* as the poetic correlative to sociable communication. It is another, explicitly literary, expression of alliance with the traditional world.

Epic form was very much on Goethe's mind while he was working on his novella cycle. Contrary to our received opposition between novel and epic, Goethe considered his own bildungsroman, written at the same time as the *Conversations,* as a kind of modern epic. "I am very much looking forward to the little stories, after the burden that a pseudo-epos such as the novel imposes," he wrote to Schiller on November 27, 1794, juxtaposing novel/epos to novella cycle.[30] In fact, Goethe's explicit interest in the social and aesthetic dimensions of epic art seems to have arisen out of his discussions with Schiller about *Wilhem Meister.* Shortly after the publication of the *Conversations,* in 1797, they began an exchange of letters that eventually resulted in one of Weimar classicism's most important poetological statements: the short essay "Über Epische und Dramatische Poesie" (On Epic and Dramatic Poetry).[31] A major manifesto of idealist art, the essay articulates Goethe's understanding of epic and reflects an aesthetic-political program developed in explicit response to the problems raised by the French Revolution. Accordingly, it allows us to read the breakdown of epic narrative in the *Conversations* in terms of the limitations not only of a traditional prerevolutionary symbolic form but also of a supposedly modern and postrevolutionary aesthetics.

Epic, for Goethe and Schiller, is the paradigm of narrative as such. This is because it exemplifies crucial features of the idealist aesthetic that privileges the education of the senses as art's fundamental social function. Three aspects of this conception are of special importance to my argument. First, its temporality: the world of the epic is a world of temporal stasis, bathed in the light of its completion. The authorial nature of the epic narrator, Schiller writes in a letter to Goethe, "corresponds nicely with the concept of *pastness,* which must be thought as standing still, and the concept of *narration;* for the narrator already knows from the outset the middle and the end, so that every moment is of the same value to him, enabling him to maintain throughout a calm freedom" (EDD 301). In epic narrative, every particular event has already been placed in relation to all other events, integrated into a narrative context consisting of beginning, middle, and end, and thus has already ceased to be an eventful event.[32] Second, the focal point of this world is its authorial creator, who invests it with meaning in order to re-present it to himself—as his world. Hence the image of the epic narrator as absolute master of his symbolic universe, as "a wise man" who "knows already in the beginning middle and end" and relates to his creation the way an omnipotent and all-encompassing God relates to the world (EDD 297). Third, this mastery of his environment is presented as an ideal of the proper relation of man to his world. The operative and highly charged term here is *Besonnenheit* (circumspection, reflection, presence of mind), which from Johann Gottfried Herder onward has meant the human capacity for interiorization and, more specifically, the ability to maintain a reflective attitude toward one's sensory experience;[33] that is, to identify my sensory experiences as *my* impressions and thus as *my* particular way of representing the world to myself.[34] To instill such *Besonnenheit* into readers and, beyond that, to teach them to develop it as a mode of relating to themselves and their environment, is the goal of epic narration. "Regarding the manner of treatment as a whole, the rhapsodist, who presents that which is fully past, will appear as a wise man who surveys past events in calm contemplation; his presentation aims to calm down his audience so that they will listen to him willingly and patiently; he will evenly distribute the interest, since he is incapable of quickly balancing out an overly lively impression" (EDD 297).

"On Epic and Dramatic Poetry" outlines the function of idealist art: to celebrate man's power of symbolic appropriation, the power to make the world his own by investing it with sense. Art provides the purest expression of this symbolic power, and the artistic genius, because of his capacity to create independent (art) worlds, epitomizes this human potential for sense-making and self-representation. But the artist is only the most accomplished practitioner of this craft, and the epic, far from being a merely poetological category, articulates the fundamental relation between humanity and the world. Every object that appears in this world bears the stamp of humanity's symbolizing power—every object is a sign centered on the self to whom it signifies. It is in this respect that the epic's ultimate referent is not just a world but *the* world, conceived of as a totality of representations, as a meaningful whole through which humanity, as in a kind of symbolic mirror, re-presents to itself its own wholeness.

The invasion that frames the *Conversations* gives rise to phenomena that escape this logic of self-representation and in this sense exceed the framework of idealist art. Moreover, it is in response to the collapse of epic discourse that the novella genre is mobilized. The frame narrative of the *Conversations* is a piece of metanarrative that explicitly, even bluntly, emplots the emergence of the novella form out of the crisis of traditional modes of representation.

This shift in genre is already indicated on the most superficial textual level, that of typography. Roughly in the middle of the frame narrative, and immediately following an intense political dispute between two characters, the orthography switches to conventions of dramatic form, with characters' speech set off in paragraphs and preceded by the speaker's name in spaced print. "On Epic and Dramatic Poetry" contrasted the epic and dramatic modes of representation with respect to temporality and affect: whereas the epic's timeless mode of enunciation induces in the listener a state of contemplative detachment, the drama makes events "wholly present," addressing an "impatiently gazing and listening" recipient fully absorbed in passionate identification with the represented events (EDD 295). The frame narrative of the *Conversations* emplots this opposition between epos and drama, thus establishing a dynamic link between represented content and representational form: the narrative is undone by the drama it reports, and the monologic speech of the epic master gives way, under the pressures exerted by the Revolution, to the cacophony of dissenting voices. The reality of revolutionary crisis, the text suggests, exceeds not only the psychic resources of the characters and the communicative resources of sociability, but also the aesthetic resources of the epic. As Goethe would write two years later: the epic narrator is "incapable of quickly balancing out an overly lively impression" (EDD 297).

Yet the dramatic mode is itself only transitional, giving way to another type of representation. Once again, the shift finds immediate typographic expression: with the move to storytelling, the typographic markers of drama disappear. Dramatic speech yields to a mode of representation that is neither epic nor dramatic, neither the monologic presentation of a completed past nor the polyvocal performance of a present conflict, but instead based on the efforts of a narrative community to work through events from the past that still haunt its members. Goethe's text, in other words, dramatizes its own generic birth, and the novella cycle emerges as the literary form uniquely equipped to respond to the forces of discontinuity and disruption associated with the French Revolution.

The New World

But what, exactly, are these forces of discontinuity and disruption? What are the "phenomena" that undo the traditional representational world of epic and sociable discourse? As already indicated, the *Conversations* emplot the French Revolution in terms of the emergence of new communicative and psychic realities: of communication predicated on novelty, immediacy, and impersonal diffusion, and of subjectivity built around affective excess.

The revolutionary irritation enters the text as a piece of news, a media event with deeply disturbing effects on its recipients. Goethe's concern with the communicative dimension of the French Revolution, and more specifically its connection to media, is already evident in his first literary response to the events in France, the fragmentary tale "Journey of the Sons of Megaprazons" (1792). A "parable of our own state" (CAF 516), the story tells of seven brothers, sent by their father on a voyage of discovery, who find themselves near an island of supposedly paradisiac qualities. While waiting for favorable winds, they converse about the "neuesten Begebenheiten [newest events]" and begin a heated discussion of the recent "seltsamen Krieg der Chranige mit denen Pygmenen [strange warfare between the cranes and the pygmies]" (RSM 589).[35] Soon the debate grows passionate and aggressive, and the ship is about to become a "Schauplatz trauriger Feindseligkeiten [scene of the saddest hostility]" (RSM 590) when a stranger appears and, asked to arbitrate between the brothers, instead administers a narcotic to them. The next morning, he suggests that their behavior was symptomatic of an epidemic that has been plaguing the region ever since an earthquake had fragmented the old island into several pieces:

> I assure you, the strange sailor replied, you were completely infected, I found you in a state of a bad crisis.
> And what malady is it? Alciphron asked, I know something about medicine.
> It is the time fever [*Zeitfieber*], the stranger said, which some people call the fever of time [*Fieber der Zeit*] . . . ; other call it the newspaper fever [*Zeitungsfieber*], which one couldn't contradict either. It is a malicious, contagious sickness, which communicates itself even through the air . . .
> What are the symptoms of this evil? Alciphron asked.
> They are strange and sad enough, the stranger replied. Human beings forget about their nearest conditions, misunderstand their truest and clearest advantages, sacrifice everything, even their desires and passions, for an opinion, which now becomes the biggest of all passions. If one doesn't intervene immediately, the thing becomes tricky, the opinion takes hold in the head and becomes, so to speak, the axis around which this blind madness rotates. . . . Then man forgets about the affairs that commonly serve his family and the state, he doesn't recognize father or mother, brother or sister. (RSM 591)

Boccaccio's pestilence has become a media plague that spreads rapidly over geographically and politically distinct areas and at least potentially affects whoever comes in contact with it. The news transmits the initially localized disease of revolutionary debate to other communicative contexts, infecting and eventually undoing them. It is the medium through which the present—this moment of democratic leveling, of the sudden guillotining of traditional bonds and distinctions—projects itself onto space and becomes a truly world-historical and inescapable event. This is precisely what happens in the *Conversations,* where the "incoming news" dissolves the traditional forms of sociability and epic discourse.

Already as modes of communication, independent of any specific content, news and sociable/epic discourse stand in stark structural tension to each other. Unlike the highly ritualized forms of sociable and epic speech, which foreground the "how" rather than the "what" of communication, news purports to have a semantic transparency and to offer an immediate presentation of facts. It thus threatens to close the referential divide between language and the world and thus to destroy the raison d'être of epic and sociable speech: the creation of an autonomous linguistic form and of a territory of meaning distinct from extrasemantic reality. Moreover, this emphasis on information rather than form and meaning is, of course, intimately connected to the feature that gives news its name: its emphasis on novelty, originality, difference. "Information," writes Luhmann, "is only information when it is new. It cannot be repeated."[36] Whereas sociable speech operates within narrowly defined thematic boundaries, continuously rehearsing formulas of communicative exchange, news accentuates difference and the break with received contexts. Hence its strict adherence to the present as the source of meaning. The communication of news operates like the Freudian writing pad, constantly overwriting and erasing old messages with new ones. Novelties are meant to be forgotten, and news is a communicative mode that abolishes past meanings rather than preserving and memorializing them. News further rests on the close temporal conjunction of event and recipient. To write news, one must invent a style that "creates the impression that something already happened, but just a moment ago."[37]

The relevant social link established through this style is thus not, as in sociable speech, between present and past or physically proximate speakers but between geographically remote subjects that become, through the communication of news, members of an imagined community defined by contemporaneousness. This intersection of geographical diffusion with temporal simultaneity implies an entirely different model of communication from that associated with epic/sociable discourse. According to John Durham Peters, the history of communication unfolds between the two opposing poles of dialogue and diffusion: communication understood as the communion of souls, on the one hand, and of the denial of dialogue and the suspension of reciprocity characteristic of the mediated dissemination of messages, on the other. This opposition underlies Goethe's juxtaposition of sociable/epic discourse with the plague of revolutionary news. The metaphor of the plague articulates the fears associated with the uncoupling of communication from face-to-face interaction and its dissemination through mediated messages unanchored in distinct and identifiable bodies, allowing for "all manner of strange couplings:

the distant influence the near, the dead speak to the living, and the many read what was intended for the few."[38]

However, the structural tension between "news" and polite discourse does not suffice to explain the former's traumatic effects in the *Conversations*. After all, the fixation on contemporaneity and novelty did not originate with the French Revolution, nor did it always have the anomic effects Goethe ascribes to it. In late seventeenth-century England, at least, the "world of print had begun its long liaison with the up to date, the latest news, and the present moment, trying to provide a sense that the printing press offered a technology for nearly instant replay of human experience."[39] Moreover, this widespread devotion to contemporaneity has been consistently and convincingly linked to the rise of the novel, not the novella.[40] Acute "awareness of the latest events and a desire for innovation and originality," writes J. Paul Hunter," contribute to the emergence of the peculiar, present-centered form of narrative that we now call (appropriately enough) the novel, and in fact the fusion of the two helps create the cultural mind that makes novels possible."[41] Is there then something distinct about the present-centeredness of the novella? Is the "news" of the "novella" a different kind of "news" from that of the "novel"?

Recall again the opening metaphor of "ill-protected gaps" and its first narrative instantiation, Luise's hysteric response to the news of the invasion. The latter's traumatic impact, we saw, derived not from its informational quality, but from the fact that Luise's erotic self-absorption made her incapable of taking in the news, of understanding and assimilating it *as a piece of information.* This inability characterizes the entire novella cycle. The "news" of the *Conversations* is, in fact, not "news" at all as commonly understood. It neither informs nor is localizable with respect to familiar contexts and received frames of references. Rather, it is an incomprehensible surd that resists integration into the fabric of psychic and socio-symbolic life, indeed, upsets and calls into question the received frames of reference as well as the forms of life these frames uphold and ground. In other words, the "news" of the novella—exemplified here by the "incoming revolutionary news"—is not a mode of communication but a challenge to it. This is the reason for its truly devastating effect on the conversible world of sociability. For if news, conventionally understood, poses a structural challenge to sociable and epic speech, it is also linked to them as a medium of communication. By contrast, the incoming revolutionary news stands outside of, and in opposition to, the conversible world of sociability. Because the object of this news entails the destruction of the contexts and forms of life on which this world depends (traditions, social and political stratification, the reign of manners, etc.), the transformation that the Revolution heralds is not a difference that the prerevolutionary world can assimilate as a distinct piece of information, as news. Revolution cannot register as a difference in that world because it entails an altogether new world.

It is this radical, countercommunicative dimension of communication that sets the modern novella apart from the genre of the novel. Novels' thirst for facts, details, news, and information, while itself responsive to the perpetual disruption of traditions in modernity, also serves a restitutive function: by reason of their worldliness and the fullness of their presentation, novels counteract the loss of context and formal life they record. Modern novellas offer no such solace. In focusing formally on an event that resists categorical identification and integration into a framing narrative, modern novellas reflect the disruptiveness of modernity within their own aesthetic structure, representing the new, not as innovation or information, but as the limit point and crisis of symbolic assimilation. At the core of the novella lies a trauma of sense, a fissure in the fabric of meaning and the system in which it operates—in short, a systemic trauma.

Nowhere is the plague of revolutionary news and its countercommunicative effects more obvious than in the political quarrel between Carl and the Privy Council: "Given the news of the day continually streaming in [*den vielen zuströmenden Neuigkeiten des Tages*], it was equally impossible to avoid political discussions. Both factions expressed their differing views and ways of thinking very heatedly and often disrupted the momentary tranquility of society" (UA 1000–1001). In the ensuing quarrel between two representatives of these factions, mutual recognition gives way to mutual death threats:

> The dispute grew ever more violent as accusations were hurled back and forth, and the two opposing parties aired every issue that had divided so many well-meaning circles in recent years. . . .
> Carl, beside himself with rage, now declared that he wished the French army all the luck in the world; and that he called on all Germans to bring an end to traditional servitude. . . .
> The Privy Councilor asserted in response that it was absurd to think that in the event of a surrender or whatever, the French would give these people even a moment's thought; instead these people would surely fall into the hands of the Allies, and he hoped to see them all hanged.
> Carl could not bear this threat and shouted that he hoped the guillotine would reap a rich harvest in Germany, too, and would not miss a single guilty head. He added a number of strong personal remarks, directed at the Privy Councilor, which were thoroughly offensive. (CR 20–21)[42]

In Carl's and the Privy Councilor's last words, the conversational world of sociability—of ego speaking like alter, of the self accommodating the other—has been shattered by a radical conflict whose ultimate aim is the destruction of the other. The scene stages what Peter France, in his study of eighteenth-century French sociability, has described as the replacement of polite decorum by hyberbolic revolutionary oratory: "In place of the salon or the academy, the revolutionary assembly. In place of the old politeness, the pathos of a new world. The real or apparent harmony of sociable living gives way to verbal battles, fight to the death. In this setting, the patterns of older rhetoric are twisted by events into something new and shocking."[43] Yet Goethe's text depicts a process of communicative self-destruction, the dissolution of speech through speech. The murder threats still participate in speech, yet with them, communication has driven itself toward its own boundaries, reached the limit point of its own existence: beyond these threats lie not more words but actions aimed at annihilating the material basis of communication itself, namely, the interlocutor.

The scene describes the near-catastrophic clash between competing forms of communication. But it also suggests that the murderous dynamic of this clash cannot be understood in communicational terms alone. If communication is shown to move toward self-destruction, this is because it arouses and is driven by forces that are not themselves linguistic: passions, affects, or desires. The Revolution brings to the fore the noncommunicative core of communication, the affective investment that underlies and drives every act of communication. This energy, the text suggests, is fundamentally erotic. For Goethe, revolutionary freedom is above all freedom of desire, and the French Revolution marks the moment when absolute desire, unfettered by social, moral, and political rules, appears as a historical force and threatens to destroy the ordered domains of the social and political. This is clear, for instance, in the description of Carl, one of the participants in the quarrel:

> It is easy to imagine that they had all been unhappy to abandon their homes, but Cousin Carl found it especially painful to leave the far bank of the Rhine. This was not because he had left a Mistress behind, as his youth, good looks, and passionate nature might have led one to believe. Instead, he had been seduced by that dazzling beauty who under the name of Liberty had won so many devoted admirers, first in secret and then publicly.
>
> Lovers are usually blinded by their passion, and Cousin Carl was no exception. They are bent on possessing one sole happiness and imagine that they can dispense with everything else. Rank, earthly possessions [*Glücks-*

güter], [and] all relations/proportions [*Verhältnisse*] seem to vanish to Nothing, while the desired good [*Gut*] becomes One, Everything. Parents, relatives, and friends become strangers to us, as we make something our own that fills us out entirely and estranges us from everything else. (CR 16; trans. modified)[44]

For the Baroness, desire operates within a rule-governed space. Intrigues may attempt to circumvent the norms of society (as in so many eighteenth-century novels of manners), but the intriguers always acknowledge the existence of these rules as the given framework in relation to which one must realize one's desire. Carl's desire, by contrast, is boundless, aimed not at a specific object but at the totality of being: "One, Everything."[45] The passage leaves no doubt about the incompatibility of this desire with the world of sociable conversation. If the organic unity of *le monde* rests on the subject's readiness to renounce total enjoyment, Carl desires just such total enjoyment, a pleasure that "fills us out entirely." To him, therefore, the social sphere—the sphere of differentiation, mediation, and sacrifice—appears only as an impediment to his desires, which he wants to dissolve "into Nothing" in order to experience the "Oneness" of full enjoyment.

Carl's desire is inherently destructive: of the other, whose demands for respect and consideration are mere obstacles on his path to full satisfaction, and of himself, insofar as the (impossible) achievement of limitless pleasure coincides with the dissolution of ego boundaries and the annihilation of the self. His case is paradigmatic. Goethe's novella cycle suggests that the implosion of the traditional socio-symbolic order results from the repeated expression of a fundamentally anomic desire, a desire that not only repudiates limits but even thrives on transgressing them. Affective excess takes the form of a will to undo all forms, to annihilate both self and other. Under the pressure of the situation, the emigrants' capacity for self-constraint yields to aggression, and the fine-tuned system of reciprocity and empathy—"in that one person says what the other is thinking"—gives way to sadistic impulses, to "Lust, ihrem Nebenmenschen tückisch etwas zu versetzen [the pleasure of dealing a malicious blow to their fellow-beings]" (UA 1001) and "dem unwiderstehlichen Reize, andern wehe zu tun [the irresistible temptation to hurt others]" (UA 999). We are dealing here with the same dark passion that the Marquis de Sade celebrated in his works, contemporaneous with Goethe's *Conversations:* the desire to transgress, to harm, to inflict pain. One hundred and twenty later, Freud's *Beyond the Pleasure Principle* would turn this "irresistible temptation to hurt others" into the cornerstone of his new theory of the subject. Aggression and sadism, Freud maintains, are attempts of the subject to discharge and deflect outward an unbearable tension stemming from within. The mind is under constant pressure from an *internal* traumatic agent, the drive, or more precisely from "the energetical real part of the drive, which can never be fully represented and keeps insisting."[46] Aggression, in this view, is the mind's response to its inability to bind and discharge this energy through verbalization. It is a way of acting out, of releasing in bodily form, an affect that exceeds the subject's capacity for psychological elaboration, exceeds, that is, his ability to make sense of, and put into words, an internal energetic pressure.

As Jacques Lacan has emphasized, Freud's discovery of something beyond the pleasure principle went hand in hand with a change in the conception of fantasy, which is now understood to be not only an expression of but also an imaginary defense against the drive. Fantasies are complex representational elaborations, responses of the mind to its overstimulation. Anticipating Freud. Goethe has his Luise demonstrate what happens when this defense breaks down:

> Luise, the Baroness's eldest daughter was made to suffer most, because she was supposed to have completely lost her head at the first alarm. She was a vivacious, impetuous and, in better days, domineering young woman, but in her confusion, indeed in a kind of trance, she had in all seriousness gathered the most useless things to be packed and had even mistaken an old family servant for her fiancé.
>
> She defended herself as well as possible; above all she didn't want to hear jokes about her fiancé. She was miserable enough to know that as a soldier in the allied army he was in constant danger and that the general disruption would delay, perhaps even entirely prevent, their marriage. (CR 15–16; trans. modified)[47]

Why this extreme and strangely sexualized response? The answer to this question is given a few pages later by the Old Man's disclosure that Luise is an avid reader of erotica.[48] Read backward, this information suggests that Luise, at the moment of hearing the news of the invasion, was absorbed in erotic daydreaming about her impending marriage. Luise's reaction to the news is thus characterized by a strange fusion of desire and anxiety. Her loss of self-control (shock, trance) and sexual confusion (mistaking the butler for her husband) results not just from the surprising news but also from the confusion between fantasy and reality brought about by the sudden appearance of the butler. In opening the door and addressing her, the butler steps, as it were, into Luise's fantasmatic space, inserting his actual body and voice into the site hitherto occupied by a figure of her imagination. Thus there opens, from within the framed space of fantasy, another frame (door) through which a new kind of object enters, an object that belongs neither to the order of fantasy (husband) nor to the order of social reality (butler) but instead represents the confusion of the two orders: the butler-as-husband.

Luise's loss of *Fassung*, or self-control, is neither a response to a threat posed to her life nor just a reaction to a cognitive surprise. It is an affect signaling the destruction of the distance that sustains desire. What overwhelms her is the unexpected reversal whereby the imagined object of her desire suddenly comes to life and addresses her. The scene, in other words, stages the collapse of desire, built on absence and framed by fantasy, under the impact of an object that, in seemingly effecting the full satisfaction of fantasy, provokes intense anxiety and a "disturbance on a large scale in the functioning of the organism's energy."[49] We have come full circle. Luise's breakdown highlights the dark underside of Carl's revolutionary enthusiasm: it shows what happens when the fantasy of absolute desire—of a pleasure "das uns ganz ausfüllt"—is suddenly fulfilled. Precisely this dialectic of desire—of a pleasure that is too much to absorb and thus is mixed with pain—leads Freud to postulate a beyond to the pleasure principle. Goethe's novella cycle provides one of the first poetic articulations of this beyond. The *Conversations* emplot the French Revolution as the emergence of a traumatic subjectivity organized around an affective excess capable of disrupting both the psychic economy of the pleasure principle and the social economy of communicative speech. The true danger posed to the system of sociability lies not in the foreign troops that invade from without but in the foreign body that erupts from within its practitioners.

The Poetics of the Novella, or, The Paradox of Exteriority

Thirty years after the publication of the *Conversations,* while discussing possible titles for a just completed story, Goethe dictated to his secretary Eckermann this famous sentence: "Wissen sie was, wir wollen es 'Novelle' nennen; denn was ist eine Novelle anders als eine sich ereignete unerhörte Begebenheit" (You know what, let us call it a "novella"; for what is a novella if not an unheard-of event that has taken place).[50] For David Wellbery, "this formulation merely accentuates what had been the salient feature of the genre since its beginning with Boccaccio and Cervantes. As its name indicates, the novella has always been directed toward the new, that is: the case (*casus*) without precedent which is therefore not yet subsumed by law or canonical narrative; the 'unheard-of' case. The stress on the question of form in the title signals, then, that what stands to issue in this text is the question of the novella form itself: How can the new be told?"[51] Wellbery highlights the fundamental feature of the genre—its engagement with novelty—but his emphasis on generic continuity underplays the transformation this engagement underwent around 1800: the stress on the countercommunicative dimension of the unheard-of event, which distinguishes Goethe's modern novellas not only from the novel but also from its generic precursors. Traditional novellas are fundamentally anecdotal, devoted to the narration of events of merely local significance. They recount episodes from the private life of an individual, "regardless of the connection of nations, or times, or the progress of humanity,"[52] explicitly locating their narratives below the representational threshold of official histories. Moreover, these episodes center around transgressions (usually sexual) that reveal the tension between the particularity of the individual and social rules. This double understanding of individuality in terms of particularity and deviation both affirms and circumscribes the significance of particularity: while the individual and his passions are shown to be fundamentally unruly, a constant challenge to society's regulatory processes, this challenge effects only a momentary and local suspension of rules, leaving the social order as a whole unchallenged. By contrast, the unheard-of transgressions of Goethe's modern novellas effect a full-blown systemic crisis, posing a threat to the survival of the organized whole in which it occurs.

Already with Boccaccio, the progenitor of the novella, narrative centers around symbolic crisis. The plague that rages through Florence threatens not only the life of its citizens but also traditional religious and cosmological schemata.[53] Yet while the plague disrupts psychic and social normality, the narrators remain unaffected, maintaining rationality and emotional control throughout the novella cycle. Goethe's radicalizes Boccaccio's model by drawing the narrators into the maelstrom of the narrated crisis, indeed, turning them into its ultimate source. The plague now becomes a plague of subjectivity, whose core, traumatic desire, threatens the group from within. This transformation has fundamental effects on both the form and content of Goethe's novellas. For one thing, communication, which in Boccaccio resists the plague, becomes in Goethe the principal medium of contagion. The *Conversations* depict the demise of the sociable world of conversation—and with it, the failure of a society built on interaction and communication—that was first recorded in the *Decameron*. Henceforth, novelistic communication, including the communicative link between author and reader, will yield to contamination by sadistic impulses, to the "pleasure of dealing a malicious blow to their fellow-beings."[54] This goes hand in hand with a new model of subjectivity and an intensification of conflict. As Tzvetan Todorov has shown, an act of transgression against customs, laws, and habits lies at the structural core of Boccaccio's novellas.[55] Yet every transgression gives rise to attempts at regulation, and in many of Boccaccio's novellas, the true narrative interest lies not in the transgression itself but in the "clever solutions and the ingenuity with which the transgressors get out from under the problem, that is, with the regulation of the case."[56] This delight in clever solutions—and thus the farcical character of many traditional novellas—disappears with the transition to Goethe. The subject matter of novellas is no longer a soluble external problem but rather an unresolvable internal secret.[57] The obstacle the protagonist encounters in his search for solutions is ultimately the subject himself, even in those cases where this obstacle assumes (according to a projective dynamic familiar from Freud's account of aggression) the form of an external impediment.

Communication that turns against itself and subjects driven by self-destructive desires are two expressions of the more general paradox of exteriority. Beginning with Goethe's *Conversations,* this paradox became the defining problematic of the novella form, and it remained so throughout the nineteenth century. Modern novellas, that is, narrate the system's encounter with its internal otherness, the confrontation between a structured whole and what Lacan has called its "extimate"—intimate yet foreign—kernel.[58] In this context, the unheard-of event around which the narrative centers, far from being some unknown yet knowable new fact, acquires a paradoxical and uncanny character, being both foreign and familiar, new and old, inside and outside. Of course, emplotment of this paradox assumes a variety of forms, depending in part on the character of the system in question. For instance, romantic novellas, with their predominant focus on subjectivity, employ such motives as incest and doubles to stage the self's confrontation with the strangeness of its own origin. At the other end of the historical spectrum, what is at issue in texts such as Joseph Conrad's *Heart of Darkness,* Franz Kafka's *In the Penal Colony,* or Thomas Mann's *Death in Venice* is the dissolution of Europe as a sociopolitical system—the discovery, in its exotic other, of the violence and transgression that grounds its presumed cultural superiority.[59]

The *Conversations* bring out the noncommunicative core of communication, its dependence on the energetic engine of affect and passion. It shows that the "conversible world" is held in place by something other than conversation, indeed, by something that is in fundamental tension with the world of speech, symbols, and representation. The *Conversations* merely highlight the paradox of exteriority that pertains to *all* communication. Luhmann argues that psychic and social systems are operationally and structurally closed, meaning that they are structured and reproduced by operations that are themselves defined by the structures thereby established.[60] In other words, the identity of systems is reducible to the identity of its operations; a system that permits different operations is a different system. The defining operations of psychic systems are thoughts and perceptions, those of social systems, communications. Consciousness and communication, then, are "independent systems . . . that determine, through their own structures, what operations will be carried out."[61] But they are "simultaneously dependent upon each other."[62] There would be no communication without people's desire to speak their minds, and no minds without language to articulate thoughts. Hence the need for a "structural coupling" of these two systems, and for a medium that "fascinates" consciousness, directing its chaotic content into an intersubjectively accessible form.[63]

In Goethe's *Conversations,* the six novellas that the group members resort to telling one another are media in precisely this sense. Their function is to reconnect consciousness and communication at a moment of crisis in which the traditional media charged with this task have broken down under the affective pressure released by the invasion. Luhmann writes:

> The mind has the privileged position of being able to disturb, stimulate, and irritate communication. The mind cannot instruct communication, because communication constructs itself. But the mind is a constant source of impulses for the one or the other turn of the operative process inherent in communication. Only the mind is capable of perception (including the perception of communication). Perceptions remain locked up in the activated mind and cannot be communicated. Reports about perceptions are possible, and, in this way, perceptions can stimulate communication without ever becoming communication, and can suggest the choice of one theme or another.[64]

Luhman's language obscures the fact that for "structural coupling" to succeed, consciousness must be in a particular state: it must *desire* to express its thoughts and perceptions, and it must *control* this desire enough to channel it into the regulated forms of public communication. Goethe's emigrants have lost precisely this self-control. The revolutionary crisis causes the overirritation of communication by consciousness. Blinded by aggressions, anxieties, and political passions, the emigrants are incapable of communicative restraint and considerations for others. Thus instead of stimulating social talk, consciousness has become a source of disturbing noise that threatens to drown out all communication. It is at this moment of structural *un*coupling, that is, in response to a crisis of medium, that the novellas are introduced.

The novellas, then, serve as functional equivalents of polite conversation under heightened postrevolutionary conditions. They are literally media, that is, intermediaries charged with reconnecting consciousness and communication at a moment when these two systems are at war. Hence the double structure of the novellas: on the one hand, they resonate with the traumatic events that caused their narration in the first place; all six novellas are built around an incomprehensible kernel, a sound, event, or act that resists understanding and echoes the dense opaqueness of desire. On the other hand, encrypted into narrative and integrated into the pragmatic context of storytelling, this dense opaqueness loses much of its paralyzing effect and instead gives rise to a desire for interpretation. Transforming the obstacle to communication into an incitement to speak, the novellas thus begin to answer the paradox of exteriority, the problem of how to respond within communication to that which exceeds it.

Enigmatic Signifiers

The first story, in Goethe's own words, a "ghost-like tale of mystification,"[65] introduces the central importance of responsiveness. Dissatisfied by countless affairs, the beautiful singer Antonelli befriends a Genovese merchant who persuades her, despite her initial resistance, to become his lover. Antonelli soon ends the relationship, however, and the Genovese falls terminally ill. On his deathbed, he repeatedly sends for Antonelli, but she refuses to see him. Shortly after his death, she begins to hear mysterious sounds, cries, bangings, shots. Initially, the sounds terrify Antonelli and her guests, all the more so because, despite investigations by police and spies, they remain unlocalizable and untraceable. As time goes by, however, the terror the sounds initially evoked subsides: "People finally grew accustomed to this manifestation" (CR 34; UA 1025). The shots change to loud applause, to which Antonelli, as a popular actress and singer, is accustomed: "There was nothing inherently frightening about it, and it could more readily be attributed to one of the admirers" (CR

35; UA 1026). "After a time this sound dissipated also, and changed to more pleasant tones. They were, to be sure, not actually melodious, but they were unbelievably pleasant and delightful. . . . It was as if a heavenly spirit wanted to draw attention by a beautiful prelude to a melody he was just about to perform. Even this tone finally disappeared and was not heard again after the whole strange affair had gone on for about a year and a half" (CR 35).[66]

The novella both echoes and alters the problematic established in the frame narrative.[67] Like the news of the invasion that upsets Luise, the sounds are terrifying because they elude cognitive or narrative integration. Incontrovertibly real, yet untraceable in source, they are effects without causes, asemantic fragments that defy representational—and thus, psychological—elaboration. Hence Antonelli's intense emotional responses, culminating in the exemplary symptom of affective overstimulation, loss of consciousness.[68] However, the problem is not simply cognitive. The terrifying nature of the sounds is intimately connected to their communicative character. Antonelli clearly believes the sounds to issue from her deceased lover and to be related to her refusal to respond to his requests—the triple refusal returns (CR 32; UA 1022) in the ghost's triple bangings (CR 33; UA 1024). The novella stages what might be called the trauma of communicative desire, at whose core lies the dense and enigmatic call of the other. The sounds are not simply physical phenomena but communications, that is, messages addressed to Antonelli and calling for a reply, and they terrify her not because they are untraceable in origin but because they are unfathomable in meaning. The sounds demand a reply, yet since they occur without the ordinary cues of communicative exchange (identity of speaker, semantic content, expressive structure), they are indecipherable and unanswerable. More significant, what is demanded is the satisfaction of a desire grown more violent and urgent in the absence of a response. The Genovese's unrequited passion survives his death, not as an otherworldly phenomenon, but as an expression of the true character of desire, which transcends the bounds of the self from which it emanates. Desire, once initiated, acquires an independent circulation in the symbolic order, and it is into the gravity of this circulation that Antonelli is pulled.

In sum, the novella emplots the riddle of desire in communication: communication, driven by desire, always expresses more than is communicable; and desire, drawn into communication to address the other, always receives less in return than it wants. Hence the central problematic of this and all the other novellas: how to respond within communication to a desire that exceeds it? Such a response must abide the unanswerability of desire and the surplus of meaning that it generates in the fabric of communication. The task is to respond to a riddle without solving it.

That this is not just a problem within the novellas is indicated by the Old Man's injunction: "no one should interpret my stories [*man soll keine meiner Geschichten deuten]!*" (UA 1016). The proper response to the stories, like the proper response to desire, will not be based on full understanding. What matters is not the illumination of opaqueness but its accommodation, not the solution to the mystery but its integration, as enigma, into the circuit of communication. The proper interpretative response will entail the recognition that there is no proper (perfect, final, ultimate) interpretation. Hence the paradoxical nature of the Old Man's injunction. However, in the context of this "ghost-like tale of mystification," which gives rise to a mad desire for interpretation both within and outside of the novella, listeners and readers alike cannot but violate the impossible injunction "not to interpret." As such, it establishes a structural similarity between story and narrative situation, desire and interpretation: just as the characters in the novella must learn to live with the unanswerability of desire that demands a reply, so the hearers/readers of the novella must learn to tolerate the impenetrability of a text that demands interpretation. In both cases, what is at stake is the ability to respond within communication to something that exceeds the resources of communication.

Significantly, the text presents two responses that fall short of this task. The second novella tells of a response that simply denies the riddle. Intent on serving the aristocratic family that has raised her, a "well-formed" (*wohlgeformte*) fourteen-year-old orphan ignores the advances of a number of suitors, when suddenly strange knockings begin to follow her every step. Disturbed by the sounds, the master of the house (*Herr vom Hause*) (UA 1028) orders their investigation. Eventually, frustrated and irritated by the failure of all enquiries to discover their source, he resorts to "a harsh expedient; he took his largest hunting whip down from the wall, and swore to beat the life out of the girl, if the knocking were ever heard again. From that time on she went all over the house and no further knocking was heard" (CR 36–37; trans. modified).[69]

Once again, a female is made to suffer the consequences of her sexuality. And yet, as with the Antonelli novella, this is not a moral tale, and the orphan girl is punished, not for an avoidable transgression, but for the transgressiveness of her femininity. The sounds that hound her are the expressions of a desire she arouses unbeknownst to her, a desire that has taken on a life of its own, independent of the subjects that provoke and express it. It is precisely this extrasubjective dimension that the master of the house ignores. His response to the problem of desire, the threat of physical punishment, thus succeeds only at the price of completely denying desire as well as the life it animates. Authority prevails by robbing the subject of her energetic core, her vitality and sexuality: "the dear child almost wasted away over the incident and looked like a ghost, although once she had been brisk and cheerful, the happiest person in the house" (CR 37).[70]

The second novella stages the traditional response to the problem of desire, its domination through brute force. The solution fails not so much because it responds to desire but because it suppresses it, thus sacrificing subjectivity as well as communication. The mirror image of this failure is the modern failure of understanding exemplified in Carl's double reaction to the problem of interpretation. On the one hand, Carl upholds a thoroughly scientific viewpoint, claiming that, given sufficient data, all phenomena are in principle fully explicable (CR 37; UA 1029–30). On the other hand, he fetishizes inexplicability, assigning true value only to phenomena that remain outside the reach of reason, interpretation, and law: "In any case . . . it seems to me that every phenomenon, like every fact, is interesting in and of itself. Anyone who explains it or relates it to other events really only does it for the fun of it and is teasing us" (CR 38).[71] Seemingly contradictory, Carl's two reactions—the denial of inexplicability and its hypostatization, science and mass culture—in fact express the same refusal to tolerate the unanswerability of desire and the surplus of meaning it generates: if science denies the limits of reason and communication, mass culture abandons them.

Against this background of failed social, political, and cultural responses, the novella cycle spells out its own complex answer, which in its final formulation involves both an ethics of renunciation and an aesthetics of sublimation. The Antonelli novella marks the first, albeit rudimentary, articulation of this answer by narrating a process of detraumatization. In the course of the story, the horror of the sounds diminishes thanks to the characters' ability to adapt to, rather than resolve, their mysterious nature. The enigma is reintegrated, through repetition, anthropomorphization, and familiarization, into the network of the known. In the last part of the story, the sounds, while still untraceable and unfathomable, have become part of a fictitious narrative that radically alters their tonality: a sound whose inhuman quality was "incredibly frightening" has been transformed into the "beautiful prelude" of a "heavenly spirit."

However, the demystification is incomplete, the riddle not so much resolved as concealed in the narratives and anthropomorphisms projected onto it. Lacking narrative closure, the story, like the sounds of which it tells, simply peters out, without granting the formal satisfaction of an ending that answers the problems raised at the beginning. Yet it is precisely as an inadequate answer to the riddle that the story sets into motion a solution to the unruliness of desire. Turned into an enigmatic signifier, unruly passions gives rise to a *hermeneutic desire* that draws on the refugees' affective excess while simultaneously channeling it into communicative forms. Precisely because they cannot resolve the mystery of the sounds and decide whether the story "was true, whether it even could be true [*wahr sei, ob sie auch wahr sein könne*]" (UA 1027), the refugees keep talking about it and talking and listening to one another. Regrouping around an explanatory hiatus, they thus associate through their collective failure of interpretation.

The Poetics of Containment

The four novellas that follow progressively develop Goethe's twofold solution to the riddle: an ethics of renunciation and an aesthetics of sublimation. The third novella, a rewriting of a French source, suggests the destructive, indeed lethal, nature of desire. Marshal de Bassompierre, a war hero and Casanova, makes the acquaintance of a beautiful shopkeeper, who proposes that the two meet by night, "with the sole condition that she be permitted to spend a night under the same sheets with me" (CR 39; UA1033). Bassompierre agrees and, since the plague is raging though the city, brings his own sheets, mattress, and blankets to the meeting. They have a lovely night together, but when Bassompierre appears a few days later for the arranged second date, he finds, instead of his lover, "two people in the room burning bedstraw and, in the firelight which lit up the whole room, two naked bodies stretched out on the table" (CR 40; UA1035).

The novella suggests an impossible solution to the riddle, namely, the extinguishing of desire in death. In place of the desired body, Bassompierre is presented with a doubled corpse, the dark mirror of his own sexual fantasy. The pathological dimensions of desire, clearly figured here in the trope of the plague, force a decision upon him. Confronted with the destructive consequence of his desire, Bassompierre must choose between death and renunciation. However, the choice is a mirage, for his retreat is instinctual and thus nonvolitional: it is not yet an ethical act. What one encounters here, in other words, is not an instance of renunciation but the brutal demand for it.

Yet there is an implicit act of renunciation in this novella, though it belongs not to Bassompierre but to his lover, who denies herself the opportunity of a second tryst. The feminine character of renunciation is brought out more fully in the next novella, the cycle's shortest. A beautiful woman has an affair with an "ancestor [*Ahnherr*]" (UA 1036) whom she loves very much. They have been meeting for several years when the man's wife finally becomes suspicious, discovers them during their sleep, and, instead of demanding satisfaction, takes "the veil from her head and spread it over the feet of the sleepers" [*ihren Schleier vom Kopfe und deckte ihn über die Füße der Schlafenden*]" (UA 1036). When the woman awakes and sees the veil, she immediately begins to mourn and lament, swearing that she will never see her lover again. Indeed, "she left him after she had presented him three gifts . . . for the three lawful daughters of his marriage and enjoined him to take the greatest care of these gifts. They were carefully preserved, and the descendants of the three daughters believed that the possession of this gift was the cause of many lucky events" (CR 41; trans. modified).[72]

Renunciation is thematically central: For the woman's gifts (*Gaben*) are above all a sacrifice (*Selbstaufgabe*), a letting go and handing over, in the form of presents, of her own pleasure. Moreover, this act is prompted by a prior act of renunciation, the paradoxical unveiling of trangression through the instrument of a veil. The totemistic afterlife of the gifts, which turn the potential disruption of family life into the source of generational continuity, establishes the restorative function of renunciation. Like the veil, the gift of renunciation restores symbolic continuity by evoking the possibility of its disruption. As such, it is a cipher that incorporates the fragility of the symbolic.[73] The gift of renunciation provides the first answer to the problem of responding within communication to what exceeds it.

Once again, however, the solution assumes a mythical or magical efficacy: the beneficial effects of the gift are simply presumed, not accounted for. The final novellas, and particularly the last one, spell out a more worldly and ethical articulation of renunciation. This final novella casts the French Revolution in terms of an oedipal conflict, narrating the emergence of a new community based on conscience and renunciation rather than power and enjoyment. Ferdinand, son of a successful but highly self-indulgent businessman, repeatedly steals money from his father, which he spends on luxurious presents for his beloved. Racked by feelings of guilt, Ferdinand embarks on a lucrative business venture for his father, confesses to his mother, and begins secretly repaying his debt. The accounts are settled again, and Ferdinand and his beloved, Ottilie, are engaged. However, Ottilie refuses to follow Ferdinand to the country to do business there. The engagement is broken off, and Ferdinand marries the daughter of his business partner, a "fine country girl," with whom he has several children.

Desire is markedly associated in this novella with paternal sovereignty and its excesses. After its link with death and the disintegration of social structure, the articulation of desire is now seen to pivot on the exercise of power and, ultimately, the mobilization of violence. Ferdinand's father combines the profligacy of pleasure and power: he spends "more than was proper on parties, gambling, and fancy clothes" (CR 56; UA 1060), narcissistically pursues only his own gratification, and enforces the law while constantly transgressing it himself. Even in his business he succeeds more by luck than by plan. The father "stuffs himself with pleasure of every sort [*sich mit Genuß allerlei Art überfüll(t)*]" (UA 1063), evoking a murderous passion of identification in his son: precisely because he wants "to be like his father" (CR 56; UA 1061) and enjoy himself the way he does, Ferdinand begins to see him as a rival (*Nebenbuhler*) (UA 1063) who constantly obstructs him.

This more specific delineation of patriarchal desire finally engenders a solution we are encouraged to accept as viable. The shift from feminine to masculine renunciation realigns renunciation with the domain of law and authority. True renunciation, the text suggests, depends upon its establishment as a principle whose authority is absolute, superseding the claims to power of all those subject to it. Only thus is the irrational reliance on magic overcome and the ethical achieved:

> I met him [Ferdinand] in later years, surrounded by a large, handsome family. . . . Even as a husband and father he made a habit of often denying himself something that would have given him pleasure; simply in order not to get out of practice of such an admirable virtue; and his sole principle of education was, so to speak, that his children must be able, even on the spur of the moment, to renounce something. . . . And so the eldest, on his own initiative, often used to allow a special piece of fruit or some other delicacy to pass. . . . He seemed indifferent to everything and permitted them almost unbridled freedom, except that once a week he would get the notion that everything had to happen on the dot. Then first thing in the morning the clocks were synchronized, everyone received his orders for the day, chores and amusements were piled up, and no one was allowed to miss a second. (CR 68–69)[74]

In subjecting himself to the principle he sets in place, Ferdinand renounces authority in favor of law. In so doing, he institutes the transcendence of paternal authority and with it, the transcendence of law and principle. The novella thus narrates what Lacan has called a shift from the real to the symbolic father, from the father as incarnation of the law to the father as its representative. This image of renunciation as encapsulated in and subject to principle is the novella cycle's final answer to the riddle of desire with which it began. And yet this response does not do away with the riddle altogether. Ferdinand's law, while based on principle and thus itself rational, is held in place by an arbitrary invocation whose irrationality registers the unanswerable character of desire.

Ferdinand's "sole principle of education" orchestrates a program of ethical training designed to free himself and his family from the constraints of desire. This is also the program of the novella cycle as a whole, which stages a shift from the revolutionary and chaotic conception of freedom as freedom *of* desire to an ethical model of freedom conceived of as freedom *from* desire. But the text does not end with the novella cycle or with the ethics of renunciation that it argues for. The *Conversations* close with a longer and highly hermetic story, programmatically titled *Märchen* (Fairy Tale), without returning to the frame narrative. With the beginning of *Märchen,* we are no longer within the generic bounds of the novella. In moving beyond the narrative frame, the text has also moved beyond the ethics of renunciation and into an aesthetics of sublimation built around the conception of poetic language as symbol.

Märchen exemplifies the indecipherability of the true symbol, as Goethe understood it: it is infinitely interpretable and inexhaustibly meaningful. It can be appreciated, Wilhelm von Humboldt writes in a letter to Goethe, only by readers who are willing "to love the form for the sake of the form. Everyone else will want to downgrade it to a mere allegory."[75] Humboldt touches here on the basic rhetorical opposition of Weimar aesthetics: on the one hand, allegory, which can be decoded and is thus rhetorical and conventional; on the other, the symbol, whose infinite interpretability is taken to be a momentary revelation of the inexpressibility of human freedom.[76] *Märchen* is symbolic in precisely this sense: "It was indeed a difficult task," writes Goethe in response to Humboldt, "to be at one and the same time meaningful and uninterpretable [*bedeutend und deutungslos*]."[77] And in a letter to Schiller we read that *Märchen* is a "product of the imagination" by means of which the "*Conversations* as it were taper off into infinity [*ins Unendliche auslaufen*]."[78]

As such, it reveals the implicit meaning of the Old Man's injunction "Don't interpret!": Do not stop interpreting! The conversion of passion into hermeneutic desire, already initiated in the earlier injunction, is now brought to completion. The unruliness of desire is transformed into the inexhaustibility of interpretation, and the ethics of renunciation is complemented by an aesthetics of sublimation. This aesthetic carries considerable ideological weight, for *Märchen,* with its aesthetics of the symbol, is a central text in the tradition of literary exegesis and analysis that Goethe himself helped to inaugurate.[79] We have moved without pause from the countryside and Carl's boundless love of freedom to the lecture halls of academia and the Germanist's inexhaustible love of Goethe.

3 ■ *Border Narratives*

Kleist's *Michael Kohlhaas*

Wilhelm Grimm did well to warn Kleist's readers against judging his stories "according to the pattern of a narrative voice that is modeled on the elegant social tone."[1] Like all of Kleist's novellas, *Michael Kohlhaas* lacks the air of a tale that can be told, to the delight of its listeners, in the conversational atmosphere of a salon. This resistance to the smoothness of conversational form is nowhere more obvious than in the margins of the text. Kleist does away with the framed tale narrative that dominates the traditional novella from Boccaccio to Goethe, and in so doing breaks with the genre's tendency to depict "fictive situations of oral communication."[2] Instead of a cycle of novellas framed by the situation of its telling, Kleist gives us a single story with clearly defined textual borders.[3]

This substitution of borders for frames does more than abolish the illusion of orality; it signals the text's pragmatic aspirations, the relation to the historical and political domain it aims to engage in. To gauge this dimension, it is necessary to note that Kleist nevertheless retains one central feature of the generic tradition. Like Goethe, he situates his story explicitly in a historical context: references to official history appear at the beginning and the end, framing the tale of Kohlhaas's rebellion. The crucial difference concerns the way inside and outside, novella and history, are related to each other. In Goethe, as we saw, the narrative logic is essentially one of mediation, of bridging a gap between embedded narrative (story of individual) and frame narrative (world history); the text assigns to literature the task of compensating for a traumatic world-historical event by restoring some measure of sociability through the act of storytelling. Read against this background, the peculiar framing in *Michael Kohlhaas* signals a programmatic departure from Goethe's narrative of compromise. Instead of de-dramatizing the gap between story and history, *Michael Kohlhaas* explicitly draws the textual borders that distinguish the novella from world history. This act of demarcation is perhaps most striking in the concluding passage in which the chronicler, in a deprecatory tone, refers to events that lie outside the world presented in the novella. After his triumphant revenge upon the Elector of Saxony, Kohlhaas is decapitated:

> So ends the hi/story [*Geschichte*] of Kohlhaas. Amid the general lamentation of the people, his body was laid in a coffin; and while the bearers lifted it from the ground to carry it to the graveyard in the outskirts of the city for decent burial, the Elector of Brandenburg called the dead man's sons to him and, instructing the Archchancellor to enroll them in his school for pages, dubbed them knights on the spot. Shortly thereafter the Elector of Saxony returned to Dresden, shattered in body and soul; *what happened subsequently there must be sought in history* [*wo man das Weitere in der Geschichte nachlesen muß*]. Some hale and hearty descendants of Kohlhaas, however, were still living in Mecklenburg in the last century. (MK/G 182–83; trans. modified, emphasis added)[4]

What does it mean for the text first explicitly to announce the end of Kohlhaas's story and then to move on, within the same paragraph, to refer to the effects of this story on Kohlhaas's descendants and on the elector? Why this double end? To begin with, note that the concluding lines extend Kohlhaas's rebellion beyond his death: while the knighting of his sons gratifies his quest for public recognition, his attack on the elector lives on in the text's withholding of information about his fate. Moreover, the full force of this narrative aggression becomes evident in the historical records to which the narrator directs the reader's attention. For if we look for *das Weitere in der Geschichte,* we learn that the actual elector disappears from the history books shortly after the events recounted in Kleist's story: "The model for Kleist's character, the elector Johann Friedrich the Magnanimous, was defeated by Emperor Charles V on April 24, 1547. . . . On May 19, 1547, he renounced his electorate for himself and his heirs in favor of his cousin Moritz, Count of Saxony."[5] Given the demiurgic tone of the concluding lines of Kleist's novella, which implicitly attribute the elector's downfall to Kohlhaas, its end can thus be read as an expression of Kleist's ambition to extend the reach of fiction into the domain of history, which he does here by inscribing Kohlhaas into it and excising the elector from it. *Michael Kohlhaas,* in short, seeks to rewrite history.

Moreover, Kohlhaas's aggression against political authority is mirrored on a discursive level in the novella's aggression against historiographic authority, as the striking repetition, within a few lines, of the word *Geschichte* suggests.[6] Repetition clearly functions here as a mark of differentiation, allowing the text to draw the line between itself and another discourse. The two hi/stories differ not only with respect to their subject matter but also in terms of genre and provenance. The *Geschichte von Kohlhaas* is the fictional text we hold in our hands as we are reading the concluding passage; the *Geschichte* we are referred to if we want to read about the elector's fate, on the other hand, is an anonymous historical text, or even historiography as such, as the extremely vague "in der Geschichte" suggests. Both texts are associated with specific styles and affective intensities. Compared to the densely dramatized end of Kohlhaas's hi/story, which terminates and fulfills, through a play of face-to-face gestures, the horse dealer's labyrinthine search for recognition and revenge, the vague reference to "the history" recorded in official history has a clearly anticlimactic effect. Thus two seemingly contradictory operations seem to intersect at the end: on the one hand, the end juxtaposes, and thus draws a line of demarcation between, aesthetic eventfulness and effete historicity; on the other, the possibility of such a demarcation seems to be denied, and the border between fiction and historiography blurred, by the casting of the story as a causal determinant of the history that follows it. The point, as we shall see, is that fiction is intended to play this causal role *as fiction;* that is, the novella's pragmatic force is made to depend upon its poetic resources.

While a full treatment of the interrelations between poetics and historicity requires a more detailed interpretation of the end, the terms of this opposition are already prefigured in the title of Kleist's novella: *Michael Kohlhaas (Aus einer alten Chronik).* What looks, on the face of it, like yet another instance of the rhetoric of factuality widespread in eighteenth-century fiction is in fact an expression of something far more subversive. The conventional reading of the title in terms of authentication is paradoxically disturbed by the very term that seems to solidify it: the preposition *aus* (from, taken from). Unlike the much more common *nach,* which would have constructed a rather loose relation of similarity between the novella and the chronicle, *aus* qualifies this relation in two additional ways: First, in pointing to an act that separates, and hence isolates, the novella from its source; and second, by emphasizing the uneven size of the two texts, implying that the novella is only part of the chronicle. The preposition thus calls attention to the fact that Kohlhaas's story derives from another narrative dealing with a broader and more general subject. Indeed, the central subject of a chronicle is the history of some town, region, or institution, not the life of a human being.[7] Individuals are mentioned in chronicles only insofar as they have some bearing on its larger subject, and thus are typically high representatives of state or church. Hence the question encoded in the title: how did a horse dealer get into the chronicle from which the narrator claims to derive his story? Simply put: how did Michael Kohlhaas enter history?

The question speaks to the conditions of possibility of a given narrative and thus involves, in David Miller's formulation, the problem of narratibility. In *Narrative and Its Discontents,* Miller defines the narratable as "the instances of disequilibrium, suspense, and general insufficiency from which a given narrative appears to arise."[8] Although Miller is exclusively concerned with the internal dynamics of narrative,[9] the title of Kleist's novella induces us to push Miller's search for "the conditions that make narrative possible"[10] back to the moment where events enter discourse. And it is precisely to this question of *historical* narratability that the narrator draws our attention in the introductory paragraph, albeit in a curiously paradoxical way. Consider the relationship between norms and historical memory in the following lines.

> Until his thirtieth year this *extraordinary* man would have been *thought the very model of a good citizen.* In a village that still bears his name, he owned a farm on which he quietly earned a living by his trade; the children with whom his wife presented him were brought up in the fear of God to be industrious and honest; there was not one of his neighbors who had not benefited from his benevolence or his fair-mindedness—*the world, in short, would have had the obligation to bless his memory, if he had not carried one virtue to excess* [*die Welt würde sein Andenken habe segnen müssen, wenn er in seiner Tugend nicht ausgeschweift hätte*]. But his sense of justice turned him into a brigand and a murderer. (MK/G 87; trans. modified, emphasis added)[11]

Husband, father, respected neighbor, and owner of a flourishing horse trade—prior to his conflict with the authorities, Kohlhaas stands out as an individual only to the extraordinary extent to which he falls in with the norms of his society. What is most curious about this passage, however, is the way the narrator inverts, in the concluding lines, the relationship between Kohlhaas's life and the novella we read. For regardless of how much the world would have had "the obligation to revere his memory," it would not have been able to do so. For the world to recall the horse trader's life, it had to be recorded. But how likely was it for a happily married trader from the sixteenth century to be mentioned in any historical record besides the baptismal registers of the church or the land registers of the town? Given the alleged historical character of the text, then, the narrator might be said to disavow what makes his story possible: it is only because Kohlhaas "carried one virtue to excess" that he can tell a story about him.

And this is not the only instance of disavowal. The claim that Kohlhaasen-brück is named after Kohlhaas, phrased in such a way as to suggest that even as a virtuous citizen, he was able to inscribe his name in history, is inconsistent with the later claim that "Kohlhaasenbrück, the place *after which the horse dealer was named,* was situated in Brandenburg" (MK/G 158; emphasis added).[12] Like a Freudian slip, the narrator's pronouncements reveal the truth they are meant to conceal: for someone like Kohlhaas, access to historical memory requires an act of transgression. To enter history, that is, Kohlhaas had to cross the borders of the law. His position in history thus resembles the fate of the "infamous men" described by Michel Foucault:

> What rescues them from the darkness of night where they would, and still should perhaps, have been able to remain, is an encounter with power: without this collision, doubtless there would no longer be a single word to recall their fleeting passage. . . . All these lives, which were destined to pass beneath all discourse and to disappear without ever being spoken, have only been able to leave behind traces—brief, incisive, and often enigmatic—at the point of their instantaneous contact with power.[13]

Like the records of the infamous men, Kleist's text is located at the point of collision between individual and authorities. Yet unlike the former, the novella explicitly extends this conflict to the discursive level, calling attention to the political mechanisms that determine historical narratability. If Kohlhaas can enter the chronicle only by violating the law, it follows that the structure of the historical record cannot be grasped without reference to the state.[14] The fiction of factuality thus functions as a device for denaturalizing the discourse of history, which is shown to be as moribund as the political institutions against which Kohlhaas rebels. Kleist's novella accordingly stages a double insurrection against two forms of historical petrification: the Saxon bureaucratic state machinery, reminiscent of the Prussian state machinery in the "Allmähliche Verfertigung," and the mausoleum of official historiography, which entombs the energetic character of contingent occurrences in the dead semiotics of the archive.

Hence the pointedly agonistic quality of the end, which marks the culmination of the novella's double insurrection. In the *Diplomatische und curieuse*

Nachlese der Historie von Ober-Sachsen, und angrentzenden Ländern (Diplomatic and Curious Supplement to the History of Upper Saxony and its Neighboring Countries) that Kleist used, the story of Kohlhaas is only a skip in the march of the powerful, a fragment that momentarily disrupts the homogeneity of official historiography. Contained within the continuity of the chronicle that encloses it, it is no more than a marginal episode. In *Michael Kohlhaas,* on the other hand, this margin is magnified to such an extent as to become a veritable countertext to the authoritative writing of history. Moved to center stage, the narrative of Kohlhaas's rebellion pushes the official history to the text's margin, where it is only cited to establish its utter insignificance. The final laconic reference to *die Geschichte* signals the culmination of this reversal, in that it triumphantly announces Kohlhaas's victory over the elector and the novella's victory over the chronicle. *Michael Kohlhaas* cites history in order to dramatize its own utterance as a breaking into another text.

This mechanism clearly resonates with the principle of revolutionary speech analyzed in the case of the Mirabeau episode, discussed in the Introduction. Mirabeau's struggle with the Master of Ceremonies returns in the guise of Kleist's struggle with the official chronicle, from which the prerogative of historical determination is wrested. Under the sign of Michael Kohlhaas, Kleist stages a narrative insurrection that doubles the political insurrection of his protagonist. Drawing their charge from an agonistic encounter with an other (elector, chronicle) whose petrified semiotic they seek to explode, *Michael Kohlhaas* and Michael Kohlhaas, the text and the protagonist, both operate as energetic signs in the precise sense indicated above. As an expression of the inexorable logic of such signs, in the final confrontation between Kohlhaas and the elector, in which Kohlhaas withholds from the elector a piece of writing the latter desperately desires, the elector suffers a deanimation equivalent to that of the Master of Ceremonies. *Michael Kohlhaas* is Kleist's thunderbolt, his stab at truly revolutionary writing.

Exceptional Narratives

An "outside begins where the expansion of a structuring force ends," Jean Starobinski writes. "Or, to put it another way: an inside is constituted when a form constitutes itself by defining its own boundaries."[15] As we have seen, this act of self-assertion assumes agonistic form in Kleist's story. The boundary, potentially also a "locus of exchange (or) of adjustment" between inside and outside,[16] functions primarily as a kind of medieval standard: contact is synonymous with conflict. This stress on confrontation signals Kleist's performative semiotics, his conception of the sign as radiating beyond the bounds of its articulation, but it does not yet tell us how the novella is to achieve this goal. To understand the dynamics of the "structuring force" that asserts itself so vehemently at the beginning and the end, it is necessary to move from an intertextual to an intratextual level, from considering the relation between the novella and other texts to analyzing the novella's internal structure. Significantly, the text features the act of border crossing as an aesthetic operation, as the carving of one form, or plot, out of another: "He rode abroad one day with a string of young horses, all fat and glossy-coated, and was *just* turning over in his mind how he would use the profit he hoped to make on them at the fairs—part of it, like the good manager he was, to get new profits, but part, too, *for present enjoyment—when* he reached the Elbe, and near an imposing castle standing in Saxon territory he came upon a toll gate that he had never found on that road before" (MK/G 88; trans. modified, emphases added).[17]

The sentence, the first after the exposition, triggers the irruption of the novelistic plot into the plot of everyday life. Kohlhaas's encounter with the toll gate initiates a series of events that quickly dissolve all bonds between the horse trader and the private sphere: he loses his wife, sells his house, sends away his children, and gives up his business. While the first part of the novella emplots this dismantling of Kohlhaas's private existence, the first sentence already points to, and in a way stages, the impending conflict through the sharp juxtaposition of two temporalities. The sentence literally confronts two forms of the present—the *Gegenwart* and the *als*—with the colon serving as a graphic boundary signaling the absence of mediation, syntactical and causal, between the two terms.

Kohlhaas's notion of the *Gegenwart* epitomizes his sense of time prior to his encounter with the toll gate. For the successful horse dealer on his way to yet another fair, time is characterized by a sense of repetitive similarity that allows for its predictability. Hence the ease with which Kohlhaas expands the notion of the present into the future: relying on his experience with earlier fairs, he assumes what has yet to be done to already be completed, forgetting about the immediate present (*gerade*) in contemplatively enjoying a present (the *Genuß der Gegenwart*) that actually lies in the future. The time of the *Gegenwart,* then, is the homogeneous time of everyday life, a time shaped by regularity, predictability, and pragmatic satisfactions, yet also marked by a certain forgetfulness of time.

The sudden appearance of the toll gate interrupts the diachronic stability of everyday life, introducing a truly new element, the unforeseen and surprising, and, along with it, a new form of temporality and affect. Unlike the *Gegenwart* of Kohlhaas's previous life, which denotes an expanse of time, the *als* that marks the sudden appearance of the toll gate stands for a much more emphatic notion of the present, for a present reduced to the magnitude of a moment. The scene, in other words, stages the intrusion of the time of the event, of time as a turning point,[18] and this will prove to be paradigmatic for the entire novella. As the dispute at the border develops into a full-fledged rebellion, the predictable narrative of everyday life gives way to a narrative marked by sudden decisions and surprising turning points.[19] The first sentence thus has a programmatic function: through it, the novella signals its own commitment to an *energetic* notion of time, one in which time is conceived of as a medium of change, rather than one of sequence, and is associated with intense affect.

But this energetic time not only stands in opposition to everyday life; it also suspends the regularities of law and political administration. Kohlhaas himself points to the interconnectedness of personal and juridico-political orders when he asserts, in his dispute with Luther, that he needs "the protection of the law if [his] peaceful calling is to prosper" (MK/G 125; MK 78). The "enjoyment of the present" is intimately connected with the ordinary administration of the law; it depends on the uncontested power of the state. And it is this power, which under normal conditions silently secures the flow of daily activities, that becomes perceptible with the toll gate incident. If Kohlhaas's initial peace of mind rests on the state's exclusive regulation of violence, his subsequent rebellion challenges this monopoly and makes transparent the violent foundation of the state.[20] Kohlhaas's actions thus inaugurate a state of exception, and the text that chronicles his exploits is an exploration of the problems posed by this state: the status of sovereignty, the relation between violence and law, and the place of the individual in the body politic.

On one level, then, the turnpike functions as a symbolic border separating the domain of daily life and ordinary administration from that of the state of exception. But the turnpike is a border in a yet more radical sense:

"What's new then? [*Was gibts hier Neues?*]" [Kohlhaas asked] when the keeper, after a good while, emerged from the house. "Sovereign privilege,' said the keeper, opening the way, "granted to the Junker Wenzel von Tronka."—"Oh?" said Kohlhaas. "So the Junker is called Wenzel?" And he contemplated the castle that with shining turrets looked out across the fields.—"Is the old master [*alte Herr*] dead?" "Died of a stroke," the tollbooth keeper replied, raising the barrier.—"A pity," said Kohlhaas. "A fine old gentleman who enjoyed traffic among people, helped trade along whenever he could [*ein würdiger alter Herr, der seine Freude am Verkehr der Menschen hatte, Handel und Wandel, wo er nur vermochte, forthalf*] and once had a stone causeway built because of a stallion of mine, back there where the road goes into the village, broke its leg." . . . "Yes, friend," he added as the keeper, cursing the weather, muttered at him to hurry up, "if that pole had stayed in the forest it would have been better for both of us." (trans. mine)[21]

The imagery of the passage casts an almost mythical light on the world prior to the border incident. It is a world of uninhibited traffic and mobility, in which individual activities effortlessly cohere into an ordered whole. At the core of this world, grounding its unity, lies the shared commitment to a single principle: a principle of fairness and symmetry, whose continuance is safeguarded by an old master, who indeed is its official representative. If this is a world of justice, justice here is also associated with the balance of nature: under the old master, the pole was a tree in the forest, firmly rooted in an organic context. The tree's transformation into a toll gate—that is, its alteration from a natural into a cultural object, from tree to sign—signals the destruction of this organic notion of justice and the dissociation of its constitutive elements. The subsequent narrative unfolds the consequences of this break: as the lived unity of justice gives way to the frenzied drafting of petitions, laws, and regulations, Kohlhaas's desire for fairness, rather than being satisfied through the intervention of a personalized authority, is detoured into an anonymous and rhizomic bureaucratic machine that endlessly obstructs and frustrates its satisfaction.

Kohlhaas's movement through the toll gate thus represents a passage, indeed a Fall, from justice to legality, and the tension between these two orders dominates the entire subsequent narrative. On the one hand, Kohlhaas's legal demand—his insistence on the restoration of his horses—implies a principle of justice based on the denial of difference, including the difference between past and present. Kohlhaas, that is, seeks to undo the Fall and restore the world to its utopian, prelapsarian state. On the other hand, the legal order in which Kohlhaas seeks redress depends upon a principle of *nonequivalence*: it is a world of formless differences and endless substitutions. The "pass" Kohlhaas is asked to produce at the border, which turns out, upon his later investigation, to be "a fairy tale" (*ein Märchen*; MK 21), is paradigmatic of this order. Like the "written permission of the court," which is itself without reality yet produces real effects (he must leave the horses behind), the laws that envelop Kohlhaas derive their force precisely from their vacuousness and their openness to endless (re)interpretations. For a law whose meaning cannot be discerned is not only unsatisfiable, its application is also, in the last instance, a matter of arbitrary decision.[22] To borrow a formulation Gershom Scholem coined with respect to Kafka: the law in Kleist's story "has *validity* but no *significance.*"[23]

Giorgio Agamben has drawn on this formulation to describe the structure of sovereignty, and with it, the violent foundation of law.[24] A sovereign who has the power legally to suspend all existing laws in order to preserve the state and its law is the purest embodiment of the extralegal violence that sustains all legal orders. For like the sovereign's words, which carry direct authority and in this sense *are* law, the legal apparatus as a whole does not rest on some substantive metanorm but is grounded ultimately in the force of its tautological self-assertion: the law is the law. And it is this extralegal dimension of the law, "this force without signification," that comes into full view with Kohlhaas's border crossing and his subsequent rebellion. Kohlhaas's rebellion, in other words, is an attack on the meaningless dimension of legality, and the story's heroic and melodramatic pathos derives from the willingness of its protagonist to take on the cynicism and arrogance of established power at the risk of his own life. But this is only half the story. For Kohlhaas's heroic fight against the violent foundation of law unleashes another, strictly complementary force without signification, a violence pertaining to the foundation of moral subjectivity. Under the paradoxical sign of Michael Kohlhaas, "one of the most righteous and most terrible human beings of his time [*einer der rechtschaffendsten zugleich und entsetzlichsten Menschen seiner Zeit]*" (MK 13), the text simultaneously explores the existential foundation of the law and the legal foundation of existence. At the center of this double exploration of foundations stands the paradox of Kohlhaas's *Recht/gefühl,* and thus his status as a moral hero.

Kant with Kleist?

Kleist took great care to dissociate his protagonist from mere criminality. The tone is set in the first paragraph, where the narrator, in a famous paradoxical formulation, declares that Kohlhaas's "sense of justice made him a robber and a murderer" (MK 13). The same emphasis on Kohlhaas's probity is evident in Kleist's divergence from the historical sources.[25] Hans Kohlhase demanded financial recompense for the withholding of his horses, whereas Michael Kohlhaas wants his rights, not his money, restored. Similarly, if the historical chronicle depicts Kohlhase as a rather crude fellow who robs and tortures innocent people, Kleist's novella carefully displaces such vileness onto Kohlhaas's followers, contrasting the exalted rebel with the rapacious mob surrounding him, in a manner completely absent from the sources.[26] What propels Kleist's protagonist into action is not greed or viciousness but moral fervor.

This stress on Kohlhaas's moralism takes on its full importance when read in conjunction with contemporary aesthetic and moral discourses. The horse dealer's dissociation from all signs of vulgarity clearly aligns him with the domain of the sublime as developed in idealist aesthetics. "Stealing," writes Schiller, "is something absolutely base, and whatever our heart may put forth in defense of a thief . . . aesthetically he will always remain a base object."[27] The aesthetic character of actions depends on the motivations that fuel them: actions done from self-interest are vulgar, while nothing is more sublime than "the heroic despair that throws into the dust all goods of life, even life himself,"[28] thus betraying an "incorruptible sense of justice and injustice."[29] Can we miss the echo of this discourse in Kleist's novella? Consider Kohlhaas's reflection that "it was his duty to do everything in his power to get satisfaction for himself for the wrong done him, and a guarantee against future ones for his fellow citizens" (MK/G 95; MK 27); his willingness to sacrifice domestic and financial security for the sake of moral duty; or his disinterest, emphasized time and again, in material goods? Whatever else Kohlhaas might be, then, he is also a sublime hero, the hero as herald of an abstract moral principle.

At stake here is not just a view of aesthetics but a new model of morality and subjectivity that Schiller derived from Kant. As we saw, Kantian moral philosophy is built on a fundamental opposition between happiness and morality, between the satisfaction of desires on the one hand, and the fulfillment of ethical demands on the other. Underlying this opposition is the conception of a subject divided against itself. The self of ordinary life—a self shaped by predilections, passions, and personal history—is in Kant's view a creature of natural causality and as such incapable of the freedom of self-legislation that is the linchpin of moral agency. Moral action requires the renunciation of this ordinary self—and with it, "life and its enjoyment" (CPrR 91)—in favor of an alternative self, one free from the constraints of natural life. In the experience of pain that accompanies such renunciation, the subject discovers the sign of his freedom and a regard (respect/*Achtung*) for himself as a moral being.

Kant's entire oeuvre following the publication of the *Critique of Practical Reason* is an attempt to narrow the gap between personal and moral subjectivity, between desire and duty. This trajectory, which already informs his turn toward aesthetic experience, finds its final and most audacious formulation in

Kant's discussion of enthusiasm as the exuberant embrace of freedom. Yet the moral passion of enthusiasm, while holding out the promise of a harmonious relationship between the moral and the sensuous, paradoxically also poses an entirely new threat to existence. If the passion of sensuous life that was the focus of Kant's earlier conception posed a threat to morality, the passion of enthusiasm *is aligned with morality and poses a threat to sensuous life.* This is so because enthusiasm is a transindividual passion, a passion mobilized by commitment to universal principle, and thus opposed to individual "life and its enjoyment." To this extent, it lies beyond the pleasure principle and carries with it the threat of violence directed both internally and externally, against the individual and the community of individuals at large. It was for this precise reason that Kant insisted on the historical development of juridico-political institutions designed to articulate and oversee the universal principle of freedom within the sphere of public life.

And Kohlhaas? Kleist's novella might be read as a compressed case study of Kantian morality that draws into contradiction its constitutive principles. The crucial difference between Kohlhaas and Kant concerns the question of renunciation. The Kantian subject renounces subjectivity, but does so at the altar, and on behalf, of reason and the community of rational agents he thereby hopes to invoke and establish. Kohlhaas, on the other hand, sacrifices both subjectivity and reason. For while the horse dealer does indeed act out of commitment to principle, this commitment, in its murderous specificity and excess, ultimately obliterates the very principle that elicits it. This dynamic is already evident in the sentence intended to establish the purity and objectivity of Kohlhaas's virtue: "the horses were not the issue—he would have been equally aggrieved had they been a couple of dogs" (MK 47). What seems a testament to Kohlhaas's commitment to justice and its underlying law of equivalent exchange proves to mean exactly the opposite, namely, Kohlhaas's *insistence on the impossibility of exchange.* For Kohlhaas demands nothing less than the restoration of his horses to the state they were in prior to his conflict with the Junker. This represents a demand not only for the recovery of property but also for the recovery of time. The horses, in other words, function for Kohlhaas as the unsubstitutable currency of, and thus as a fundamental contradiction in, his conception of justice.[30]

This contradiction constitutes the essential problem of his moral heroism. While justice depends on the balancing of equivalents, and thus on an independent measure of value (i.e., on a currency), Kohlhaas's insistence on the restoration of his horses implies a principle of justice based on the balance of identicals whose exclusive value lies in their simple identity. Kohlhaas's murderous rampage is the result of his fervent embrace, to the point of collapse, of this paradoxical principle. At the heart of his madness lies the utter denial of difference: between equivalents (*these* horses), between past and present (*prior* to the conflict), and ultimately between instance and law, singularity and principle.

The impossibility of this conception of justice materializes in the surreal bodies of the horses, whose numerous physical transformations clearly defy biological laws.[31] In the denial of symbolic distance—the horses, literally, *are* the issue—the horses are conflated with a transcendent meaning that disfigures and denatures them. This incongruity between matter and sense is the source of the horses' comic, slapstick quality,[32] a comic pathos that also attests to Kleist's deep materialism, revealing the impossibility of an organic identity between body and meaning, singularity and universality. Fallen, downcast creatures, the horses carry nothing less than the burden of civilization incurred in their passage through the toll gate.

Yet Kohlhaas's particularization of justice, while a reversal, perhaps a perversion of Kantian moral procedure, nonetheless points to two difficulties inherent in the latter. The first has to do with the problem of universalization, with the difficulty of fashioning a principle of action that is at once universal in scope and specific in application. Kohlhaas's initial understanding of his suffering in universal terms, as an injustice done to him as well as to his "fellow citizens" (MK/G, 95; MK, 27), implies the properly Kantian recognition of a world of equivalently autonomous agents. But whereas in Kant this recognition forms the basis of moral actions that align the individual with the welfare of everyone, in Kohlhaas the passage to action results in his blatant *withdrawal* from all communal obligation, and in an egotistical quest for justice that mercilessly destroys everything and everybody in its way. Kohlhaas's moral narcissism draws attention to the problem of pure practical judgment. To act morally, the subject must bridge the gap between the universality of the moral law on the one hand, and the irreducible specificity of the context of action on the other. But this requires two types of calculation that would seem impossible to conclude: the generation of a maxim of universal applicability, and the assessment of the consequences of its universal application. Derrida has described this predicament in terms of the aporia of legal decision. The decision of the judge is at once subject to rule and ruleless. This is so because a purely formal deduction would require infinite information, whereas the actual decision of the judge is always carried out in a finite moment of urgency, in the "night of non-knowledge."[33] Kohlhaas's fall into immoral action highlights the difficulty, perhaps even structural impossibility, of accomplishing the double operation required by moral action, a difficulty that is heightened by the formal and "empty" character of Kantian law: precisely because the categorical imperative tells us only *that* we must universalize our actions but not *how* to do so in a specific situation, we never know if we have properly translated the abstract injunction to do our duty into a concrete universal norm.

The second, closely related problem has to do with the unique form of rational passion required for adherence to moral principle. If the proper object of this passion is the universal law of freedom, the passion itself resides less in individual subjectivity than in the self as universal, in what I have called the impersonal personality, and to this extent, it exceeds the resources of the individual to contain it. As we saw, Kant's *Contest of the Faculties* betrays a certain ambivalence about this passion. On the one hand, Kant insists on the necessity of regulative legal structures, betraying a more skeptical view of the sufficiency of reason to regulate the attachments to which it gives rise than one finds in the earlier *Critique of Practical Reason.* On the other hand, he also underscores, again in contrast to his earlier writings, the role of passion as an affective substrate of, and motivational force behind, moral activity. Kohlhaas's collapse of the universal into the particular and his subsequent embrace of violence may thus be seen as an elaboration of a strain of excess that belongs to the dynamic of moral agency and, more specifically, to a moral enthusiasm unmoored from the regulatory framework of both reason and institution.

This excess surfaces early on in the novella, in Kohlhaas's reflections on his return from Dresden, where he has been informed that the permit the Junker requested from him was "a mere fairy tale:"[34] A few weeks later, with the string of horses he had brought with him sold to his satisfaction, "he returned to Tronka Castle without any other bitter feeling besides that of the universal destitution of the world" (kehrte er, ohne irgend weiter ein bitteres Gefühl, als das der allgemeinen Not der Welt, zur Tronkenburg zurück) (MK 21). Note the absence of proportion in Kohlhaas response to the incident, his predisposition to take a relatively small incident as indicative of the "allgemeine Not" of the world, two terms that have strong ontological overtones.[35] After all, all that has happened so far is that a "scraggy" (MK 21) Junker has falsely assumed the right to withhold two of Kohlhaas's horses; a troubling incident, to be sure, especially for someone whose existence depends on the legal protection of his trade, but hardly the kind of event that by itself warrants a judgment on the rottenness of all things earthly.

Kohlhaas's ontological despair resurfaces a few pages later, this time also betraying its aggressive potential. After reading the court's impudent answer to his resolution, he "was foaming with rage."

> Whenever he heard a sound in the courtyard he looked, his breast filled with a repugnance such as he had never experienced before, toward the gate, expecting to see the Junker's men appear and, perhaps even with some excuse, hand the starved and emaciated horses back to him; *the only case in which his soul, well-schooled by the world, was not prepared for anything that entirely corresponded to its feeling* [*der einzige Fall, in welchem seine von der Welt wohlerzogene Seele, auf nichts das ihrem Gefühl völlig entsprach gefasst war*]. Shortly afterwards, however, he heard, from a friend who had travelled that way, that the nags were as heretofore being used on the field at Tronka Castle with the Junker's other horses; *and through the midst of his pain at perceiving the world in such monstrous disorder flickered the inward contentment at seeing his own breast now in order* [*und mitten durch den Schmerz, die Welt in einer so ungeheuren Unordnung zu erblicken, zuckte die innerliche Zufriedenheit empor, seine eigne Brust nunmehr in Ordnung zu sehen*]. (MK 47; trans. mine, emphasis added)

The passage clearly articulates Kohlhaas's desire to avenge himself for the wrongs done to him, and thus adds to his moral feeling a more pathological sentiment. But *Rechtgefühl* and revenge are not the only forces that impel him to act. The repetition of the earlier existential condemnation—"the general destitution of the world" now having become the world's "monstrous disorder"—returns our attention to the presence of another affect, which, on its resurfacing, has changed its epistemic status: what used to be only a vague *feeling* has now crystallized into a perception, "the pain at *seeing* the world in such monstrous disorder." Hence also the extraordinary affective investment in Kohlhaas's look at the gate. The fear sustaining his gaze is directed against the possibility of a perception that by spoiling Kohlhaas's image of the world's "monstrous disorder" would also destroy his "inward contentment at seeing his own breast now in order." Kohlhaas's jubilant reaction thus derives from his relief at having encountered an external confirmation of his own ontological despair. The conflict with the Junker enables him to transform his unease *in* the world into an unease *with* the world, and Kohlhaas clings with such anxiety to the result of this transformation because it liberates him from an internal split from which he had suffered up to this moment.

The psychic dynamic that articulates itself in this passage constitutes the subjective correlate to Kohlhaas's drive toward specificity already seen in relation to the object of his legal dispute, the horses. Just as Kohlhaas there identifies his rights with the restoration of *these* horses, so here he identifies his *entire* existence with his quest for justice. For as the passage unmistakably states, Kohlhaas's embrace of moral action coincides with the disappearance of any psychic conflict ("seine eigne Brust nunmehr in Ordnung zu sehen"), which is displaced onto the outside (the *ungeheure Unordnung* of the world). And this split between internal harmony and external disorder persists throughout Kohlhaas's rebellion, which is characterized by both extreme violence and the absence of feelings of remorse, doubt, or guilt. This is a complete reversal of the Kantian picture. If, for Kant, morality is inherently conflictual, and the moral subject is necessarily divided against itself owing to its dual nature, in Kleist, moral passion enables the subject to overcome his lack of identity. The result of this reversal is a monstrosity, namely, a subject that is, from the point of view of Kant's dualistic moral psychology, utterly inconceivable: for if Kohlhaas's violent particularization of justice disqualifies him as a moral subject, his willingness to sacrifice himself for his moral quest makes it equally impossible to conceive of him as a pathological subject in the Kantian sense.

Kohlhaas's passion is thus neither universal nor subjective, but *extrapersonal*. Hence its destructiveness with respect to both principle and self. On the one hand, mobilized by commitment to principle, Kohlhaas's passion casts him along a trajectory that exceeds and annihilates the self. On the other hand, incapable of channeling this universal passion into a universal maxim, his actions immediately exceed the bounds of principle from which they sprang. Kleist's protagonist is propelled by an enthusiasm that has unmoored itself from the regulatory framework of both reason and subjectivity. Inhabiting the truly inhuman realm beyond morality and the pleasure principle, Kohlhaas is not so much an individual subject as he is the conduit for an extrasubjective energetic force. In other words, he is a perverse inflection of Kant's impersonal personality.

Melodrama

Kohlhaas's moral particularism is mirrored in an important structural feature of Kleist's narrative, a tendency toward disambiguation, polarization, and simplification, which I propose to call its *melodramatic* dimension.[36] The plot of *Michael Kohlhaas* is built on stark contrasts and polarization, with the conflicting parties functioning as semantic carriers of moral extremes, not as psychologically graduated characters: while Kohlhaas, this apparent "paragon of a good citizen," represents "justice," Hinz and Kunz von Tronka, his main opponents, are pure and simple "villains." At significant turning points in the narrative, this dualism often crystallizes into a hyperbolic and melodramatic rhetoric, one that recurs, as the following examples show, throughout Kleist's writings:

> . . . and she was just about to sink to the ground when a Russian officer, hearing her piercing screams, appeared on the scene and with furious blows of his sword drove the dogs back from the prey for which they lusted. To the Marquise he seemed an angel sent from heaven. He smashed the hilt of his sword into the face of one of the murderous brutes, who still had his arms around her tender waist. (*The Marquise of O . . .* , 144)[37]

> Don Fernando, this godly hero, was now standing with his back to the church; on his left arm he held the children, in his right hand his sword and with every blow he struck one of his attackers down, his blade flashing like lightning [*Mit jedem Hieb wetterstrahlte er einen zu Boden*]; a lion could not have defended itself better. (*The Earthquake in Chile*, 221)[38]

> Gustav buried his face in his hands. Oh! he screamed without looking up, and the earth seemed to give way under his feet: is this true, what you are telling me? He put his arm around her body und gazed into her face, his heart rent with anguish [*und sah ihr mit jammervoll zerrissenem Herzen ins Gesicht*]. "Oh", cried Toni, and these were her last words, "you should not have mistrusted me!" And so saying, the beautiful soul expired [*Und damit hauchte sie ihre schöne Seele aus*]. (*The Betrothal in St. Domingo*, 259)[39]

In these melodramatic sequences, Kleist's tendency toward disambiguation, toward extreme symbolic reduction, manifests itself most clearly. The represented world is stripped of all qualifications and gradations and reduced to a few basic elements: heroes and villains, gods and dogs. As a result, the texts are charged with an extraordinarily high level of affective energy; the melodramatic rhetoric of the absolute, of total, pure choices between extremes, exerts a pressure on the narrative that makes it radiate with intensity. Consider, for the first and paradigmatic occurrence of this rhetoric in *Michael Kohlhaas,* the description of the horse dealer's attack on Tronka Castle:

> He fell upon the castle with this handful of men at twilight on the third night, charging down the toll keeper and the gatemen as they stood in con-

versation beneath the gateway, and, as the barracks in the castle grounds, which they pelted with fire, burst into flame, Herse dashed up the spiral staircase into the tower, where he surprised the warden and the steward, half-naked and playing at cards, with cut and thrust, while Kohlhaas dove upon Junker Wenzel in the castle. The angel of justice thus descends from heaven. (MK 63; trans. mine)[40]

The passage stages a carefully constructed moment of cathartic violence. Coming after, and putting an end to, a series of outrageous injustices, Kohlhaas's attack produces a number of gratifying reversals: from passivity to activity, from repetition to an aim-oriented narrative, and from moral corruption to a moment of moral integrity. This effect is heightened by a sudden shift in scale. Inscribing Kohlhaas's action into a drama of religious dimensions, the hyperbolic phrase "angel of justice" radically changes the parameters for evaluating his attack: the object of his rebellion is no longer a circumscribed crime but "the monstrous disorder of the world." This exalted religious register continues in the metaphors of light and darkness that frame the entire episode, infusing it with apocalyptic significance. In short, the staging of the episode, the register of its language, and the choice of its metaphors conspire to turn Kohlhaas's attack on the Tronkenburg into a cosmic drama, a struggle for the very possibility of truth and meaning.

Melodrama is first of all drama. Kohlhaas's stormy attack on the Tronkenburg; Don Fernando and the Count's fencing against the mob; Gustav's kneeling over and embracing of the dying Toni—such scenes epitomize the melodramatic urge toward externalization, gesture, and spectacle. The melodramatic moment is quintessentially a moment of enactment, of making things visible and acting them out. In Kleist, this pressure toward externalization typically culminates in scenes of spectacular violence. Kohlhaas's attack on the Tronkenburg illustrates the interweaving of melodrama and violence, semantic reduction and physical confrontation: violence is experienced as pleasurable, because it radically simplifies the semantic universe, replacing the web of contradictory legal arguments with the neat opposition between good and bad, friend and foe. In other words, melodrama functions as a narrative analogue of the violence of condensation and reduction that defines Kohlhaas's moral narcissism.

The confluence of melodrama and moral struggle is not accidental. According to Peter Brooks, melodrama as a genre emerged during the last decades of the eighteenth century in response to a pervasive sense of social and political collapse:

The origins of melodrama can be accurately located within the context of the French Revolution and its aftermath. This is the epistemological moment which it illustrates and to which it contributes: the moment that symbolically, and really, marks the final liquidation of the traditional Sacred and its representative institutions. . . . [Melodrama] comes into being in a world where the traditional imperatives of truth and ethics have been violently thrown into question, yet where the promulgation of truth and ethics, their instauration as a way of life, is of immediate, daily, political concern.[41]

Hence the intrinsic connection between melodrama and French Revolution. "When the revolutionary Saint-Just exclaims, 'Republican government has as its principle virtue; or, if not, terror' he is using the manichaeistic terms of melodrama, arguing its logic of the excluded middle, and imagining a situation—the moment of revolutionary suspension—where the word is called upon to make present and to impose a new society, to legislate the regime of virtue."[42] Both Revolution and melodrama represent attempts at resacralizing the law at a moment where its traditional institutions (monarch and church) and their performative magics have lost much of their currency, and both respond to this loss with a heightened rhetoric, charging language to make visible, indeed create, a new system of belief. Melodramatic hyperbole, in short, is the rhetorical sign of a foundational crisis.

This is precisely the constellation we find in Kleist's novella. But Kleist pushes the logic and rhetoric of melodrama to the point where its internal contradictions come to the fore. What becomes visible thereby is not only the destructive, indeed terroristic, core of revolutionary activity and the melodramatic rhetoric it draws on, but also the violence in the foundation and operations of established law. Consider in this context Kohlhaas's self-stylization at the peak of his rebellion:

> In the manifesto which he scattered abroad on this occasion, he called himself a "viceroy of the Archangel Michael, come to punish with fire and sword, for the wickedness into which the whole world was sunk, all those who should take the side of the Junker in this quarrel." And from the castle at Lützen, which he had taken by surprise and in which he had established himself, he summoned the people to join with him to build a better order of things. With a kind of madness, the manifesto was signed: "Done at the Seat of Our Provisional World Government [*Weltregierung*], the Chief Castle at Lützen." (MK/G 121)[43]
>
> . . . on a morning when two of his men were to hang for violating orders and looting in the neighborhood, they decided to draw it [Luther's notice]

to his attention. He was just returning from the place of execution, with the pomp that he had adopted since the proclamation of his latest manifesto—a large archangelic sword was borne before him on a red leather cushion ornamented with gold tassels, while twelve men with burning torches followed after. (MK/G 123)[44]

Kohlhaas conceives of himself not simply as a rebel fighting the existing political-legal order but also, and above all, as the ruler of a "provisional world government," subject only to God's authority. He assumes, in other words, the attributes of sovereignty, and it is hardly accidental that the passage shows him exercising one of the defining privileges of sovereign power: the power of life and death over his subjects. Lacking a state to rule, however, Kohlhaas seeks to install the legal-political order in his own person, becoming, as it were, his own city-state. In embracing the language and imagery of sovereignty, the horse dealer seeks to legitimate his own violence and to present himself as a ruler entitled to wield the sword of justice. But this attempt at self-legitimation clearly fails, and his ever more fantastic trappings and rituals of sovereignty end up highlighting, through their excessiveness, what they were supposed to conceal: that Kohlhaas's assumption of sovereignty is fictitious, his violence extralegal and illegitimate.

Kohlhaas's fantastic self-stylizations dramatize the essential contradiction of the melodramatic project, its "urge toward resacralization and the impossibility of conceiving sacralization other than in personal terms."[45] But the text also suggests the political and linguistic reasons for this failure. Kohlhaas's self-legitimation falters not just because his violence defies legality but, more important, *because its force exceeds the rhetoric of sovereignty invoked to legitimate and contain it.* Unbeknownst to himself, Kohlhaas embodies a form of *bare* sovereignty that abandons the fantasy of legitimacy and written law, thus articulating the "validity without significance" (Scholem) that underpins the legal order. Yet since this force is impersonal and structural, a violence that holds in place a structured order, his attempt at containing it within the boundaries of his own person necessarily fails, resulting, on the one hand, in a hyperbolic body, and on the other, in a violence that constantly exceeds the self and strikes at others. Kohlhaas's increasing madness and the text's ever more fantastic melodramatic rhetoric result from his impossible identification with an impersonal force. In assuming the sovereignty of the law for himself, Kohlhaas has aligned himself with an extrasubjective force that exceeds—and thus confuses or displaces (*verrückt*)—personal subjectivity.[46]

Melodramatic hyperbole thus functions in Kleist as the rhetorical mirror of an extrapersonal force. This might explain its pervasiveness throughout the writings of Kleist, for whom, as our reading of "Allmähliche Verfertigung" showed, passion and language outstrip the bounds of the individual and in that sense are impersonal. Melodrama provides a linguistic conduit into the nonlinguistic, thus allowing access to the affective energies stored in collective movements. Kohlhaas's manifestos exemplify this linguistic resource in abundance. And just as Kohlhaas, through his manifestos, focuses the amorphous energies of the people, thereby constituting the scattered crowd as a collective force, so Kleist, through the melodramatic rhetoric of his novella, aims at harnessing, and ultimately commandeering, the passions of his reading public. Melodrama, and the dynamic of the energetic sign on which it rests, is a constitutive element of Kleist's media politics, or what has been called his *Federkrieg* (war of the pen).[47]

The connection between the idiom of excess and questions of sovereignty is at the center of one of the more famous and notorious explorations of legal violence, that of Carl Schmitt, whose work has often been connected with Kleist's, especially in recent years.[48] Indeed, the logic of radical disjunction operative in melodrama's stress on polarization is the modus operandi of the political according to Schmitt. Schmitt's *The Concept of the Political* (1927) begins with the contention that the liberal distinction between state and society no longer holds for the twentieth century. The point of this assertion, however, is less to claim the omnipotence of the state than to underscore the ubiquity of the political. Schmitt sees the political not as a subsystem among other subsystems (economy, art, law, etc.) but as a specific type of relation that at least potentially penetrates the whole of society. The fundamental criterion of the political "is the distinction between *friend* and *foe*."[49] Unlike other binary oppositions such as good/bad (morality) or ugly/beautiful (aesthetics), the political opposition between friend and foe is intrinsically existential: the foe is the other whose existence poses a threat to my own existence. Hence Schmitt's emphasis on violence as the ultimate truth of the political: "The concept of the foe implies the eventuality of struggle. . . . The notions friend, foe, and struggle gain their meaning from the fact that they keep in contact with the real possibility of physical annihilation. The war is a consequence of enmity, for the latter is the negation of the other's *being* [*seinsmäßige Negierung eines anderen Seins*]. War is only the most extreme realization of enmity."[50] However, violence is for Schmitt not only the operative mode of political life but its enabling condition; it is the foundation of the political order. Violence is the transcendence of the state: first, because violence puts in place, and thus transcends, the legal apparatus (state), and, second, because in doing so, it establishes the state as an entity that transcends the conventions, laws, and rules that it oversees and regulates. Schmitt's name for this transcendence is, of course, the sovereign, who has the power legally to suspend the law in order to preserve the state and its law in times of exceptional danger.[51]

Kleist's conception of the political is both similar to and more complex than Schmitt's. The integration of specific acts of violence into organized state violence also structures many of Kleist's texts. Kohlhaas's local feud with the Junker, for instance, develops into a rebellion against Saxony and eventually results in an international conflict that polarizes Saxony, Brandenburg, Poland, and the Holy Roman Empire.[52] Thus, whereas Schiller conceived of the state in universalist terms, as the representative of humanity, Kleist and Schmitt emphasize its role as the nexus of power. An aggressive force among other forces, the state is, quite simply, the sublimation of a successful concentration of power within a given territory.

It is the character of this sublimation that sets Kleist apart from Schmitt. Kohlhaas's failed rebellion brings out the structural and impersonal dimension of bare sovereignty that Schmitt's nostalgic fixation on the figure of the sovereign tends to occlude. While Schmitt locates violence exclusively in the sovereign, Kleist treats it as an impersonal energetic force whose principal conduit is the individual. More precisely, political power rests in Kleist on the double foundation of anarchic passion and its structuring in the symbolic machinery of the state. The problem is, of course, that in Kleist's novella, these two dimensions are initially opposed to each other: while the rebel Kohlhaas is charged with the energetic force of extralegal violence, the legal-political order is a petrified bureaucratic mechanism drained of vitality. *Michael Kohlhaas* is a tale about the revitalization—and thus, refoundation—of the political order, a narrative project that finds its climactic expression in a final scene of sacrifice, apotheosis, and the perfection of justice. But it is also, as we shall see, a meditation on the necessary role of art as a medium of transmission from individual passion to political representation.

Bare Sovereignty

Kohlhaas's manifestos represent a first instance of such a medium, but they are not the model Kleist adopts. Kleist's narrative insurrection follows a different logic from Kohlhaas's political insurrection, which remains caught in the impossible task of representing, indeed, embodying, a force that is beyond signification and legitimation. The inadequacy of Kohlhaas's conception of justice, already evident in his fantastic self-stylizations, becomes fully visible in the failure of his rebellion in Dresden.

With Kohlhaas's move to Dresden, the structure of the narrative and his position within it change radically.[53] As the plot becomes more complex,[54] Kohlhaas's opponents gain the upper hand, skillfully tapping the emerging subplots to drive the horse dealer out of the text. The "Herren Hinz und Kunz," for instance, succeed in their struggle against Kohlhaas precisely by channeling the actions of other*s*: first those of the mob, whose near-rebellion, "aroused throughout the land . . . a feeling that was highly prejudicial to the successful outcome of his [Kohlhaas's] case" (MK 98); and then of Nagelschmidt, whose actions the "crafty lords were clever enough" (MK 100) to employ against him. In short, the melodramatic narrative of rebellion, shaped by stark contrasts and direct physical confrontation, is replaced by a narrative of intrigue, where success depends primarily on the ability of actors to manipulate information, to "plot" in the sinister sense of the word.

That Kohlhaas is ill at ease with this new plot is evident in the way the novella loses sight of him. After being the focus of narrative attention in the first two sequences, he is increasingly pushed to the periphery of the text that bears his name, reduced either to a mere object of discussion or to the restricted role of interrogee, subject to the rules of speech imposed upon him by the authorities.[55] The text also figures the marginalization of its hero spatially, through his confinement to the domestic realm he had forgone, at the beginning of the story, to launch his rebellion. Kohlhaas's imprisonment is a sign of narrative regression. It attests to the tendency of the Dresden plot to cancel out the plot of rebellion, to undo the narrative trajectory that has filled the empty signifier "Michael Kohlhaas" with historical significance.

The logic of the Dresden episode resonates with the failure of energetic speech at the end of the "Allmähliche Verfertigung." Dresden, that is, is much more than a geographic locus: it is the topographic name for a legal apparatus that petrifies the force of the energetic sign, thus threatening both Kohlhaas's rebellion and the narrative insurrection that Kleist launches under the name of his protagonist. The discussions at the court of Dresden, which demonstrate the incapacity of the legal order to generate a consistent judgment on Kohlhaas's case, show that the former rests on a principle of nonequivalence that is diametrically opposed to the horse dealer's own conception of justice. A world of formless differences and endless substitutions, the law in Dresden is open to endless (re)interpretations, thus denying Kohlhaas precisely the solid-ity and self-identity he so desperately seeks. The arbitrary decision with which the Elector of Saxony terminates the discussion about Kohlhaas's case is not an accidental feature, however, but instead points to what I have called the paradox of exteriority: the fact that the foundation of a system is itself not held in place by any of the operations that define the system. The elector's arbitrary decision foregrounds this impossibility of complete formalization, thus highlighting the nonsemantic force, the violence, at the heart of the legal order.[56]

And yet, at issue in the Dresden episode is not simply the petrifying Saxon bureaucracy and its lack of justice but also the deficiency of Kohlhaas's rebellion to make up for this lack and energize the decrepit state machinery. Put differently, the problem of sovereignty permeates both the official legal order and the revolt against that order. Note that it is Kohlhaas himself who brings about the disastrous turn of events in Dresden. His manifestos, these performative acts of self-legitimation, turn against the horse dealer, making him the victim of the very impersonal force he had sought to commandeer. Kohlhaas cannot control the warrant for the campaign of justice he himself issued, because in invoking the law, he invokes an extrasubjective entity that can be taken up and invoked by everyone. In other words, Kohlhaas falls victim to the necessarily transcendent (i.e., extra-individual) character of law he seeks to embody and circumscribe within his own person.

The first instance that exemplifies this mechanism is the mass riot in Dresden, which "aroused a feeling throughout the land, even among the more moderate and better class of people, that was highly dangerous to the success of his suit" (MK/G 144; MK 98). The riot is fueled by the people's identification with Kohlhaas, who has become in their eyes "the avenging angel who chastised the oppressors of the people with fire and sword" (MK/G 134; MK 87). If this is the language of Kohlhaas's rebellion, it now, however, produces nothing but dead letters: "As soon as he heard this, the Chamberlain went across to the knacker at a jump that set his helmet plume nodding and tossed him a bag of money; and while the latter scraped the hair back from his forehead with a lead comb and stared at the money in his hand, Sir Kunz ordered a servant to untie the horses and lead them home. The man left a group of his family and friends in the crowd at his master's summons and did, in fact, with a red face, step over a large pile of dung at the horses' feet and go up to their heads" (MK/G 142).[57]

The scene stages in inverted form the trajectory of the energetic sign encountered earlier. Whereas Mirabeau succeeds in channeling the amorphous energies of communal dissent into a sign that revolutionizes the symbolic order, Kohlhaas is forced to witness the people's fragmentation of his quest for justice into a morass of meaningless details: the plume of the helmet, the leaden comb, the great pile of dung. What follows in the wake of this collapse is the deadening of the sign of justice through the devaluation of its currency: the horses. "The Count answered: 'Sir, they [the horses] *are* dead: dead in a legal sense [*in staatsrechtlicher Bedeutung*] because they have no value, and will be so physically before they are fetched from the knacker's yard to the von Tronka stables" (MK 99). Thus when the crowd, like the narrative, has dispersed, all that remains of the action are Kohlhaas's horses, drained of any symbolic value and reduced to sheer matter: "[D]eprived of all care and attention they became the laughingstock of street urchins and loiterers" (MK 98).

The disastrous consequences of Kohlhaas's writing are even more striking in the case of the "other, more important storm. . . . whose lightning the crafty lords were clever enough to draw upon his [Kohlhaas's] luckless head" (MK 100):

> A man called Johan Nagelschmidt, one of the band whom the horse dealer had collected and then turned off again after the Electoral amnesty, had some weeks later rounded up a part of this rabble, which shrank from nothing, . . . with the intention of carrying on for himself the trade Kohlhaas had taught him. This ruffian announced, partly to scare the sheriff's officers on his heels, and partly to get the peasantry to take a hand in his rascalities as they had done with Kohlhaas, that he was Kohlhaas's lieutenant [*Statthalter*]; . . . the result of this being that the incendiary crew were able to masquerade, in manifestoes very much like Kohlhaas's that Nagelschmidt had posted up, as honest soldiers assembled together for the sole purpose of serving God . . . all this, as has just been said, done not at all for the glory of God nor out of attachment to Kohlhaas, whose fate the outlaws did not care a straw about, but to enable them to burn and plunder with the greater impunity and ease. (MK/G 146)[58]

In these passages, Kleist's text dramatizes the logical impossibility of the conception of justice Kohlhaas seeks to embody. The crux of this idea is encapsulated in the word *Statthalter*,[59] which points to the double void on which Kohlhaas's rebellion so precariously rests: the lack of legal, official justice, and the evacuation of his own personhood and, therefore, of any claim to legitimacy. As for the first, we have already seen how Kohlhaas, in assuming the prerogatives of sovereignty, positions himself as God's *Statthalter*, thereby substituting himself for the elector. The Nagelschmidt episode brings out the weakness of Kohlhaas's performative self-authorization. Since his sovereignty is merely the product of the manifesto, it is enough to duplicate the manifesto to duplicate its effects. The lack of institutional support, in other words, makes him dependent upon a convention that can be appropriated by anyone who wishes to. Nagelschmidt, "with the ingenuity he had learnt from his master" (MK/G 146; MK 100), simply exploits this mechanism, unfolding the dynamic character of what Derrida calls "supplementarity."[60] The *Statthalter* is replaced by another *Statthalter,* and the attempt to fill the void of justice ends up increasing it.[61]

Moreover, this mechanism is exacerbated by a second feature of Kohlhaas's rebellion, which I have called his assumption of *bare* sovereignty. After all, it might be argued that in invoking divine authority, Kohlhaas does in fact place himself in a very real institutional context, that of a religious crusade and, beyond that, in the traditional context of religiously motivated unrest. The problem is that his actions undermine this contextualization and disengage his invocation. For while Kohlhaas speaks the language of divine justice, his actions, unbeknownst to him, speak another language—that of bare sovereignty. Kohlhaas's illegitimacy follows from his failure to articulate or exemplify any recognizable concept of justice; and this failure is due, in turn, to his assuming the prerogatives of pure sovereignty, which abandons the fantasy of warrant and legitimacy for the rule of force. From this perspective, Kohlhaas's melodramatic manifestos seek, through appeal to divine legitimacy, to reign in the bare force of legality he has embarked upon. They are attempts to personalize and make meaningful an extrapersonal force that is without signification.

It is against this background that the death sentence becomes readable as the staging of an unsuccessful closure that terminates Kohlhaas's first search for justice.

> No sooner had the fellow delivered the horse dealer's answer to the Governor of the Palace than the Lord Chancellor was deposed, the President, Count Kallheim, was appointed head of the court in his place, and, by an order in council of the Elector, Kohlhaas was arrested, put in chains, and thrown into the Dresden dungeon. On the evidence of the letter, a copy of which was posted at every street corner, he was brought to trial; and when he answered "Yes!" to a councilor who held the letter up in front of him at the bar and asked him if he acknowledged the handwriting as his own, but looked down at the ground and said "No!" when he was asked if he had anything to say in his own defense, Kohlhaas was condemned to be tortured with red-hot pincers by knackers' men, to be drawn and quartered, and his body burned between the wheel and the gallows (MK/G 156–57).[62]

The enormous acceleration of the narrative; the infamous character of the announced death; Kohlhaas's radical demotion from agent to object—each of these features on its own would suffice to prevent a satisfactory narrative closure; together, they make a mockery of it. The passage not only fails to provide the narrative with a full and final meaning but actively dismisses the desires and questions it had generated: Kohlhaas's search for justice—ridiculed by the powers of corruption; his demand for recognition as a legal subject—denied by a death sentence that pronounces him an outlaw;[63] and his quest for a heroic existence—nullified by his reduction to complete passivity. This, then, is an ending that retroactively annuls the meaningfulness of the narrative that led to it. It dismisses as failure not only Kohlhaas's melodramatic rebellion but also, it would seem, Kleist's attempt to create, under the sign of Michael Kohlhaas, a truly revolutionary text.

Repetition

So what does it mean that precisely at this point, when everything seems to be over and done with, the Elector of Brandenburg, in the manner of a deus ex machina, "intervened to pluck [Kohlhaas] from the fist of arbitrary power; in a note presented to the Chancery of State in Dresden, he claimed him as a subject of Brandenburg" (MK/G 157)? Note that the new sequence is staged as an act of *repetition,* as a going over again of a ground already covered. On his way from Dresden to Berlin, Kohlhaas once again crosses the border between Saxony and Brandenburg:

> Now just at this time the Elector of Saxony, at the invitation of the High Bailiff, Count Aloysius von Kallheim, who in those days owned broad estates *along the Saxon border,* had gone to a great stag hunt at Dahme that had been got up for his entertainment. . . . [T]he entire company, still covered with the dust of the hunt, were seated at table and being served by pages, while lively music sounded . . . when Kohlhaas and his escort of horsemen came riding slowly up the road from Dresden. For the illness of one of his little children, who were quite frail, had made it necessary for the [group] to hold up for three days in Herzberg. . . . The Elector, with his shirt open at the throat . . . said "Let's go and offer this goblet of wine to the unfortunate fellow, whoever he may be." . . . [T]he entire company had already streamed out of the tent with refreshments of every kind in their hands when the High Bailiff came toward them in evident embarrassment and begged them to stay where they were. When the Elector asked him in surprise what had happened . . . the Bailiff . . . stammered out that it was

Kohlhaas who was in the wagon; at this piece of news, which none could understand, for it was public knowledge that the horse dealer had departed six days ago, the Chamberlain, Sir Kunz . . . emptied his goblet of wine into the sand . . . and while the Knight Friedrich von Malzahn, respectfully saluting the company, whom he did not know, *passed slowly through the tent ropes running across the road* and continued on his way toward Dahme, the ladies and gentlemen, at the Bailiff's invitation, returned inside the tent. (MK/G 159–60; emphasis added)[64]

The new narrative, which begins as repetition, accomplishes what the old one (rebellion, Dresden episode) was incapable of achieving: the accommodation of Kohlhaas's desires. However, this accommodation is linked to the displacement of agency from Kohlhaas to the two authorities that intervene on his behalf; the Elector of Brandenburg and a mysterious gypsy soothsayer, who bears a resemblance to his deceased wife. Kohlhaas's success is thus dependent on the foreclosure of the solipsistic vision of morality and history that guides his rebellion. He achieves his goals only after he yields to the narrative logic of two interwoven, yet relatively independent, stories: the legal story about his demand for his rights, which depends on the decisions and writings of the Elector of Brandenburg and the emperor; and the story of revenge and aggression, which centers around the soothsayer's prophecy.

The radical break in narrative structure that occurs with the intervention of the Elector of Brandenburg has been a recurrent issue in the critical literature, starting with Ludwig Tieck's debunking of the anti-realistic stance of the final sequence as a "phantastische Traumwelt" (fantastic dreamworld).[65] More recently, Roland Reuß has proposed a sophisticated reading that culminates in the identification of the soothsayer as the novella's allegory of its own poetic character. The limitation of this interpretation is obvious in its omissions. Not even in passing does Reuß comment on the other half of the ending, on the story involving the Elector of Brandenburg. If Reuß ignores the political dimension of Kleist's novella, Wolf Kittler's work conversely sidesteps all formal and representational questions. There exists, then, a strange division of labor in recent Kleist scholarship: while Reuß focuses on the figure of the gypsy, interpreting the novella in terms of artistic self-referentiality, his new-historicist counterpart Wolf Kittler instead concentrates exclusively on the figure of the Elector of Brandenburg, reading Kleist's story as a straightforward propagandistic pamphlet for the Prussian state.

That Kleist's novella should give rise to two such diametrically opposed interpretations is no accident. The critical divide echoes the novella's narrative bifurcation, its splitting, in the last sequence, into two narrative strands. Kittler and Reuß each simply ignore the strand that does not fit their readings, gaining interpretative univocality at the price of overlooking the dyadic structure of the novella. The obvious question then arises, what is the relation between these two paths, between elector and soothsayer, between propaganda and self-referentiality, and between politics and poetics? The introduction of the elector as a deus ex machina suggests a first answer. Cast as an explicity poetic gesture, the intervention marks a moment of logical compression that recalibrates the narrative, which from this point on moves inexorably toward the final orgy of satisfaction. Compared to the frustration of narrative at the end of the Dresden episode, the aesthetic teleology of the final sequence thus assumes the character of an energetic interpolation. In other words, the break with the realist mode that initiates the novella's final sequence signals a shift in the text's underlying semiotic model from the constative to the energetic. On the reading I want to suggest, politics (elector) and poetics (soothsayer) are presented not as distinct domains but as interwoven and interdependent articulations of the energetic sign: if politics is concerned with the reorganization of impersonal energies into the fabric of civic life, the poetic gives expression to the unmanageability of the energetic, to its asemantic, and thus unnamable, dimension, a trajectory that culminates in Kohlhaas's ingestion of the prophetic sign.

Let me first turn to the undoing of constative language, which is evident in the text's subversion of the referential pretensions of the chronicle fiction. The chronicle is only the extreme generic manifestation of a mimetic principle that underlies all realistic narratives: the claim that events predate and determine their representation. "Narrative," writes Peter Brooks, "always makes the implicit claim to be in a state of repetition, as a going over again of a ground already covered: a *sjuzet* repeating the *fabula*."[66] If mimetic repetition serves to ground the sign in an extraverbal referent, Kleist's intratextual repetition—the retelling of an already reported episode—functions to subvert the latter's purported realism. Put differently, the novella does not simply abandon constative language but instead submits it to a rhetorical replication through which it releases its fictional kernel. Consider in this context the text's ever more complex play with historiographical discourse. On one hand, and in perfect agreement with historiographic rhetoric, the narrator increasingly disrupts the flow of narration, underscoring the difference between textual report and reported events. "Where he [the Elector of Saxony] actually went, and whether in fact he arrived in Dessau, we shall not attempt to say, as the chronicles which we have compared oddly contradict and cancel one another on this point" (MK/G 179). The novella, which up to this point was presented as part of a single chronicle ("Aus einer alten Chronik"), is now said to be compiled from several sources. The stress on compilation takes the text one step further away from historical reality, but in a manner that underscores, rather than weakens, its claim to historical truth: history, it now seems, speaks to us through the voice of a conscientious historian who compares and checks his sources, omitting from his report what cannot be ascertained without doubt.

However, this historiographic rhetoric is mocked elsewhere. "Now it happened that at this time the Polish crown was involved in a dispute with the House of Saxony, *over what we do not know,* and pressed the Elector of Brandenburg repeatedly to make common cause with them against the Saxons" (MK/G 157; trans. modified, emphasis added). The obvious absurdity of this statement—the allegedly unknown causes of the war are recorded in every history book—reveals the concession of ignorance, this ultimate gesture of integrity and reliability, to be a rhetorical mask that hides a gesture of cunning authorial manipulation.[67] Many more instances of manipulation could be cited, but none is perhaps more revealing than the text's foregrounding of chance and accident, signaled by one of Kleist's hallmark sentences: "Es traf sich aber daß" (It happened that). To cite only a few instances, "Es traf sich aber daß" Poland is in conflict with Saxony (MK 113); the elector is stag hunting on the border with Brandenburg (MK 115); and the Chamberlain chooses the real gypsy woman to contact Kohlhaas, when in fact he was only looking for someone resembling her (MK 134). Unlikely by themselves, these events are even more improbable in light of the series they constitute. The chance occurrences form decisive turning points in a narrative chain that "happens to" result in Kohlhaas's final satisfaction. The narrative continuity of the final sequence, in other words, hinges on the concatenation, without causal relation, of highly improbable events; the climactic closure, this orgy of fulfilled desire, is accomplished through the *absence* of internal motivation.

This "chancing" undoubtedly affects the text's representational status. The forced causality exposes what Roland Barthes has called the "mainspring of narrative," namely, "the confusion of consecution and consequence, what comes *after* being read in narrative as what is caused *by.*"[68] If the smooth blending of sequentiality with causality is the source of narrative's ability to "discover" meaningful designs in temporal sequences, the forced causality of Kleist's text, by contrast, denaturalizes historical reason: meaning here is marked as the effect of authorial imposition and aesthetic sovereignty.

Ironically, then, it is under the cover of a decisively realistic rhetoric that the novella introduces a type of narrative that undercuts the distinction between telling and told, between *fabula* and *sjuzet*. The seemingly coincidental encounters, and the meaning that emerges from them, are not the product of chance, but the effect of sentences that bring these events into collision. The text, that is, assumes a generative role: it no longer speaks *of* something, but, rather, speaks something, brings it about through the force of its own utterance. The force at issue here is that of energetic impersonal speech, and indeed the rhetoric of the impersonal (i.e., the idiom of "Es traf sich daß"), while on the face of it a familiar trope of traditional realism, is employed here as the modality of authorial imposition, which subverts the constative in favor of the generative and energetic axis of language. It is precisely this collapse of mimesis that the narrator announces in what is perhaps the most enigmatic statement of the entire novella, a sentence that, I am tempted to say, tells us how to read and, above all, how not to read *Michael Kohlhaas*:

> and as probability is not always on the side of truth, *it just so happened that* [*Es traf sich daß*] something had occurred here which we do report; nonetheless, anyone who so pleases we must concede the liberty to doubt it: the Chamberlain had committed the most appalling of blunders, for in the old rag seller whom he had picked up in the streets of Berlin in order to imitate [*nachahmen*] the gypsy woman, he had *encountered* [*getroffen*] the mysterious gypsy woman herself, whom he had *wanted to imitate* [*die er nachgeahmt wissen wollte*]. (MK 134; trans. mine, emphasis added)

The rhetoric of historiography is a ruse; the appeal to the Aristotelian distinction between history and poetry, ostensibly meant to underscore the factual and mimetic character of the narrated events, collapses when read in the light of the Chamberlain's "most appalling of blunders": the blunder of understanding the gypsy woman's mysterious art in terms of imitation. What the Chamberlain treats only as a means for imitating reality turns out to be identical with that reality; the gypsy in Berlin is the same as the gypsy in Jüterbock, just as the novella is indistinguishable from the history it tells.

Soothsaying

Nowhere is the novella's rejection of constative language more manifest than in the figure of the soothsayer.[69] This is not to say that the soothsayer is an allegory of the novella's own operations, nor that soothsaying as such is opposed to constative language. After all, soothsaying is, in the first instance, a form of truth saying, and is thus a type of constative speech, albeit one that elevates the constative to the level of the uncanny. Prophetic speech is simply true speech about the future, and the occurrence of what it prophesizes is evidence both of its authenticity and of the inevitability of the future it presages. Thus understood, the representationalism of soothsaying, with its elision of temporality, stands in direct opposition to the energetic model of speech discussed so far, and the claim that Kleist's novella conceives of its own pragmatic aspirations on the model of prophetic speech would seem, on the face of it, untenable.

Perhaps it is difficulties of this kind that account for the tendency in critical discussions of the soothsayer to avoid questions of historical causality in favor of an almost exclusive focus on matters of self-referentiality. To be sure, there are good reasons to conceive of the soothsayer's "mysterious art" (geheimnisvolle Kunst) in autological terms: her inhuman, artificial appearance, epitomized in "her gaze, cold and lifeless, as from eyes of marble" (MK 129);[70] the sudden and almost magical reversal she effects with regard to the struggle between Kohlhaas and the Elector of Saxony; her disruption of the historical chronotype, bound up with the novella's foregrounding of its textual character; the similarity between her and Kohlhaas's dead wife Lisbeth, which constitutes the most obvious example of the novella's employment of parallelism, a rhetorical figure that for late eighteenth-century aesthetics was *the* defining feature of art;[71] and finally, the fact that in Kleist's time, the figure of the gypsy had already become a literary topos, a stereotypical metaphor for the fantastic and the poetic.[72] But to read the soothsayer only as a figure of the poetic without any reference to questions of historical causality is to misconstrue Kleist's conception of the poetic, according to which the latter is directly implicated in the realms of politics and history. The poetic is for Kleist a conduit of the energetic, a medium through which what lies beyond language, and drives it, is drawn into its midst, and poetic speech, conceived in these terms, is neither constative nor simply self-referential. This is nowhere more evident than in the text's rewriting of soothsaying, that quintessential trope of poetic self-reflexivity and constativity.

To begin with, the art of soothsaying is explicitly introduced as a challenge to political sovereignty. According to the Elector of Saxony, who recounts the first and only encounter between the political authorities and the soothsayer,

> the Elector of Brandenburg and I encountered a gypsy woman on the third day of our meeting in Jüterbock. Now the Elector, who has a very lively

spirit, *had decided to destroy, through a joke played on her in front of all the people, the reputation of this bizarre woman, whose mysterious art had just been made, in an unseemly manner, the subject of conversation at dinner.* Walking up to her table with folded arms, he demanded a sign from her, one that could be put to the proof that very day, to confirm the truth of the fortune she should tell; otherwise, he declared, though she were the Roman Sibyl herself, he would not believe one word she said. (MK 128; emphasis added)[73]

The Elector of Brandenburg responds to a threat to his sovereignty: the gypsy's ability to predict history interferes with, and indeed curtails, his political prerogative to make it. Where mystical speech describes the future, political authority is reduced to the role of a handmaid, executing a reality it can neither alter nor master. But the elector's attempt to ridicule the gypsy backfires as her prediction comes true, while her second prediction, which bears on the political fate of the Elector of Saxony, becomes instrumental in Kohlhaas's revenge on the Saxon ruler. Thus the prophetic art, rather than functioning as a trope of self-reference, serves as an emblem and instrument of Kohlhaas's attack on the authorities. Indeed, Kleist's use of the soothsayer mirrors on this point the historical status of the predictive arts during Kohlhaas's time. As Reinhart Koselleck has pointed out, "the genesis of the absolutist state is accompanied by a continuous struggle against all manner of religious and political predictions. The state enforced a monopoly on the control of the future by suppressing apocalyptic and astrological readings of the future."[74] Depicting a moment of constituting sovereignty in early modernity, Kleist folds the figure of the soothsayer, a historical threat to the state's emerging monopoly of power, into his own conception of art as an energetic, and thus political, force.

As mentioned earlier, soothsaying traditionally understood is truth saying, a constative utterance concerning the future, and as such has no causal efficacy, that is, no productive energetic dimension. In Kleist, on the other hand, soothsaying is charged language not because it is *about,* but because it is designed to *affect,* the future, and it achieves this task precisely when it is misunderstood in constative terms. Let us once again look at the decisive scene in the marketplace. To the challenge of the Elector of Brandenburg, who demands from the gypsy a sign,

measuring us at a glance from head to foot, she said that this was the sign: the big roebuck that the gardener's son was raising in the park would come to meet us in the market place where we were standing, before we should have gone away. Now the roebuck, you must understand, was intended for the Dresden kitchen and was kept under lock and key inside an enclosure surrounded by high palings and shaded by the oaks of the park; and since the park as a whole, as well as the garden leading into it, was also kept carefully locked because of the smaller game and the fowl they contained, it was impossible to see how the beast could fulfill the strange prediction and come to meet us in the square. Nevertheless, the Elector was afraid there was some trick in it, and after a short consultation with me, since he was absolutely bent on exposing the ridiculousness of everything she had to say, he sent to the castle and ordered the roebuck slaughtered then and there and the carcass dressed for dinner on one of the next days. Then, turning back to the woman, before whom all this had been openly done, he said, "Well, now! What kind of fortune have you got to tell me?" (MK/G 170–71)[75]

And in fact, after the gypsy foretells the contrasting political futures of the two electors—one openly proclaimed and predicted to be glorious and successful (Elector of Brandenburg), the other withheld and written down but supposedly disastrous and deadly (Elector of Saxony)—the sign of proof called for by the Elector of Brandenburg does appear:

"But at that very moment, I confess to my immense relief, the knight whom the Elector had sent to the castle reappeared and reported to him, with a broad grin, that two hunters had killed the roebuck under his very eyes and hauled it off to the kitchen. The Elector jovially put his arm around mine with the intention of leading me from the square, and said, 'Well, do you see? Her prophecy was just an ordinary swindle, not worth the time and money it cost us!' But what was our surprise when a shout went up, even before these words were fairly out of his mouth, all around the square, and everybody turned to see a huge butcher's dog trotting toward us from the castle yard with the roebuck that he had seized by the neck in the kitchen as fair game: and . . . he let it fall to the ground three paces from us—and so in fact the woman's prophecy, which had been her pledge for the truth of everything she said, was fulfilled, and the roebuck, dead though it was, to be sure, had come to meet us in the market place. The lightning that plummets from a winter's sky is no more devastating than this sight was to me, and my first endeavor, as soon as I got free of the people around me, was to discover the whereabouts of the man with the feathered bonnet [i.e., Kohlhaas] whom the woman had pointed out to me. . . . And then, friend Kunz, a few days ago, in the farmhouse at Dahme, I saw the man with my own eyes!"— And letting go the Chamberlain's hand and wiping his sweating face, he fell back on the couch. (MK/G 173)[76]

The common reading of the prophecy in terms of magical speech remains blind to the energetic dimension of speech as such, and to the concentration of this dimension in the prophetic. Not the prediction as such, but the elector's attempt to avoid it—and thus, his belief in its truth-bearing nature—leads to the fulfillment of the prophecy. The force of the prophecy, in other words, rests on the elector's failure to register his own role in the scene of prediction, and it is owing to this blindness, and to his corresponding obsession with matters of truth and fact, that he is transfixed and enervated by the dynamic of prophecy. Like Mirabeau's "thunderbolt," which leaves the master of Ceremonies in a state of complete mental bankruptcy (*Geistesbankrott*), the "lightning" of the prophecy strikes down and deanimates the elector. The elector's misapprehension of the prophetic delivers him over to the literalness of its content: he quivers, faints, and suffers stroke after stroke, prefiguring the decline the gypsy had predicted for him. Like the chamberlain who commits the "terrible blunder" of mistaking the gypsy woman for a mere imitation, the elector falls prey to mimetic illusion.

Finale (1): The Self-Fashioning of Politics

The various threads of reading I have traced so far converge in the novella's spectacular finale. Unlike the rushed and aborted end of the Dresden episode, the novella's finale celebrates the rhetorical force of narrative closure and enacts an orgy of satisfaction. This second, successful closure, it is now clear, is made possible by a transfer of agency from Kohlhaas to the text. Where the horse dealer's melodramatic pamphlets fail, the novella's energetic self-interpolation, mediated through its two fictionalized conduits, the Elector of Brandenburg and the soothsayer, succeeds. The complexity of the finale derives from the fact that it presents us, *within* a space marked as fictional, with a double ending in which the political and the aesthetic are portrayed as independent, yet interrelated, dimensions of historical life. While the political, represented in the figure of the Elector of Brandenburg, is concerned with fashioning the public body and with structuring the anarchic elements of the sovereign state, the aesthetic, allegorically figured in Kohlhaas's swallowing of the prophecy, foregrounds the uncontainability of energetic signs, whose force radiates beyond the bounds of meaning and articulation.

The intervention of the Elector of Brandenburg determines the first—political—end of the novella, which emerges through a complex rewriting of melodrama. The ending shows how the state can marshal the popular passions aroused by Kohlhaas's revolt, and translate the subversive ferment of dissatisfaction into a spectacle that reinforces, rather than challenges, existing political hierarchies. This recasting of melodrama as propaganda presents the aesthetic as an integral part of the self-fashioning of the political. The aestheticization of politics, already signaled in the openly fictional insertion of the Elector of Brandenburg as deus ex machina, culminates in the highly choreographed spectacle of Kohlhaas's execution. And a spectacle it is:

> When he arrived at the scaffold, he found the Elector of Brandenburg and his suite, which included the Archchancellor Sir Heinrich von Geusau, sitting their horses in the midst of an immense crowd of people; on the Elector's right stood the Imperial Attorney General, Franz Müller, with a copy of the death sentence in his hand; on his left, his own attorney, Anton Zäuner, with the Dresden court's decree; *in the center of the half-open circle, which the crowd completed*, stood a herald with a bundle of articles in his hand, and the two black horses, sleek with health and pawing the ground with their hooves. . . . When Kohlhaas, with his guard, advanced up the knoll to the Elector, the latter said, "Well, Kohlhaas, this is the day on which justice is done you. Look here, *I am giving you back everything that was taken from you by force at Tronka Castle*, which I as your sovereign was duty bound to restore to you: the two blacks, the neckerchief, gold gulden, laundry—everything down to the money from the doctor's bill for your man Herse who fell at Mühlberg. Now are you satisfied with me?"
>
> At as sign from the Chancellor the decree was handed down to Kohlhaas, who . . . read it through with sparkling eyes; and when he found that it contained a clause condemning the Junker Wenzel von Tronka to two years' imprisonment, his feelings overcame him and, crossing his hands on his breast, he knelt down from afar before the Elector. . . .
>
> The Elector called out. "Kohlhaas, the horse dealer, now that satisfaction has been given you in this wise, you on your side prepare to satisfy His Majesty the Emperor . . . for breach of the public peace!" Taking off his hat and tossing it on the ground, Kohlhaas said he was ready to do so; he lifted the children from the ground one more time and hugged them tightly; then, giving them to the bailiff of Kohlhaasenbrück, who weeping silently, led them away from the square with him, he advanced to the block. (MK/G 180–82)[77]

Note the stress on visibility and externality in this passage. To the three groups participating in this spectacle—reader, protagonists, and anonymous crowd—the scene is fully legible: Kohlhaas reads the court's verdict, the readers know what he is reading; and the crowd, though without direct access to this information, nevertheless sees Kohlhaas's reaction to his reading, his kneeling down in front of the elector. In the world of this text, then, saying is a way of making visible, of making things public. And this transparency of linguistic and corporeal signifiers, which here symbolizes a spectacular moment of justice, the theatrical fulfillment of Just Power, is also presented as a conclusion to the narrative sequence: the spatial closure of the ideological circle ("in the center of the half-open circle, which the crowd completed") corresponds to and coincides with the temporal closure of the narrative circle, the restoration of everything that was taken from Kohlhaas, the return to the fullness that predates time and narrative.

For there can be no doubt that the two black horses, restored after a textual process of disintegration and decorporealization to their original material fullness, stand as emblems of a regained paradise of justice and identity. Kohlhaas's mythical conception of justice—his demand for the recovery of time—is granted narrative reality: the horses, emaciated and shabby "objects of ridicule for the ragamuffins and the idlers" (MK/G 143) in Dresden, reappear in Berlin "sleek with health and pawing the ground with their hooves," mirroring the "shiny-coated string" (MK/G 89) of the novella's opening scene.[78] Moreover, if the tree's denaturalization into a toll gate initiated the dissociation of an organic notion of justice into a system of arbitrary signs, the public spectacle in Berlin restores the balance of the natural and political order. The endless chain of bureaucratic deferrals and obfuscations now yields to a law whose presumed principle of fairness and symmetry is safeguarded by, and embodied in, a personalized agency.[79]

Thus the spectacle in Berlin presents Kohlhaas's mythical conception of justice as political reality; the fantasmatic is granted reality, the prelapsarian cast as historical fact. But it is not just Kohlhaas's desire that is at stake here, for this fantastic scene of individual wish fulfillment is part of a carefully orchestrated political phantasmagoria staged for the people ("in the center of the half-open circle, which the crowd completed"). More precisely, Kohlhaas's satisfaction is an element in a theater of compensation that establishes both the justice of the state and its singular prerogative in the administration of law and violence. This is the principal meaning of Kohlhaas's decapitation: "At the same time he [the Elector of Brandenburg] pointed out how necessary it was, in view of Nagelschmidt's continuing outrages, which the outlaw, with unheard of audacity, had even carried as far as Brandenburg, to make a horrible example of Kohlhaas [*wie notwendig . . . die Statuierung eines abschreckenden*

Beispiels wäre]" (MK 127). The individual is sacrificed to the juridico-political order, his death reduced to an example that substantiates the rule of law. And yet, even this sacrifice, this subsumption of the particular under the general, is presented as an element in an economy of exchange that recalibrates the balance of justice. If Kohlhaas submits to the death sentence, the scene suggests, it is only in exchange for the state's attentiveness to his demands and complaints. Kohlhaas's death is thus absorbed into a more encompassing arrangement that establishes the justice of the sovereign state. The public spectacle in Berlin stages the aesthetic production of sovereignty through the sacrifice of the individual.

The political is thus shown to rest on a double foundation: on an anarchically energetic element, and on the domestication of that element through the machinery of the state. It is propaganda, aesthetically conceived, that is the instrument of this institutional reconstitution. Art is shown to be an integral part of political operations, a constitutive moment in the self-fashioning of the political as an energetic sign. The fact that we, the readers, know that the spectacle of justice presented to the crowd in Berlin is a ruse intended to deter the people from challenging the state's monopoly of violence is therefore not an argument against this arrangement but a mechanism that enables the text, and us, to observe a (political) system whose vitality depends on its ability to fold asemantic passion into its symbolic operation.[80] The aesthetic propaganda of the Elector of Brandenburg continues the subversion, not just of the constative, but of the opposition between fiction and truth saying that marks the end of the novella. A pantomime of the constative, the fiction of the truth of justice staged in the public spectacle is neither simply true nor false; rather, it is an energetic sign that transforms the political landscape through its power to commandeer the passion of the impersonal. For can there be any doubt that the symbolic depth of the final tableau—that "half-open circle, which the crowd completed"—attests to a revitalized and unified body politic, and thus precisely to the kind of political community whose creation Kleist deemed necessary if Prussia was to survive the French invasion? The ending shows how the state can assemble the passions aroused by Kohlhaas's actions, and channel the people's seditious agitation into a spectacle that unifies the masses and thus strengthens existing political hierarchies. The fictional blueprint is indispensable in this scenario. Art brings about the unified *Gemeinschaft* by producing it as object of desire. Who knows, the crowd that witnesses the "voluntary" decapitation of its former "avenging angel" might just be ready to follow its hero's sacrifice when the moment calls for it. In other words, it might just be the community that Kleist envisioned in his most vicious anti-Napoleonic pamphlet, "Was gilt es in diesem Kriege?" ("What Is at Stake in This War"): "A community [*Eine Gemeinschaft*], which no German heart can survive, and that will be brought down only with blood that darkens the Sun."[81]

It is worth remarking that the revitalization of the political proceeds through the sacrifice of the sexualized body and the conversion of sexual into political energy. Note that the bankruptcy of the Saxon state is depicted in terms of the feminization of its leader: rather than mastering, the Elector of Saxony is mastered by his passions and desires (he blushes, faints, and makes political decisions based on romantic attachments).[82] Similarly, as we have seen, Kohlhaas's rebellion—and with it, the restoration of the political—depends on the obliteration of his wife and her transformation into an ethereal apparition. And finally, in the execution scene at the end of the story, Kohlhaas's daughters are notably absent, while the dubbing of his sons suggests the creation of a phallic symbolic order based on patrilineal ascendancy. The sexualized body, we might speculate, is the politically weak body, because it directs energy away from the *political* distinctions between friend/foe and sovereign/subject to the sexual distinction between masculine and feminine. Kohlhaas's (and Kleist's) struggle for the revitalization of the political depends upon the destruction of femininity and the inauguration of a phallic order.

Finale (2): Ingesting the Sign

The public spectacle concludes with the revitalization of the juridico-political order through the sacrifice of the individual. But this is not the conclusion of Kleist's novella. Hidden from public view, there unfolds another more private spectacle of revenge, through which the anarchic passion of the individual inscribes itself into history. If the public spectacle accomplishes, through a series of regulated symbolic gestures, the incorporation of the individual into the body politic, the private drama enacts, through the physical incorporation of the symbol, the triumph of aesthetic over political sovereignty.

> The Elector called out, "Kohlhaas, the horse dealer, now that satisfaction has been given you in this wise, you on your side prepare to satisfy His Majesty the Emperor, whose attorney stands right here, for breach of the public peace!" Taking off his hat and tossing it on the ground Kohlhaas said he was ready to do so: . . . He had just unknotted his neckerchief and opened his tunic when he caught sight, a short way off, of the figure that he knew with the blue and white plumes, standing between two knights whose

bodies half hid him from view. Kohlhaas, striding up in front of the man with a suddenness that took his guard by surprise, drew out the capsule, removed the paper, unsealed it and read it through; and looking steadily at the man with the blue and white plumes, in whose breast fond hopes were already beginning to spring, he stuck the paper in his mouth and swallowed it. At this sight the man with the blue and white crest was seized by a fit and fell unconscious to the ground. Kohlhaas, however, while his dismayed companions bent over him and raised him from the ground, turned around to the scaffold where his head fell under the executioner's ax.

Here ends the story of Kohlhaas. . . . Shortly thereafter the Elector of Saxony returned to Dresden, shattered in body and soul; what happened subsequently there must be read in history. Some hale and hearty descendants of Kohlhaas, however, were still living in Mecklenburg in the last century. (MK/G 182–83; trans. modified)[83]

Note the progressive narrowing of narrative scope: The focus shifts from an open political spectacle to a drama of revenge known to very few. The reader becomes the exclusive witness to a scene that involves only three parties: Kohlhaas, the soothsayer, and the Elector of Saxony. Ultimately, however, even the reader is excluded. When Kohlhaas in the end faces the elector and ostentatiously swallows the note, the reader, like the elector, has no knowledge of what the soothsayer has written on it. In fact, instead of the content (the date of the elector's fall from power) being disclosed, we are redirected to another text.

Kohlhaas's consumption of the prophecy attest to the persistence of an affective surplus that cannot be satisfied within the economy of exchange associated with the public spectacle. His unpredictable interruption of the execution ceremony—he steps forward "with a suddenness that took his guard by surprise"—is a step beyond the limits of legal subjectivity accorded to him within the public spectacle. In the first place, Kohlhaas wants more than his rights—he wants to *hurt* his enemy: "Noble Sir, if your sovereign should come to me and say, 'I'll destroy myself and the whole pack of those who help me wield the scepter'—destroy himself, mind you, which is the dearest wish of my soul—I would still refuse him the paper, which is worth more to him than his life, and say, 'You can send me to the scaffold, but I can make you suffer, and I mean to'" (MK/G 166). He accomplishes his goal by directing his aggression not at the physical body of his enemy, as in the first part of the novella, but instead at the object of the elector's desire. In ingesting the paper, which as Kohlhaas well understands, "is worth more to him [the elector] than his existence [*ist ihm mehr wert . . . als das Dasein*]" (MK 123), Kohlhaas destroys the very thing that sustains the elector's fantasy life, thus consuming his desire and vitality. The destructive force of this devitalization far exceeds the devitalization accomplished in the state's beheading of Kohlhaas: deprived of his desire, the elector is deanimated and stripped of all function and form, a heap of refuse and detritus ejected after his passage through the digestive system of Kohlhaasian power. In this sense, the act of swallowing is a conversion of prophecy into revenge.

Yet this act also functions as a textual mirror of Kleist's insertion of the text of *Michael Kohlhaas* into history. In eating the prophecy, Kohlhaas literally incorporates the symbol, thus inverting the process of sublimation that underpins all projects of *Bildung*, whether individual or collective. It is precisely this materialization of the sign—its absorption into the body of the individual—that brings about the sign's historical realization: its incorporation into the body of history. For the prophecy is said to contain the answer to three questions: "the name of the last ruler your house shall have, the year in which he shall lose his throne, and the name of the man who shall seize it for himself by force of arms [*den Namen des letzten Regenten deines Hauses, die Jahreszahl, da er sein Reich verlieren, und den Namen dessen, der es, durch die Gewalt der Waffen, an sich reißen wird*]" (MK/G 172; MK 129–30). For answers to these questions, the narrator refers the reader to historical chronicles ("wo man das Weitere in der Geschichte nachlesen muß"). Through the placement of this reference directly after Kohlhaas's swallowing of the prophecy and the elector's subsequent collapse, the text clearly suggests a causal relationship between Kohlhaas's aggression and the real elector's subsequent fate, between fictional narrative and historical chronicle. If the model for Kleist's character, the elector Johann Friedrich the Magnaminous, renounced his electorate for himself and his heirs shortly after his defeat by Charles V—and the year 1547, when this occurred, is one of the key dates in Saxony's history, known to most of Kleist's readers—this was so, the end suggests, because the fictional Kohlhaas used a fictional piece of paper to take revenge on him. The dismissive reference to "das Weitere" is thus not a self-referential gesture through which the text demarcates itself from its outside but, on the contrary, a device that signals the novella's impact on this outside, its power to transcend the borders of its own utterance.

This is not to say that Kleist's fiction is strictly analogous to soothsaying. Rather, the text confers the historical and epistemic authority of soothsaying upon the art of literary speech. Note that the elector's decline results not from the prophecy as such but from its swallowing—that is, from Kohlhaas's substantiation, one might even say: transubstantiation—of the letter of prophecy.

As we have seen, soothsaying is a form of truth saying and thus a type of constative speech. Kohlhaas's consumption of the prophecy signals an attack on this use of language and the reduction of constative to energetic speech. In ingesting the paper, Kohlhaas destroys, together with the letter of the prophecy, the possibility of distinguishing between word and meaning on which constative speech, and thus the prophecy's function as *Wahr-sagung,* depends. And yet, this fictional destruction of the referential dimension of the prophecy coincides with the historical realization of its meaning: the end of Kohlhaas's *Geschichte,* which is Kleist's invention, brings about the end of the elector, which is documented in actual *Geschichte.* Kleist's text thus effects, within a space marked as fictional, a shift from fiction to history through the incorporation of the sign and the somatization of meaning. Kohlhaas's swallowing of the paper marks the climactic realization of the project outlined in the "Allmähliche Verfertigung"—to recover the materiality of the sign. The finale of *Michael Kohlhaas* celebrates the historical force of energetic speech, of signs that, in opening themselves to the vitality of the body, produce change in the matter and meaning of history.

But this celebration of energetic speech also coincides with the death of the individual who functions as its vehicle. The end of Kleist's novella radicalizes the mechanism of the Kleistian bottle encountered in the "Allmähliche Verfertigung":

> Whereupon, well content with himself, he [Mirabeau] sat down.—As to the Master of Ceremonies, we must imagine him bankrupted by this encounter of all ideas. For a law applies rather similar to the law which says that if a body having no electricity of its own enters the zone of a body which has been electrified at once the latter's electricity will be produced in it. And just as in the electrified body, by a reciprocal effect, a strengthening of the innate electricity then occurs, so our speaker's confidence, as he annihilated his opponent, was converted into an inspired and extraordinary boldness. (GP 407)[84]

Unlike Mirabeau, who lives on to witness his opponent's historical demise, Kohlhaas outlives his foe only indirectly, through his descendants and his name. Kleist's novella carries the inhuman logic of his electrical metaphor to its conclusion. What matters according to this model is not the individuality of the subject but his ability to relinquish himself to the historical eventfulness of his own speech. Indeed, history is of fundamental importance to Kleist. It is no coincidence that Kleist aligns his hero with the trajectory of the Elector of Brandenburg and against the representative of Saxon power, Brandenburg's and hence Prussia's, historical enemy. In other words, *Michael Kohlhaas* is Kleist's prophecy, understood as Kohlhaas himself understands prophecy, not as a claim concerning the future but as an instrument of historical change. Just as Kohlhaas succeeds through rendering illegible what must be read, so Kleist seduces through a poetic concentration that both promises and frustrates decipherment. Kleist constructs a text whose singular intensity is designed to enlist the passions of his readers in the formation of a Prussian national community. Yet in the end, his ambition is perhaps no less than to lose and preserve himself in the impersonal monumentality of his writing, to bequeath to history a labyrinthine code whose key is always Kleist himself.

Conclusion

The Big Either

Each of the texts discussed in the preceding pages reads the French Revolution as the historical manifestation of a unique moral passion focused on the principles of human freedom and justice. In its intensity and extrasubjective orientation, this passion exceeds, and thus disrupts, the operations of ordinary life: the rituals of sociability, the utilitarian calculus of pleasures and profits, and the regulative economy of law and authority. Moral passion is thus linked to foundation, and, paradoxically, to foundational crisis and the state of exception. The moment of crisis brings to the fore what I have called the paradox of exteriority, the fact that the foundations of systems lie outside the systems in question. The fundamental form of this paradox, for all three authors, is located in a tension pertaining to subjectivity. The passion for freedom projects the subject along a trajectory that transcends the narrow confines of self-interest and interiority: the subject of moral passion is therefore necessarily a split subject; he is paradoxically situated outside of himself, or, to put it in Freudian terms, beyond the pleasure principle.

In Kant, this "beyond" makes itself felt in a complication of progress, which is no longer thought in terms of a linear developmental narrative but instead revolves around moments of rupture and crises. While the passion for freedom, identified by Kant as enthusiasm, reveals the historical efficacy of moral principle, this manifestation also discloses a transgressive dimension of moral practice. For the principle to become historically effective, it needs to be taken up, indeed passionately embraced by a subject, yet the passion that thereby mobilizes it is itself unprincipled and thus inclined toward unruliness and ultimately violence. Kant's remedy is legalistic: the passionate embrace of principle is to be tempered by the disciplinary apparatus of the state. In Goethe, the "beyond" threatens above all the everyday world of civility and communication. The Revolution is shown to unleash the absolutism of desire, of desire freed from all social and political constraints and tyrannically insisting on its own satisfaction, beyond even the boundaries of the self. The restitution of civility and the symbolic order here falls to art and the sublimation of desire it effects: the conversion of the freedom *of* desire to the freedom *from* desire. Finally, in Kleist, the "beyond" operates both in the domain of desire and law, the individual and the universal. Indeed, each term of the two oppositions stands as the "beyond" of the other. Kohlhaas's passionate embrace of justice not only draws into senseless particularity the universality of the law it invokes, it also exceeds, and ultimately destroys, the limits of individual subjectivity. Moreover, through the ritual of public decapitation, this excess achieves the status of political sacrifice: the individual, as exemplar of the particular, is sacrificed to the universal law of justice.

The problem of foundation first articulated in the works of Kant, Goethe, and Kleist found full expression in the literary and philosophical traditions of the following century. On the one hand, the paradox of exteriority became the defining problematic of the novella form, the dominant genre of nineteenth-century Germany literature. Modern novellas narrate the system's encounter with its internal otherness, the confrontation between a structured whole and what Lacan has called its "extimate"—intimate yet foreign—kernel.[1]

On the other hand, the concern with rupture, freedom, and the existential moment became the fulcrum of a philosophical critique of progress that culminated in an all-pervasive sense of crisis, including the crisis of philosophy itself. The progenitor of this last tradition is Kierkegaard, and it is in his work that literary and philosophical strands momentarily intersect. Not only does Kierkegaard write what may be called philosophical novellas, but his most sustained attack on modern life is articulated in an interpretation of a novella whose narrative turns on, of all things, a comparison between the Age of Revolution and his own time.

In the spring of 1846, Kierkegaard published *En literair Anmeldelse,* a book-length review of the novella *Two Ages* by the Danish writer Thomasine Gyllembourg. Divided into two stories set in the 1790s and 1840s respectively, *Two Ages* contrasts the high-flung idealism of the revolutionary age with the present period, suggesting that what the latter lacks in passion and intensity, it makes up for in civility and taste. In Kierkegaard's reading, Gyllembourg's rather pedestrian story becomes the foil for a full-scale attack on modern life. The present age, Kierkegaard charges, is one of unqualified reflection and dead signs. Private conversations or public announcements, the conduct of lovers or the workings of the state, commerce, or art—all modern phenomena have become subject to the devitalizing operations of reason. Kant's bureaucratic rationalization of passion seems to have worked all too well: not only does the unruliness of passion no longer threaten the progress of reason, but the institution charged with implementing the universal—the state—has come to operate independently of the life of the individual, as a bureaucratic machine responsive to nothing but its own internal logic. Kleist's sublime spectacle of the sacrifice of the individual to the universal, then, has given way to the daily routine of modern bureaucratic rule. Thus, in a move that at once repeats and reverses the logic of the preceding texts, Kierkegaard calls for a renewal of sacrifice, but this time it is reason, not passion, that is to be surrendered. The senseless march of progress, he maintains, can be interrupted only through the suspension of reflection and the embrace of religious passion.

"Reflection," Kierkegaard's term for the malady of reason, is unusually compendious in scope in his definition of it. In all of its multifariousness, however, its consequences are always the same: the leveling of difference and the devitalization of meaning. Reflection is above all an instrument of untrammeled abstraction, the machinery of homogenization and quantification. Its principal victim is thus individuality:

> Anyone can see that leveling has its profound importance in the ascendancy of the category "generation" over the category "individuality." Whereas in antiquity the host of individuals existed, so to speak, in order to determine how much the excellent individual was worth, today the coinage standard has been changed so that about so and so many human beings *uniformly* make one individual: thus it is merely a matter of getting the proper number—and then one has significance. . . . The trend today is the direction of mathematical equality, so that in all classes about so and so many uniformly make one individual. (TA 85)

As the individual registers not as an array of qualities but as a calculable quantity, significance becomes a question of magnitude rather than of excellence. The relevant individual in the present age, Kierkegaard seems to suggest, is no longer the concrete human being but the accumulated mass—that is, the group—to which the individual numerically contributes. One can see here the elements of a critique of representative democracy, conceived of as a political framework that, paradoxically, makes the public representation of the individual qua individual (i.e., outside the group or class to which s/he belongs) impossible.

The metaphor of "coinage" is not incidental. As in the realm of political representation, so in the realm of economics, value and quality have undergone a process of desubstantialization. In place of the irreducible material value of metal coins, value has taken on the abstract form of paper money: "Just as in our business transactions we long to hear the ring of real coins after the whisper of paper money, so we today long for a little primitivity" (TA 75). The ascendancy of paper money, however, is only the emblem of a more general economy of substitution. Desubstantialization is not confined to the realm of commerce but equally affects the play of desire. The age's fixation on money, for instance, is indicative of the rule of reflection, which dissolves all relations but that of substitution: "But an age without passion possesses no assets [*valuta*]; everything becomes, as it were, transactions in representatives. . . . So ultimately the object of desire is money, since it is itself a representative or an abstraction" (TA 75; trans. modified). To desire money is to desire, not an actual object, but the possibility of its substitution, or rather, possibility as such. For the age of unqualified reflection, Marx observes, money, "the common form into which all commodities as exchange values are transformed, i.e., the universal commodity,"[2] also becomes the universal object of desire.

Like Marx, Kierkegaard conceives of the internal logic of money as "inherently universalistic, necessarily devouring all sources of value other than money as pure exchange-value" (TA 151). Yet for him, capitalism and commodification are the symptoms of a deeper malaise of reason. Substitution, economic or otherwise, rests on the annulment of the principle of contradiction intrinsic to the operations of reflection:

> The present age is essentially a sensible age, devoid of passion, and therefore it has nullified the principle of contradiction. . . . The existential expression of nullifying the principle of contradiction is to be in contradiction to oneself. The creative omnipotence implicit in the passion of absolute disjunction [*Disjunctions-Lidenskap*] that leads the individual resolutely to make up his mind is transformed into the extensity of prudence and reflection—that is, by knowing and being everything possible to be in contradiction to oneself, that is, to be nothing at all. (TA 97)

Reflection distinguishes, but its distinctions are indifferent to value. Devoid of the "creative omnipotence implicit in the passion of absolute disjunction," the subject of reflection constantly creates distinctions without being able to choose one side of the distinction over the other. His, therefore, is a formless world of differences that do not make a difference, a world populated by equivalents and structured, not by the asymmetrical either/or of absolute disjunction, but by the uniform "and" of infinite reflection.

Reflection's lack of evaluative differentiation is at the heart of the evacuation of meaning in modern communication. The "and" of infinite equivalents finds its linguistic expression in the ubiquity of what Kierkegaard terms "chatter":[3]

> What is it to chatter? It is the annulment of the passionate disjunction between being silent and speaking. Only the person who can remain essentially silent can speak essentially, can act essentially. Silence is inwardness. Chattering gets ahead of essential speaking, and giving utterance to reflection has a weakening effect on action by getting ahead of it. But the person who can speak essentially because he is able to keep silent will not have a profusion of things to speak about but one thing only, and he will find time to speak and to keep silent. (TA 97)

In his "Allmähliche Verfertigung," Kleist had developed a model of history built on the agonistic tension between the finite time of the individual and the infinite time of community. Novelty, meaning, and life depend upon the seizure of time and historicity, the victory of individual thought in the contest of expression, of utterance over communication. In the present age, impersonal discourse—communication—has won the day, and "chatter" is the condition of its dominion. And yet, chatter does have a subject, though a strange one: the public and its official organ of expression—the press:

> For leveling really to take place, a phantom must first be raised, the spirit of leveling, a monstrous abstraction, an all-encompassing something that is nothing, a mirage—and this phantom is the public. Only in a passionless but reflective age can this phantom develop with the aid of the press, when the press itself becomes a phantom . . . The public is the actual master of leveling, for when there is approximate leveling, something is doing the leveling, but the public is a monstrous nonentity. . . .
>
> Only when there is no strong communal life to give substance to the concretion will the press create this abstraction "the public," made up of unsubstantial individuals who are never united or never can be united in the simultaneity of any situation or organization, and yet are claimed to be a whole. The public is a corps, outnumbering all the people together, but this

corps can never be called up for inspection; indeed it cannot even have so much as a single representative, because it is itself an abstraction. (TA 90–91)

If someone adopts the opinion of the public today and tomorrow is hissed and booed, he is hissed and booed by the public. A people, a general assembly, a community, a man still have a responsibility to be something, can know shame for fickleness and disloyalty, but public remains public. A people, an assembly, a person can change in such a way that one may say: they are no longer the same; but public can become the very opposite and is still the same—public. (TA 92)

Phantom, mirage, nonentity—the public is the true subject of the age of reflection precisely because it corresponds to no one in particular. And yet it is only through identification with this phantom subject, Kierkegaard seems to suggest, that the individual of the present age gains access to the world and his experience of it. In this identification, however, the individual exchanges his interior particularity for an impersonal simulacrum. His experiences, therefore, are no longer his own, indeed the possibilities of experience are not possibilities *for* him, since they are not possibilities *for* anyone. And this is precisely the problem: the subject of the present age lives in a world that abounds with differences and possibilities, yet the only relation he can bear to it is that of uninvolved spectatorship.[4] As Robert Musil puts it in his epitomy of this crisis, his great novel *The Man Without Qualities:* "A man without qualities consists of qualities without man."[5]

Two Ages registers a profound transformation of the sense of crisis. In Kant, Goethe, and Kleist, crisis was associated with the disruption of daily life brought about by the excess of passion and the overinvestment of ideas with affect. In Kierkegaard, by contrast, crisis arises from the evacuation of passion from everyday life. The subject of the present age inhabits a world of dead signs, of words, ideas, and rituals drained of affect and divested of energy, and it is this devitalization of symbolic life that gives rise to a pervasive sense of indifference and emptiness. The reign of reason results, paradoxically, in a crisis of meaninglessness. In his attack on modern life, Kierkegaard thus discovers the paradox of exteriority pertaining to meaning: the foundation of meaning lies outside the instrumentality of reason and the symbolic. It is to be found, not along the axis of concepts and universals, but along the axis of the individual and the particularity of human life. Meaning, in other words, is conceived of here purposefully rather than instrumentally; it is a function, not of the hierarchy of concepts and their objects, but of the passionate investments in the projects and plans of a particular subject.

This is why Kierkegaard reads the present age against the foil of the Revolution. For in the revolutionary age, which Kierkegaard understands as the age of passion and enthusiasm, the barren machinery of disjunction is transformed into the true engine of decision and action. The either/or of undifferentiated possibilities gives way to the asymmetric either/or of crisis, which is, as we have seen earlier, ultimately always the either/or of life and death. The point not to be missed is that this decisive moment is neither extraordinary nor limited to great events; rather, revolutionary decisiveness is a normative virtue of authentic life: "The presence of the crucial either/or depends upon the individual's own impassioned desire directed toward acting decisively, upon the individual's own intrinsic competence, and therefore a competent man covets an either/or in every situation because he does not want anything else" (TA 67; trans. modified).

Like Kant, then, Kierkegaard sees in revolution the revelation of moral passion, except that in his case, the stamp of morality does not derive from the presence of principle and reason but is expressed directly in the energy of an intrinsically ethical passion: "The age of revolution is essentially passionate; therefore it is essentially revelation, revelation, by a manifestation of energy" (TA 66). It is through the investment of this passion that the transformation of empty into full disjunction, of infinite possibility into actuality, is effected. In this sense, Kierkegaard represents a move from a Kantian—and, more broadly, Enlightenment—ethics of rule and principle to an anti-rationalist ethics of crisis and decision, which is already prefigured in Kleist's work and would become a dominant theme in early twentieth-century philosophical and political thought. Indeed, a short quotation from *Two Ages* might stand as a motto for the tradition in question: "It must come to a decision, but this, in turn, is the liberating factor; for decision is the little magic word that existence respects" (TA 66; trans. modified).

An exasperated sense of the impossibility of such liberation defines the early twentieth-century German and European novella tradition. In texts such as Conrad's *Heart of Darkness* (1902), Mann's *Death in Venice* (1912), and Kafka's *In the Penal Colony* (1919), the genre's concern with the absence of foundation and the crisis of meaning has moved beyond the local boundaries of subjectivity and nationhood: the sustainability and legitimacy of occidental culture as a whole is called into question.[6] All three novellas emplot the breakdown of the Enlightenment topography of center and periphery, of the centrality and sovereignty of reason, on the one hand, and the marginality and anomie of the primitive, on the other.

At the same time, a similar sense of crisis gave rise to a frenzy of foundational work in mathematics, scientific methodology, and philosophy itself.[7] An ultimate suspicion of the inadequacy of such attempts and the principal unavailability of foundation conventionally understood found expression in the works of Wittgenstein and Heidegger. In Wittgenstein, the discovery of the absence of foundation occurs as a moment of revelation, orienting philosophy toward the restitution of life and meaning in ordinary practice, freed from the governance of foundation. For the Heidegger of *Being and Time,* the groundlessness of the world discloses itself first of all in the minuscule crises that result from the breakdowns of ordinary functioning: the hammer whose head falls off, a flat tire, the ladder without rungs, and so on. The petrification of the world thus revealed is to be resolved through an inversion of the relation between individual and community, existential and historical time, death and progress. If, for Kleist, the vitality of life and history depends upon the individual's seizure of time—the decisive moment of utterance and action—against the horizon of his urgent finitude, for Heidegger, the authenticity of life depends upon the individual's passionate, yet terrified, embrace of finitude itself, indeed, of his death.

With Benjamin and Schmitt, finally, the critique of progress and the valorization of crisis is brought back to the domain of politics and law, indeed to the question of revolution. Like Kleist, Benjamin and Schmitt embrace the violence of revolution as its central and fundamental truth: revolutionary violence reveals the groundlessness of law and meaning and is itself unveiled as the source of spiritual and political salvation respectively. Schmitt, aligning himself explicitly with the Kierkegaardian panegyrics of exception,[8] is the champion of decision in its anti-democratic, indeed totalitarian, guise. "Sovereign is he who decides on the exception"—thus the famous opening sentence of his *Political Theology.*[9] The sovereign is the purest embodiment of the unfoundedness of law, the truth of which he exemplifies in his decision, in moments of exceptional danger, to legally suspend the law in order to preserve the state and its law. For Schmitt, the grounding of law in violence exemplified in the figure of the sovereign is a structural feature of every judicial act insofar as every such act *applies*—and thus goes beyond—established law;[10] indeed, it holds true for political life as such, which is nothing but a battle between ultimately unfounded principles. This is why Schmitt thinks that dictatorship is not only as legitimate as any other form of political organization but is indeed the purest expression of the truth of law and sovereignty. Schmitt's embrace of totalitarianism is a matter of principle.[11]

Despite his fascination with Schmitt's work, Benjamin's notion of violence is more complicated, and it is ultimately at odds with Schmitt's. For Benjamin, "violence" as such has no meaning; it is not a monolithic entity but instead depends on its orientation, provenance, and the context of its invocation. Indeed, the various forms of political and state violence that engage Schmitt are all illegitimate for Benjamin. Against this authoritarian violence, which is either law-making or law-preserving, Benjamin counterposes his notion of divine violence, which is the bloodless violence of messianic transformation.[12] Authoritarian violence is purely instrumental, in that it upholds the law and principles of an extant sovereignty; this is why Benjamin insists, somewhat paradoxically, that under conditions of the rule of law, the state of exception *is* the rule.[13] Divine violence, on the other hand, is eschatological and serves only the moment that it itself engenders. As such, it is the only legitimate form of sovereignty: "Divine violence, which is the sign and seal but never the means of sacred execution, may be called sovereign [*waltende*] violence."[14] This violence is one of finality and the end of time. The true crisis, for Benjamin, is the irruption of revelation; the pure state of exception is the messianic destruction of history.

Notes

Introduction. Energetic Signs

1. The most important exceptions are Gillespie, "Kleist's Hypotheses of Affective Expression"; Kowalik, "Kleist's Essay on Rhetoric"; Rohrwasser, "Eine Bombenpost"; and Neumann, "Stocken der Sprache." My reading of Kleist's essay is in dialog with two recent attempts to describe Kleist's media politics and his agonistic conception of "intersubjectivity." Blamberger, "Agonalität und Theatralität," locates Kleist's oeuvre in the tradition of moral skepticism (Montaigne, La Rochefoucauld, Castiglione), which conceives of the subject in pragmatic rather than expressive terms, meaning that the quality of actions is to be measured by its effectiveness in a world conceived of as fundamentally agonistic and extramoral. The duel, for Kleist, thus becomes the paradigm of both intersubjectivity and self-actualization. Despite many agreements, my reading differs from Blamberger's in that it stresses the importance for Kleist of the *eventfulness* of agonistic encounters. As the second and third anecdotes show, what matters for Kleist is not simply the victory of one subject over another but the effect of this agonistic act (or speech act) of self-preservation on the (textual, political, social) context in which it takes place. Moreover, this performative conception of the sign as radiating beyond the bounds of its articulation is intimately connected with the impersonal energies sedimented in the sign and thus depends on the impossibility of what Blamberger calls the "Steuerung der Selbstrepräsentation" (32) in moral skepticism. Dotzler, "Federkrieg," analyzing Kleist's anecdotes and journalistic activities in terms of media politics, stresses the role of effectiveness and intervention in Kleist's work. Kleist's literary politics is said to level the difference between literature and information in favor of the sheer positivity of speech. Speaking, for Kleist, is a way of usurping power, a way of launching a *Federkrieg*, or war of the pen, in which the

control of discourse is tantamount to control tout court. What matters is thus not the content or truth of discourse but "das factum brutum seiner Existenz" (61). While I agree with Dotzler's attempt to highlight the extrasemantic dimension of Kleist's conception of speech, I do not believe that this dimension is adequately captured in terms of sheer facticity. Effective language, for Kleist, is precisely not limited to the material dimension of the sign (Dotzler's "sheer positivity") but carries what is generally referred to as the force of language, a force that generates material effects without itself being reducible to "sheer" (whatever that might be) positivity. Despite this disagreement, Dotzler's argument on Kleist's media politics and his editorship of the *Berliner Abendblätter* is extremely interesting and adds an important institutional dimension to my own discussion of the "Allmähliche Verfertigung," which was, of course, first published in the *Abendblätter*.

2. See de Man, "Aesthetic Formalization," and Schneider, "Deconstruction of the Hermeneutical Body."

3. See also Wellbery, "Contingency," esp. 242–50.

4. "Oft sitze ich an meinem Geschäftstisch über den Akten, und erforsche, in einer verwickelten Streitsache, den Gesichtspunkt, aus welchem sie wohl zu beurteilen sein möge. Ich pflege dann gewöhnlich ins Licht zu sehn, als in den hellsten Punkt, bei dem Bestreben, in welchen mein innerstes Wesen begriffen ist, sich aufzuklären. Oder ich suche, wenn mir eine algebraische Aufgabe vorkommt, den ersten Ansatz, die Gleichung, die die gegebenen Verhältnisse ausdrückt, und aus welcher sich die Auflösung nachher durch Rechnung leicht ergibt." AV 535.

5. "Der Franzose sagt, l'appétit vient en mangeant, und dieser Erfahrungssatz bleibt wahr, wenn man ihn parodiert, und sagt, l'idée vient en parlant. . . . Und siehe da, wenn ich mit meiner Schwester davon rede, welche hinter mir sitzt, und arbeitet, so erfahre ich, was ich durch ein vielleicht stundenlanges Brüten nicht herausgebracht haben würde." AV 535.

6. "Nicht, als ob sie [die Schwester] es mir , im eigentlichen Sinne sagte. . . . Auch nicht, als ob sie mich durch geschickte Fragen auf den Punkt hinführe, auf welchen es ankommt, wenn schon das letzte häufig der Fall sein mag. Aber weil ich doch irgend eine dunkle Vorstellung habe, die mit dem, was ich suche, von fern her in einiger Verbindung steht, so prägt, wenn ich nur dreist einmal den Anfang mache, das Gemüt, während die Rede fortschreitet, in der Notwendigkeit, dem Anfang nun auch ein Ende zu finden, jene verworrene Vorstellung zur völligen Deutlichkeit aus, dergestalt, daß die Erkenntnis, zu meinem Erstaunen, mit der Periode fertig ist. Ich mische unartikulierte Töne ein, ziehe die Verbindungswörter in die Länge, gebrauche doch wohl eine Apposition, wo sie nicht nötig wäre, und bediene mich anderer, die Rede ausdehnender, Kunstgriffe, zur Fabrikation meiner Idee auf der Werkstätte der Vernunft, die gehörige Zeit zu gewinnen. Dabei ist mir nichts heilsamer, als eine Bewegung meiner Schwester, als ob sie mich unterbrechen wollte; denn mein ohnehin schon angestrengtes Gemüt wird durch diesen Versuch von außen, ihm die Rede zu entreißen, nur noch mehr

erregt, und in seiner Fähigkeit, wie ein großer General, wenn die Umstände drängen, noch um einen Grad höher gespannt." AV 535.

7. The attempt in Greiner, "Mediale Wende," to read Kleist's conception of speech in terms of Kant's aesthetic theory completely overlooks this agonistic dimension. Greiner sees the relation between speaker and other in analogy to the relation between imagination and intellect in Kant's conception of the beautiful. Given Kleist's own use of military metaphors, it is difficult to see how Greiner can claim that speaker and other stand in a nonhierarchical relationship to each other (166), and how this relationship can be described as play, let alone as a harmonious one. Similarly unconvincing is Greiner's interpretation of Kleistian speech in terms of Kant's "interesseloses Wohlgefallen" (165–66). Mirabeau and the fox, for instance, are highly interested in the outcome of their speech: they want to strike down the other and indeed to kill him off through their speech. Kleistian speech occurs in, and produces, moments of crisis and emergency, which is to say that it moves toward a decision and in this sense is diametrically opposed to the ideally unending play of the faculties in Kant's conception of the beautiful.

8. The distinction made by Rohrwasser, "Eine Bombenpost," between "wohlwollendem" (first and second anecdotes) and "feindlichem Gegenüber" (third and fourth anecdotes) overlooks the fact that the combative metaphors are introduced at the end of the first anecdote and thus already refer to the sister. For Kleist, the other as such is an opponent. Neumann, "Stocken der Sprache," underscores this agonistic dimension but overvalues the role of sexual difference in Kleist's conception of speech; the thesis that speech in Kleist emerges "im Spannungsfeld der Geschlechterdifferenz" (14) seems rather questionable in view of the intensification of antagonism in the second and third anecdotes, which deal exclusively with men.

9. "Ich mische unartikulierte Töne ein, ziehe die Verbindungswörter in die Länge, gebrauche doch wohl eine Apposition, wo sie nicht nötig wäre, und bediene mich anderer, die Rede ausdehnender, Kunstgriffe, zur Fabrikation meiner Idee auf der Werkstätte der Vernunft, die gehörige Zeit zu gewinnen." AV 405–6.

10. See Peters, *Speaking into the Air.*

11. I shall discuss the political, psychological, and narrative dimension of the term, as well as its connection to the notion of decision in more detail in the following chapters. For the moment, it suffices to point out the peculiar temporality of crisis, which is a "processual concept that moves toward a decision. It indicates that period of time in which a decision is due but has not yet been made," Koselleck writes ("Krise," 619). The pointedness of this time is intimately linked to its *finitude.* What gives the time of crisis its peculiar urgency is the perception that it will (and should) not last forever. Accordingly, a crisis has the temporal structure of a *finite progress:* it runs its course, and it runs it inevitably to its end. This finite temporality is at the center of Kleist's "Allmähliche Verfertigung" and, beyond that, of all the texts I discuss in this book.

12. "Ich glaube, daß mancher große Redner, in dem Augenblick, da er den Mund aufmachte, noch nicht wußte, was er sagen würde. Aber die Überzeugung, daß er die ihm nötige Gedankenfülle schon aus den Umständen, und der daraus resultierenden Erregung seines Gemüts schöpfen würde, machte ihm dreist genug, den Anfang, auf gutes Glück, hin zu setzen. Mir fällt jener 'Donnerkeil' des Mirabeau ein, mit welchem er den Zeremonienmeister abfertigte, der nach Aufhebung der letzten monarchischen Sitzung des Königs am 23ten Juni, in welcher dieser den Ständen auseinander zu gehen anbefohlen hatte, in den Sitzungssaal, in welchem die Stände noch verweilten, zurückkehrte, und sie befragte, ob sie den Befehl des Königs vernommen hätten? 'Ja' antwortete Mirabeau, 'wir haben des Königs Befehl vernommen'—ich bin gewiß, daß er bei diesem humanen Anfang, noch nicht an die Bajonette dachte, mit welchen er schloß: 'ja, mein Herr' wiederholte er, 'wir haben vernommen'—man sieht, daß er noch gar nicht recht wußte, was er will. 'Doch was berechtigt sie' fuhr er fort, und nun plötzlich ging ihm ein Quell ungeheurer Vortsellungen auf—'uns hier Befehle anzudeuten? Wir sind die Repräsentanten der Nation.'—Das war es was er brauchte! 'Die Nation gibt Befehle und empfängt keine.'—um sich gleich auf den Gipfel der Vermessenheit zu schwingen. 'Und damit ich mich Ihnen ganz deutlich erkläre'—und erst jetzo findet er,was den ganzen Widerstand, zu welchem seine Seele gerüstet dasteht, ausdrückt: 'so sagen Sie Ihrem Könige, daß wir unsre Plätze anders nicht, als auf die Gewalt der Bajonette verlassen werden.'—Worauf er sich, selbst zufrieden, auf einen Stuhl niedersetzte." AV 536–37.

13. "'Wir sind die Repräsentanten der Nation.'—Das war es was er brauchte!"

14. I am referring here primarily to the work on the ideological origins of the French Revolution done by François Furet and Keith Baker. See Furet, *Interpreting the French Revolution,* and Baker, *Inventing the French Revolution* and "Sovereignty." I discuss these questions in detail in Chapter 1.

15. "Man liest, daß Mirabeau, sobald der Zeremonienmeister sich entfernt hatte, aufstand, und vorschlug: 1) sich sogleich als Nationalversammlung, und 2) als unverletzlich, zu konstituieren." AV 537.

16. "Worauf er sich, selbst zufrieden auf einen Stuhl niedersetzte.—Wenn man an den Zeremoniemeister denkt, so kann man sich ihn bei diesem Auftritt nicht anders, als in einem völligen Geistesbankerott vorstellen, nach einem ähnlichen Gesetz, nach welchem in einem Körper, der von dem elektrischen Zustand Null ist, wenn er in eines elektrisierten Körpers Atmosphäre kommt, plötzlich die entgegengesetzte Elektrizität erweckt wird. Und wie in dem elektrischen dadurch, nach einer Wechselwirkung, der ihm inwohnende Elektrizitäts-Grad wieder verstärkt wird, so ging unseres Redners Mut, bei der Vernichtung seines Gegners zur verwegensten Begeisterung über." AV 537.

17. "Vielleicht, daß es auf diese Art zuletzt das Zucken einer Oberlippe war, oder ein zweideutiges Spiel an der Manschette, was in Frankreich den Umsturz der Ordnung der Dinge bewirkte." AV 537.

18. "Man kennt diese Fabel. Die Pest herrscht im Tierreich, der Löwe versam-

melt die Großen desselben, und eröffnet, daß dem Himmel, wenn er besänftigt werden solle, ein Opfer fallen müsse. Viele Sünder seien im Volke, der Tod des größesten müsse die übrigen vom Untergang retten. Sie möchtem ihm daher ihre Vergehungen aufrichtig bekennen. Er, für sein Teil gestehe, daß er, im Drange des Hungers, manchem Schafe den Garaus gemacht; auch dem Hunde, wenn er ihm zu nahe gekommen; ja, es sei ihm in leckerhaften Augenblicken zugestoßen, daß er den Schäfer gefressen. Wenn niemand sich größerer Schwachheiten schuldig gemacht habe, so sei er bereit zu sterben. 'Sire', sagt der Fuchs, der das Ungewitter von sich ableiten will, 'Sie sind zu großmütig. Ihr edler Eifer führt Sie zu weit. Was ist es, in Schaf erwürgen? Oder einen Hund, diese nichtwürdige Bestie? Und: quant au berger,' fährt er fort, denn dies ist der Hauptpunkt: 'on peut dire'; obschon er noch nicht weiß was? 'qu'il méritoit tout mal'; auf gut Glück, und somit ist er verwickelt; 'étant'; eine schlechte Phrase, die ihm aber Zeit verschafft: 'de ces gens là', und nun erst findet er den Gedanken, der ihn aus der Not reißt: 'qui sur les animaux se font un chimérique empire.'—Und jetzt beweist er, daß der Esel, der blutdürstige! (der alle Kräuter auffrißt) das zweckmäßigste Opfer sei, worauf alle über ihn herfallen, und ihn zerreißen." AV 538.

19. This "plague" refers in the last instance to what Carl Schmitt called the paradox of sovereignty, that is, the fact that the legal order rests on a moment of violence. In Kleist's time, this problem was discussed under the rubric of a right to rebellion and in terms of the question of popular sovereignty. Both issues—Is there a right to revolution? Who legitimates the sovereign?—acquire heightened significance in the context of the French Revolution. I discuss Kant's and Kleist's treatment of these questions, and their relation to a more general crisis of foundation, in Chapters 1 and 3.

20. Put differently, my work attempts to articulate the connection between the legal-political concept of the *state* of exception and a model of subjectivity characterized by linguistic and affective *states* of exception. The need for such an articulation is particularly obvious with respect to Kleist's writings, where the depiction of extreme political situations (war, revolution, rebellion) regularly opens the stage for scenes of extreme violence (*Penthesilea, Michael Kohlhaas, Earthquake in Chile, Hermannschlacht, Robert Guiskard*, etc.). In a compelling recent article, Manfred Schneider, "Welt im Ausnahmezustand," discusses Kleist's excessiveness against the background of legal and natural-legal conceptions of war and conflict. Kleist, Schneider argues, dismantles the traditional thought about war from Cicero to Pufendorf, which sees in the latter an exceptional state that, for all its exceptionality, is nonetheless bound to and regulated by codes of behavior that ultimately rest on the assumption of a law-governed and predictable natural order. In Kleist, on the other hand, war is "überall das Präludium . . . zum restlosen Unwahrscheinlichwerden der Welt" (105), "der Vorlauf für die Überschreitung, für das Außerkraftsetzen aller Erklärung, für das Dunkel- und Hilfloswerden der Welt unter der unbekannten, unberechenbare Gewalt" (114). As Schneider observes, in

this state of affairs, which he identifies with the structure of the state of exception (114–15), Kleist's characters are regularly driven by extreme affects and behave as if they were "von einem anderen Schauplatz her gesteuert, sie haben kein Bewußtsein" (118). My discussion of the impersonality of the energetic sign and its relation to the problem of sovereignty attempts to explore in more detail the systematic connection between affect, politics and law in Kleist's work. See also Chapter 3.

21. Austin, *How to Do Things with Words*, 6, 5.

22. Derrida, *Limited Inc*, 9.

23. Butler, *Excitable Speech*, 27.

24. Ibid., 159.

25. Derrida, *Limited Inc*, 9.

26. Felman, *Scandal of the Speaking Body*, 65.

27. Ibid., 67 (Felman's emphasis.)

28. Ibid., x.

29. Butler, "Afterword," in ibid., 118–19.

30. Obviously, not every sign induces a revolution. For a sign to unleash its revolutionary potential, the conventionalized linguistic and extralinguistic contexts that hold it in place and bind its charge must already be in flux. This is exactly what happens in Mirabeau's case. Mobilized by diffuse popular discontent and the passions of communicative exchange, Mirabeau's speech moves the symbolic cornerstone of the ancien régime, the notion of royal sovereignty, and installs it as the foundation of a revolutionary order; yet his speech can effect this transformation only because the edifice of conventions that have kept the term "sovereignty" in place have already begun to crumble.

31. For a rich documentation of responses to the French Revolution, see *Französische Revolution: Berichte und Deutungen,* ed. Günther; on the debate about the right to resistance, see Beiser, *Enlightenment, Revolution, and Romanticism;* on German Jacobinism, see Stephan, *Literarischer Jakobinismus in Deutschland.*

32. From Schiller's announcement to the journal *Horen,* which he coedited with Goethe. The journal's opening issues contained both Schiller's *Letters on the Aesthetic Education of Man* and Goethe's *Conversations of German Emigrants.* I discuss the political role of this journal and the relation between Schiller's and Goethe's text in Chapter 2. "Ankündigung," in Schiller, *Werke und Briefe,* 8: 1002.

33. The phrase "aesthetic turn" is taken from an influential essay by Marquard, "Kant und die Wende zur Ästhetik."

34. On the conceptual link between the French Revolution and German Idealism, see Henrich, *Aesthetic Judgment,* 85–99, and Pinkard, *German Philosophy.*

35. See also Pinkard, *German Philosophy,* 82–85.

36. See Hegel, *Phänomenologie des Geistes,* VI. B. III, "Die absolute Freiheit und der Schrecken." The classical study of Hegel's relationship to the French Revolution is Ritter, *Hegel and the French Revolution.*

37. This is also the common denominator behind a number of essays in the re-

cent *Cambridge Companion to German Idealism,* ed. Ameriks. For a comparison of Kant's and Hegel's theoretical and practical philosophy from this perspective, see Guyer, "Absolute Idealism," 37–57, and Pippen, "Hegel's Practical Philosophy," 180–200. Larmore, "Hölderlin and Novalis," 141–60, explores the attempts to overcome Kantian dualism in the works of Hölderlin and Novalis.

38. Hegel, *Vorlesungen über die Geschichte der Philosophie,* 18: 41.

39. For a discussion of the violent dimension of Schiller's organicism, see my "Of Beautiful and Dismembered Bodies."

40. Wellbery, "Enden des Menschen," 601.

41. Hegel's dialectic was strongly influenced by Goethe's botanical studies, according to Förster, "Bedeutung," an article that has strongly influenced my discussion of Hegel's organicism.

42. Hegel, *Phänomenologie des Geistes,* 52.

43. Pippen, "Hegel's Practical Philosophy," 188. See also Pinkard, *German Philosophy,* 59–60, which explicitly identifies Kant's fact of reason as "an expression of the Kantian paradox" and underscores its importance for post-Kantian idealism.

44. Pippen, "Hegel's Practical Philosophy," 194.

45. Nagel, *View from Nowhere.*

46. See Förster, "Bedeutung." My discussion of Goethe's method and its relation to Kant and Hegel follows closely Förster's account.

47. Förster, "Bedeutung," 335.

48. Ibid., 186.

49. Wellbery, "Enden des Menschen," 601.

50. Ibid., 634.

51. Ibid., 633 (Wellbery's emphases).

52. Ibid., 634.

53. Ibid., 632.

54. Note in this context also that Friedrich and Natalie, the two figures of supplementarity, are brother and sister of Lothario, the master of the Tower Society

55. For a more detailed account of the emergence of the modern German novella, see my "La forma e il caso" and "A Case of Individuality," 101–5. The only analysis of the novella in terms of its relation to philosophies of history appeared in a book devoted to the historical *novel.* "Historical Novel or Historical Novelle," the third chapter of Humphrey, *Historical Novel as Philosophy of History* (25–55), reads nineteenth-century poetological statements about the novella against the background of contemporary (1960s and 1970s) philosophical discussion on the nature of historical narratives (Danto, Walsh, etc.). Humphrey's argument is lucid and informative, but is clearly intended to indicate a gap in scholarship, rather than to close it by itself. The title of the first chapter in Swales, *German Novelle,* "The Novel as Historical Genre," is misguiding in this context, since Swales uses the term "historical" only to indicate that he is interested, not in the novella as an ideal form, but in how specific shorter narratives were shaped by "the traditional

normative presence of the genre expectation" (12). Swales's study nonetheless is to be recommended as one of the most evenhanded discussions of nineteenth-century novellas. Ingo Breuer's rich and illuminating essay "Schauplätze jämmerlicher Mordgeschichte," situates Kleist's engagement with history in the context of the generic tradition of the novella. Breuer shows that around 1800 the category of the "novella" covers a wide variety of shorter narrative forms that include fictional and nonfictional texts (anecdotes, moral tales, case history, news). More important than the novella's distinction from other fictional or nonfictional genres, according to Breuer, is its stress on historical veracity and its opposition to genres that appeal strongly to the reader's imagination (199–207). Kleist's work both follows and undermines this realistic mode of narration by exposing the rhetorical means through which literature produces *effects* of historicity and veracity (214–25): "Damit tritt das Erzählen von Novellen und Geschichten aus dem Bereich der Historiographie und des evidenten Exemplums heraus in den Bereich einer ästhetischen Fiktion, *indem* die Historia als vorgestellte und inszenierte Wirklichkeit vor Augen gestellt wird—und damit auch ein 'Hiatus von Historie und Fiktion' sowie die Auseinanderentwicklung von Rhetorik und Poetik" (224–25). For my own discussion of Kleist's "rhetoric of facticity," see Chapter 3.

56. See Koselleck's *Futures Past* and work on historical semantics represented in the six volumes of the dictionary *Geschichtliche Grundbegriffe.*

57. "Unser Zeitalter scheint uns aus einer Periode, die eben vorübergeht, in eine neue nicht weniger verschiedene zu führen." Humboldt, *Das achtzehne Jahrhundert*, in *Werke*, 1: 398.

58. Meier, *Greek Discovery of Politics*, 190.

59. "Es ist die Novelle eine Anekdote, eine noch unbekannte Geschichte . . . die an und für sich schon einzeln interessieren können muß, ohne irgend auf den Zusammenhang der Nationen, oder der Zeiten, oder auch auf die Fortschritte der Menschheit und das Verhältnis zur Bildung derselben zu sehen. Eine Geschichte also, die, streng genommen, nicht zur Geschichte gehört." Schlegel, "Nachricht von den poetischen Werken des Johannes Bocccaccio" (1801), quoted in Polheim, *Theorie und Kritik*, 12.

60. August Wilhelm Schlegel, *Vorlesungen über die schöne Literatur und Kunst (Lectures on Literature and Art)* (1803–4), cited in Polheim, *Theorie und Kritik*, 21.

61. F. D. E. Schleiermacher cited in ibid., 22.

62. Goethe, *Werke*, ed. Trunz, 6: 744 (conversation with Eckermann, January 29, 1827).

63. Wellbery, "Afterword," 294.

Chapter 1. Revealing Freedom

1. For a discussion of Kant's problems with the Prussian government, see Vor-länder, *Immanuel Kant*, 140–53.

2. Page numbers refer to the English and German versions of Kant's "Renewed Question." Quotations are from the bilingual edition of the essay in Kant, *Conflict of the Faculties / Streit der Fakultäten*, trans. Gregor (CF). The pagination of the English translation is cited first (and since the edition is bilingual, even short quotations sometimes span three pages), followed by that of the *Akademieausgabe* (AA), 7: 5–116. If there is only one citation, the translation is mine, and the pagination is that of AA.

3. The difficulty in upholding this barrier becomes obvious in Kleist's *Michael Kohlhaas,* where the return of the repressed gypsy prediction will enable the protagonist to satisfy his thirst not only for justice but also for vengeance. See Chapter 3.

4. Schneewind, "Autonomy," 332–33; Henrich, *Aesthetic Judgment,* 24–25.

5. See also Allison's claim in *Idealism and Freedom* that Kant's argument leaves open "the epistemic possibility that our putative freedom is illusory, that we are automata rather than agents" (141).

6. We confront here in very specific terms the paradox of foundation, what I earlier called the paradox of exteriority. What is at issue is the foundation of freedom. For Kant, as is well known, freedom consists of the free adherence to moral principle and to the actions that proceed from it. The first paradox is that the free adherence to principle manifested in the expression of enthusiasm is itself necessarily unprincipled. The expression of enthusiasm is by its very nature as affect irrational and hence unsusceptible to law and principle. Moreover, this unprincipled dimension is not an accident of human psychology; it is not a by-product but an integral aspect of freedom. To the extent that freedom requires the absence of determinacy, it tends toward causelessness and ultimately toward chaos. Kant, of course, tries to constrain the forces of chaos in a conception of freedom as principled action—that is, action governed and preceded by an invocation of principle—yet submission to principle is not itself governed by that or any other principle. Instead, it is a free expression of commitment. Viewed as such, enthusiasm is the affective correlate of the principle that prompts it, and it is only by virtue of this specific sort of affect that moral principle becomes operative. The second paradox concerns the foundation of Kant's model of teleological history: the discovery of the relevant concept of man according to which the unfolding of history is to proceed is a matter of historical accident. Put differently, teleological history, while understood as the principled unfolding of a concept, rests on a historical event that both in its irreducibly circumstantial and unpredictable character and in its energetic dimension falls outside the purview of the conceptual. As we shall see, it is this irrational and chaotic character of enthusiasm that prompts Kant's insistence on institutional mediation of its expression and his favoring of a strict top-down approach to social and political reform.

7. On the semantics of "epoch," see Kalweit, "Szenerien der Individualisierung," and Riedel, "Epoche. Epochenbewußtsein," who also discusses Kant's "Renewed Question."

8. Foucault, *Politics of Truth,* 84–85. See also Foucault's discussion of the "Renewed Question" in the same volume, 83–101.

9. Ibid., 86.

10. Kant's foregrounding of revolutionary enthusiasm was also a polemical intervention into a social field characterized by rather different descriptions of the present. According to Beiser, *Enlightenment, Revolution, and Romanticism,* for instance, Kant's essay indicates less about his own time than it does about his senile detachment from it. "By the late 1790s, however, such a proof [of enthusiasm as *Geschichtszeichen*] had already become very dated. The revolutionary wars had greatly diminished public sympathy for the Revolution. Sadly, the aging Kant had grown out of touch with history" (38). Beiser's first point—that the political climate in Europe in the late 1790s was vehemently anti-revolutionary—is well taken and indisputable. By 1798, the ideas and events of the Revolution were not simply forgotten, as Beiser suggests, but had become powerful ideological weapons in the Franco-Prussian confrontation. In Germany, following Friedrich von Gentz's translation in 1793 of Burke's *Reflections on the Revolution in France,* a number of conservatives had launched a full-scale dismissal of the Revolution, arguing that violence was the necessary outcome of the revolutionaries' "metaphysical" approach to politics, that is, of their attempt to organize historical realities according to abstract principles. The reactionary Prussian government under Friedrich Wilhelm II gladly picked up on these suggestions in order to implement an even more repressive public policy, tightening censorship laws, outlawing group meetings, and cracking down on all forms of expression contrary to official doctrine. In short, the Revolution and the conservative backlash had engendered an attitude that, in the years to come, would increasingly shape Prussian politics and German culture: the identification of ideas as political weapons and the ensuing pressure on politics to become ideological. Gentz, the main conservative voice in the 1790s, put the matter succinctly in a letter to Metternich in 1806: "Against an enemy like the one the Revolution has brought to this age our military and political skills cannot prevail . . . we shall soon be destroyed unless we bring entirely new weapons into the field" (quoted in Srbik, *Metternich,* 1: 112).

Gentz's "new weapons" point to the enormous transformation Prussia would undergo in response to the Napoleonic threat. This transformation included military reforms that revolved around the idea of an army of citizen-soldiers that would be inspired and mobilized by patriotism—that is, by a suicidal enthusiasm for the sublime idea of the nation. It is of course precisely this nationalist interpretation of enthusiasm that interested Kleist and made him write, among other things, a pamphlet entitled "Was gilt es in diesem Kriege?" ("What Is at Stake in This War"). There is no doubt then that in the Prussia of 1797–98, support for the revolution had "greatly diminished," and not just for the reason Beiser quotes. But the point is that Kant wrote his "Renewed Question" partly *in response* to this anti-revolutionary climate of emerging nationalism. In highlighting enthusiasm as the "event of our time," Kant does not misrecognize his time, as Beiser would have it, but engages in a struggle over descriptions that seek to determine what the present is. This is why no aspect of Kant's reading is more important than his claim that the meaning of the present is not available as a prediscursive fact, but depends on the nomological description—on the philosophical reading—of historical occurrences: enthusiasm becomes the event of our time only when it is conceived of as a *sign* of history. On the ideological weapon of Napoleonic France, see Sheehan, *German History*, 366. On the sobering effects of this policy on the prorevolutionary groups in Germany, see Blanning, *French Revolution in Germany*, chap. 7. For the conservative reaction to the French Revolution, see Valjavec, *Entstehung der politischen Strömungen*, 302–28; Aris, *Political Thought in Germany*, chap. 8 (on Gentz); and Beiser, *Enlightenment, Revolution, Romanticism*, chap. 12. The Prussian military reforms are discussed in Craig, *Politics of the Prussian Army*, chap. 2, and Kittler, *Geburt des Partisanen*. For the kinds of rhetoric and politics that begin but do not end with these reforms, take, e.g., Scharnhorst's assertion that the goal of the reforms was "to raise and inspire the spirit of the army, to bring the army and the nation into a more intimate union and to guide it to its characteristic and exalted destiny" (cited in Craig, *Politics of the Prussian Army*, 41).

11. Foucault, *Politics of Truth*, 99.

12. Ibid., 97.

13. The distinction between *Begebenheit* and *Eräugnis* is explicit in an earlier draft: see the so-called Kraków fragments printed in *Kant-Studien* 51 (1959–60): 6. In the published version, Kant makes the same point through the emphasis on the spectatorship of the enthusiasts and uses the term *Eräugnis* (an event that is seen) to capture the circumstantial nature of the progress made possible by enthusiasm, as we shall see. On the distinction between *Begebenheit* and *Eräugnis*, see Fenves, *Peculiar Fate*, 246–54.

14. Since the identification of an event is only possible on the basis of a distinction, and since every distinction requires a description of some kind (which can be wholly unconscious), the Revolution as an observed event is already an event under description, a sense-event.

15. The literature on Kant's attitude toward revolutions and the French Revolution is extensive. I found Korsgaard, "Taking the Law into Our Own Hands," and Fehér, "Practical Reason in the Revolution," most helpful. For the evolution of Kant's thought about revolutions, see Henrich, "Kant über die Revolution," and Burg, *Kant und die Französische Revolution*. Burg's "Die Französische Revolution als Heilsgeschehen," on the other hand, is very superficial. Not only is any religious interpretation of Kant's text untenable, but, even more problematical, Burg fails to distinguish properly between the Revolution and the reaction to it, thus missing Kant's major point.

16. On this distinction, see Fish, "Force," 503, who then of course goes on to deconstruct it.

17. Benjamin, "Critique of Violence," in *Reflections*, 277–300. Derrida, "Force of Law," forcefully brings out this performative dimension of law-preserving violence. For a very clear discussion of this performative aspect, see also Santner, *My Own Private Germany,* esp. 9–12, and the essays on Derrida collected in *Deconstruction and the Possibility of Justice*, ed. Cornell et al.

18. Korsgaard, "Taking the Law," 309.

19. Wittgenstein, *Philosophische Untersuchungen / Philosophical Investigations,* 25/25e.

20. Kant's discussion of radical evil and the execution of the king has become a favorite topic of deconstructive criticism. The best treatments are Fenves, *Peculiar Fate,* 271–77; Rogozinski, "It Makes Us Wrong"; and Joos, *Kant et la question de l'autorité,* 161–211.

21. The illegitimacy or legitimacy of the king's trial is still a subject of debate today. See Fehér, *Frozen Revolution,* 97–113.

22. Fenves, *Peculiar Fate,* is the most sustained and thorough reading of Kant's essay. Fenves is interested in the intersection of "world-history" and metaphysics in Kant's work, and he traces this crossing in and through three texts: Kant's *Universal Natural History and Theory of the Heavens;* his "Idea for a Universal History"; and the "Renewed Question." According to Fenves, it is in these relatively marginal texts that the "fate" of reason announced by Kant in the opening paragraph of the *Critique of Pure Reason* is most clearly spelled out. This "fate," Fenves argues, consists ultimately in reason's inability to ground itself, that is, to ground transcendental freedom. On this reading, "world-history" names the attempt by reason to account for "the appearance of the world in the first place" (2). Since this appearance is said to take place in language, Fenves's study is crucially concerned with Kant's language. Essentially, Fenves reads those "passages where the presentation outdoes the basic thesis it is supposed to illustrate" (2) as indicative of Kant's failure to ground freedom, and to answer the metaphysical questions reason is fated to ask. One result of this approach is that Fenves understands Kant's "primacy of practical reason" in terms of a primacy given to the "practice of reading philosophical diction" (4). Thus Kant's interest in progress and republicanism becomes an interest in reading signs that would make it possible to ground these notions. Unlike Fenves, I maintain that Kant's moral and pragmatic concerns cannot be reduced to matters of reading, and for two reasons: First, Kant is concerned not just with the *reception* but also with the *production* of Geschichtszeichen. Second, this linguistic production is itself bound up with political and pragmatic interests, and ultimately with Kant's attempt to help built a republican constitution. Moreover, while Fenves focuses on the instability of language, I am mostly concerned with the instability of the affective state on which Kant rests his model of history: enthusiasm. Notwithstanding these differences, I am deeply indebted to Fenves's brilliant reading, and especially to his comments on the status of communication, participation, and enthusiasm in Kant's work.

23. Lyotard, *Enthousiasme.*

24. Korsgaard, "Taking the Law," 319.

25. Žižek, *Plague of Fantasies,* 221.

26. On Kant's theory of freedom, see Allison, *Kant's Theory of Freedom,* and id., *Idealism and Freedom,* esp. 129–43.

27. For Deleuze, an "event" is neither a mere word nor a mere state of affairs but an action-under-description, or, as he calls it, a sense-event. Thus while Deleuze conceives of language in determinative rather than representational terms, he situates this pragmatic notion of language in the wider context of an ontological argument aimed at recasting "Being" as "Becoming" and "Event." Language as fluctuating sense (rather than as solid representation) mirrors the nonsubstantial dimension of all change, the birthing or becoming that occurs in every passage from one state of affairs to another, but that is not reducible to any of them. Deleuze and Guattari call this presence-in-process "pure sense-event" in *What Is Philosophy?* and describe it as an "unhistorical vapor" or virtual reservoir inherent in, but not exhausted by, any determinate occurrence (101). "This is what we call the Event, or the part that eludes its own actualization in everything that happens. . . . The event is pure immanence of what is not actualized or of what remains indifferent to actualization, since its reality does not depend upon it. The event is immaterial, incorporeal, unlivable: pure *reserve*" (156). For an excellent discussion of Deleuze's concept of language and event, see Patton, "World Seen from Within." Schaub, *Gilles Deleuze im Wunderland,* has recently presented a powerful interpretation of Deleuze's theory of time and event in its relationship to the philosophical tradition. See in particular 93–98, where Schaub discusses the difference between Kant's notion of the sublime and Deleuze's philosophy of the event.

28. Arendt, *On Revolution,* chap. 1.

29. Ibid., 38.

30. Ibid., 34.

31. Negri, *Potere costituente,* 8; my trans.

32. See Böckenförde, "Verfassungsgebende Gewalt."

33. On this last point, see Sieyès's observation, cited in Baker, *Inventing the French Revolution,* 287, that the constituent will of the people "alone is power; the others are only authorities."

34. On the religious and metaphysical connections, see Schmitt, *Verfassungslehre,* 77–80; on the link between Montesquieu and Sieyès, see Sauerwein, "'Omnipotenz' des pouvoir constituant," 27.

35. Negri, *Potere costituente,* 19.

36. On the verbalization of power in the French Revolution, see Furet, *Interpreting the French Revolution,* esp. 46–47. "Since the people alone had the right to govern—or at least, when it could not do so, to reassert public authority continually—power was in the hands of those who spoke for the people. Therefore, not

only did that power reside in the word, for the word, being public, was the means of unmasking forces that hoped to remain hidden and were thus nefarious; but also power was always at stake in the conflict between words, for power could only be appropriated through them, and so they had to compete for the conquest of that evanescent yet primordial entity, the people's will" (49). See also Hunt, *Politics, Culture and Class,* 19–123. On the problem of sovereignty during the French Revolution, see Baker, *Inventing the French Revolution,* 252–305, and id., "Sovereignty."

37. Baker, *Inventing the French Revolution,* 247.

38. Sieyès, *What Is the Third Estate?* 126.

39. Furet, *Interpreting the French Revolution,* 51.

40. Sieyès, *What Is the Third Estate?* 29. As for the nation's character outside history: "We must conceive of the nations of the world as being like men living outside society or 'in a state of nature,' as it is called" (127–28).

41. See the work by Furet and Baker.

42. Sieyès, *What Is the Third Estate?* 124.

43. "The right of lawgiving originates in the people but derives from the monarch [*Das recht der Gesetzgebung ist beym Volke originarie aber beym monarchen derivative*]," Kant observes (AA 19: 503, refl. 7734); and see also refl. 7713 (AA 19: 498).

44. Korsgaard, "Taking the Law," 310.

45. "Nothing seems more natural than that if the people have rights, they also have force [*Gewalt*]; but precisely because they cannot establish a legitimate force, they have no strict right but only an ideal one [*Es scheint nichts natürlicher, als das, wenn das Volk rechte hat, es auch eine Gewalt habe; aber eben darum, weil es keine rechtmäßige Gewalt etablieren kann, hat es auch kein strictes recht sondern nur ein ideales*]," Kant also writes (AA 19: 504, refl. 7737).

46. Kant's wavering has been noted by several scholars: e.g., Reiss, "Introduction," 29; Fehér, "Practical Reason in the Revolution," 212; and Burg, *Kant und die Französische Revolution,* 215–17.

47. See on this also Fehér, "Practical Reason in the Revolution," 212.

48. Agamben, *Homo Sacer,* 41. But see Agamben's entire discussion of constituting power and sovereignty, which also touches on the work of Arendt and Negri, esp. 39–49.

49. Arendt, *On Revolution,* 184–85. The passage is also cited in Agamben, *Homo Sacer,* 41.

50. See also PP 101, and Kant's refl. 7725: "By comparison the law (ex voluntate comuni) is impeccable, holy [*Dagegen ist das Gesetz (ex voluntate comuni) untadelhaft, heilig*]" (AA 19: 500).

51. This is the essence of right according to Kant. "This moral cause inserting itself is twofold: first, that of the *right,* that a nation must not be hindered in giving itself a civil constitution, which appears good to the people themselves" (CF 153/85).

52. Marx and Engels, *Collected Works,* 5: 73–74.

53. In fact, Kant's theatrical reading of the Revolution might be said to be even more aestheticizing than Aristotle's discussion of tragedy in the *Poetics.* Whereas Aristotle gives equal weight to tragic action and its imaginative reception, Kant foregrounds enthusiasm at the expense of the historical drama, which is reduced to a mere stage set. In other words, Kant's reading of the Revolution as tragedy seems calculated to deprive the political events in France of any tragic depth.

54. "Das Überschwängliche für die Einbildungskraft (bis zu welchem sie in der Auffassung der Anschauung getrieben wird) ist gleichsam ein Abgrund, worin sie sich selbst zu verlieren fürchtet." KU 103; my trans.

55. Balke, *Staat nach seinem Ende,* 254.

56. Delekat, *Immanuel Kant,* 283. According to Delekat's fascinating discussion, the distinction between *auctor legis* and legislator is of religious origin. A fundamental point of reference in this context is the tension between positive and natural law, exemplified most clearly, according to Delekat, in the relation between the Decalogue, which is mediated by Moses and addressed to the people of Israel, and natural laws that are thought to derive directly from God (283–86).

57. "A law (a morally-practical one) is a proposition which contains a categorical imperative (a command). One who commands (*imperans*) through a law is the *lawgiver* (*legislator*). He is the author (*auctor*) of the obligation in accordance with the law, but not always the author of the law. In the latter case the law would be a positive (contingent) and chosen law. A law that binds us a priori and unconditionally by our own reason can also be expressed as proceeding from the will of a supreme lawgiver, that is, one who has only rights and no duties (hence from the divine will). But this signifies only the idea of a moral being whose will is law for everyone, without his being thought as the author of the law." MM 381.

58. Baker, "Sovereignty," 852.

59. "When a people are united through laws under a suzerain, *then* the people are given as an object of experience conforming to the Idea in general of the unity of the people under a supreme powerful Will" (emphasis added). As Korsgaard, "Taking the Law," 65, helpfully comments: "What makes a people unified is that there are procedures under which they are unified, procedures that make collective decisions and actions possible, and give them a general will."

60. Sieyès, *What Is the Third Estate?* 124.

61. The spectatorial position also allows the enthusiasts a different relation to the sovereign voice within them. The wholly pleasurable nature of enthusiasm suggests a conception of freedom that is no longer bound up with the sacrificial logic so prevalent in Kant's earlier descriptions of moral feeling (respect, sublimity). As is well known, it was precisely this sacrificial logic that became the focus of the psychoanalytical critique of Kant's moral theory, which interpreted the latter in terms of obsessional masochism (Freud) or perverse sadism (Lacan). Both Freud's and Lacan's readings turn on the phantasm of an absolute master who de-

mands our pain and sacrifice, and thus on the very notion of sovereignty whose vicissitudes I have traced above. It is precisely the absence of this phantasm that accounts for the wholly pleasurable nature of enthusiasm. The joy of enthusiasm is the affective sign of a nonsacrificial relationship between subject and law, one in which the otherness of freedom is no longer experienced in terms of a punishment inflicted on the subject by some fantasmatic Master but as a mysterious gift coming from a place that is both in the subject yet beyond his volition and control. Enthusiasm, then, attests to a mode of freedom that combines self-legislation with lack, autonomy with respect for otherness, and activity with receptiveness.

62. As, for instance, in Kant's famous discussion about the duty of truth-speaking. See his "On a Supposed Right to Lie from Philanthropy" (1797).

63. Weber, *Institution and Interpretation*, 143.

64. "Nun behaupte ich dem Menschengeschlechte *nach den Aspecten und Vorzeichen unserer Tage* die Erreichung dieses Zwecks und hiemit zugleich das von *da an nicht mehr gänzlich rückgängig werdende Fortschreiten* desselben zum Besseren auch ohne Sehergeist vorhersagen zu können." CF 159/88; emphasis added.

65. The passage is somewhat ambiguous about the event that is supposed to become a bearer of progress: is it the Revolution or its reception?

66. I am alluding here to Kleist's story "Die Verlobung in Santo Domingo" (The Betrothal in Santo Domingo).

67. Descombes makes a similar argument in his excellent *Barometer of Modern Reason*, 31.

68. Fenves, *Peculiar Fate*, 265.

69. Fehér, "Practical Reason," 210.

Chapter 2. The Poetics of Containment

1. See Moretti, *Way of the World.*

2. On the dominance of the novella form in German culture, see my "La forma e il caso." The claim that the *Conversations* inaugurate the novella tradition in Germany is generally accepted both in the older (Wiese, Fricke, Polheim, Swales) and more recent (Neumann, Aust, Paulin, Schlaffer, Holland) literature on the subject. See in particular Henel, "Anfänge der deutschen Novelle." However, only one author has linked this generic observation to historical transformations of subjectivity and social structures. Neumann, "Anfänge deutscher Novellistik," perceives Schiller's "Verbrecher aus verlorener Ehre" and Goethe's *Conversations* as the dual origins of the modern German novella. According to Neumann, Goethe's novella must be read against the background of the radical changes in the eighteenth century that brought about both a new model of subjectivity, based on free will and emphatic self-expression and an increasing rationalization of all forms of society under the impact of science and the capitalist

economy. While I agree with Neumann's claim that Goethe's novella cycle addresses the crisis brought about by changes associated with the French Revolution, I disagree with his characterization of this crisis and thus with most of his readings of the novellas. In particular, I do not think that the novellas thematize subjectivity in view of new scientific (novellas 1 and 2), communicative (3 and 4), and economic structures (5 and 6). Inexplicability, for instance, is only one, and not the most disturbing, aspect of the sounds in the first two ghost stories, which are less interested with the limits of scientific explanation, as Neumann claims, than with the force of address and with communicative desire. Indeed, as my reading here will show, I believe that in all six novellas, what is at stake is the relation between desire and communication, language, and drive.

3. Starobinski, *Blessings in Disguise*, 203.

4. "In jenen unglücklichen Tagen, welche für Deutschland, für Europa, ja für die übrige Welt die traurigsten Folgen hatten, als das Heer der Franken durch eine übelverwahrte Lücke in unser Vaterland einbrach, verließ eine edle Familie ihre Besitzungen in jenen Gegenden und floh über den Rhein." UA 995.

5. For Luhmann's theory, see above all his *Social Systems.*

6. Wellbery, "Luhmann's Conceptual Design," 17, speaks aptly in this context of Luhmann's "stance or attitude of non-romantic marginalism."

7. For an excellent outline of the history of the concept of psychic trauma from Charcot to Freud, see Forrester, *Seductions of Psychoanalysis,* 192–206.

8. See Fischer and Riedesser, *Lehrbuch der Psychotraumatologie,* 58–120.

9. The distinction between accidental or historical and structural trauma is a crucial and often overlooked dimension of Freud's theory. Essentially, up to *Beyond the Pleasure Principle,* Freud subscribed to an accidental notion of trauma, which he understood to result from the subject's encounter with an external traumatic agent, so that it might or might not happen. In *Beyond the Pleasure Principle,* Freud identifies a second, internal source of trauma resulting from the drive itself, or, more precisely, in Paul Verhaeghe's words, from "the energetical real part of the drive, which can never be fully represented and keeps insisting" (56). In contrast to the first kind, this trauma is structural and unavoidable, something every human being has to deal with. For an excellent account of the differences between these two kinds of trauma, see Verhaeghe, *Beyond Gender,* 49–65.

10. According to Freud, anxious expectation and anticipation are protective mechanisms that enable the subject to bind and contain incoming stimuli. Traumatic events always take the subject by surprise. See his *Inhibition, Symptom, Anxiety,* in *SE* 20: 166; *GW* 14: 197–98.

11. "[B]ei dem ersten Schrecken ganz aus der Fassung geraten sei, in Zerstreuung, ja in einer Art von völliger Abwesenheit die unnützesten Sachen mit dem größten Ernste zum Aufpacken gebracht, ja sogar einen alten Bedienten für ihren Bräutigam angesehen habe." UA 996.

12. For a detailed discussion of the German novella from Goethe to Mann along these lines, see my "La forma e il caso."

13. Bakhtin, *Dialogic Imagination,* 16. As Bakhtin makes clear, this reliance on tradition is not just a matter of content or sources but a formal feature of epic discourse: "The epic relies entirely on this tradition. Important here is not the fact that tradition is the factual source for the epic—what matters rather is that a reliance on tradition is immanent in the very form of the epic, just as the absolute past is immanent in it" (ibid.).

14. I take the term "conversible world" from Russo, "Editor's Preface." For a contemporary account of sociability, see Friedrich Daniel Ernst Schleiermacher, "Versuch einer Theorie des geselligen Betragens," which was written in 1796, the same year Goethe's *Conversations* appeared. There has been good recent work on sociability. See France, *Politeness and Its Discontents; Yale French Studies* 92 (1997); and Luhmann, "Interaktion in Oberschichten," 136–61. See also Simmel, "Soziologie der Geselligkeit," and Barthes, "La Bruyère."

15. "Aber dasjenige kann ich von dem Zirkel erwarten, in dem ich lebe, daß Gleichgesinnte sich im Stillen zueinander fügen und sich angenehm unterhalten, indem der eine dasjenige sagt, was der der andere schon denkt." UA 1007.

16. "J'ai mal à votre poitrine" (I have a pain in your chest), Madame de Sévigné writes to her sick daughter (quoted in Julien, *Jacques Lacan's Return to Freud,* 86).

17. Schleiermacher, "Versuch einer Theorie," 169–70.

18. Ibid.

19. On the distinction between "inland" and "outland" in sociability, see Barthes, "La Bruyère," 227.

20. "Wie sehr hütete man sich sonst in der Gesellschaft irgend etwas zu berühren, was einem oder dem andern unangenehm sein konnte! Der Protestante vermied in Gegenwart des Katholiken irgend eine Zeremonie lächerlich zu finden; der eifrigste Katholik ließ den Protestanten nicht merken, daß die alte Religion eine größere Sicherheit ewiger Seligkeit gewähre." UA 1008.

21. Schleiermacher, "Versuch einer Theorie," 175–76.

22. Simmel, *Soziologie,* 396.

23. Russo, "Editor's Preface," 2.

24. Simmel, "Soziologie der Geselligkeit," 12.

25. Furet, *Revolutionary France,* 11.

26. "In jenen unglücklichen Tagen, welche für Deutschland, für Europa, ja für die übrige Welt die traurigsten Folgen hatten, als das Heer der Franken durch eine übelverwahrte Lücke in unser Vaterland einbrach, verließ eine edle Familie ihre Besitzungen in jenen Gegenden und floh über den Rhein, um den Bedrängnissen zu entgehen, womit alle ausgezeichneten Personen bedroht waren, denen man zum Verbrechen machte, daß sie sich ihrer Väter mit Freuden und Ehren erinnerten, und mancher Vorteile genossen, die ein wohldenkender Vater seinen Kindern und Nachkommen so gern zu verschaffen wünschte." UA 995.

27. On epic distance and the contrast between (dramatic) content and (tranquil) form, see, Redfield, *Nature and Culture in the Iliad,* 36–39; on tradition and epic resistance to change, see Nagy, *Greek Mythology and Poetics,* esp. 18–36, 294–303, as well, of course, as Bakhtin's work.

28. "There is no place in the epic world for any openendedness, indecision, indeterminacy." Bakhtin, *Dialogical Imagination,* 16.

29. Redfield, *Nature and Culture,* 38.

30. "Zu den kleinen Erzählungen habe ich große Lust, nach der Last, die einem so ein Pseudo-Epos, als der Roman ist, auflegt." UA 1510.

31. For the complex history of Goethe und Schiller's "Über Epische und Dramatische Poesie," which was published only in 1827, see the editor's comments in the German edition, 1133–35. Since the German edition of this essay is more comprehensive, I shall mostly quote from that. Unless otherwise noted, translations are mine.

32. See also Bakhtin's comments on the completeness of epic time: "This past is distanced, finished, and closed like a circle . . . within this time, completed and locked into a circle, all points are equidistant from the real, dynamic time of the present; insofar as this time is whole, it is not localized in an actual historical sequence; it is not relevant to the present or the future; it contains within itself, as it were, the entire fullness of time." *Dialogic Imagination,* 19.

33. On Herder, see Mücke, *Virtue and the Veil.*

34. See Bosse, "The Marvelous and Romantic Semiotics," esp. 224–34.

35. "Ich kann sie versichern versetzte der fremde Schiffer, sie waren vollkommen angesteckt ich traf sie in einer heftigen Crysis.

"Und was für eine Krankheit wäre es denn gewesen fragte Alciphron? Ich versteh mich doch ein wenig auf die Medizin.

"Es ist das Zeitfieber sagte der Fremde das einige auch das Fieber der Zeit, nennen und glauben sich noch bestimmter auszudrücken, andere nennen es das Zeitungsfieber, denen ich auch nicht e[n]ntgegen sein will. Es ist eine böse ansteckende Krankheit die sich sogar durch die Luft mitteilt. . . .

"Was sind denn die Symtome dieses Übels fragte Alciphron.

"Sie sind sonderbar und traurig genug versetzte der fremde, der Mensch vergißt sogleich seine nächsten Verhältnisse, er mißkennt seine wahrsten seine klarsten Vorteile, er opf[e]rt alles, ja! seine Neigungen und Leidenschaften einer Meinung auf die nun zur größten Leidenschaft wird . . . nun vergißt der Mensch die Geschäfte: die sonst den seinigen und dem Staate nutzen, er sieht Vater und Mutter Brüder und Schwestern nicht mehr."

36. Luhmann, *Gesellschaft der Gesellschaft,* 1003.

37. Luhmann, *Realität der Massenmedien,* 54.

38. Peters, *Speaking into the Air,* 37.

39. Hunter, *Before Novels,* 167.

40. See ibid., esp. 167–95; McKeon, *Origins of the English Novel,* 46–50; Davis, *Factual Fictions,* 42–84; and Anderson, *Imagined Communities,* 22–36.

41. Hunter, *Before Novels,* 167.

42. "Durch mehreres Hin-und Widerreden ward das Gespräch immer heftiger und es kam von beiden Seiten alles zur Sprache, was im Laufe dieser Jahre so manche gute Gesellschaft entzweit hatte. . . .

"Karl, der sich im Zorn nicht mehr kannte, hielt mit dem Geständnis nicht zurück: daß er den fanzösischen Waffen alles Glück wünsche, und daß er jeden Deutschen auffordere, der alten Sklaverei ein Ende zu machen. . . .

"Der Geheimrat behauptete dagegen, es sei lächerlich zu denken, daß die Franzosen nur irgend einen Augenblick, bei einer Kapitulation oder sonst für sie sorgen würden, vielmehr würden diese Leute gewiß in die Hände der Alliierten fallen und er hoffe sie alle gehangen zu sehen.

Diese Drohung hielt Karl nicht aus und rief vielmehr: er hoffe, daß die Guillotine auch in Deutschland eine gesegnete Ernte finden und kein schuldiges Haupt verfehlen werde. Dazu fügte er einige sehr starke Vorwürfe, welche den Geheimrat persönlich trafen und in jedem Sinne beleidigend waren." UA 1004.

43. France, *Politeness and Its Discontents,* 4–5. Here one might evoke Carl Schmitt, for whom divisiveness, conflict, and the struggle to death are the defining features of the political, indeed, the antagonistic truth upon which all social order rests. Or one could draw on the more empirical work of Niklas Luhmann and Hans-Ulrich Gumbrecht, who have analyzed the French Revolution in terms of the dissociation of interaction and society (Luhmann) and the end of the Enlightenment model of communication based on dialog and the free play of opinion (Gumbrecht). See Luhmann, *Social Systems,* 425, and Gumbrecht, "Outline of a Literary History."

44. "Ungern hatte, wie man leicht denken konnte, die ganze Gesellschaft ihre Wohnungen verlassen, aber Vetter Karl entfernte sich mit doppeltem Widerwillen von dem jenseitigen Rheinufer; nicht daß er etwa eine Geliebte daselbst zurückgelassen hätte, wie man nach seiner Jugend, seiner guten Gestalt und seiner leidenschaftlichen Natur hätte vermuten sollen, er hatte sich vielmehr von der blendenden Schönheit verführen lassen, die unter dem Namen Freiheit sich erst heimlich, dann öffentlich so viele Anbeter zu verschaffen wußte, und, so übel sie auch die einen behandelte, von den andern mit großer Lebhaftigkeit verehrt wurde.

"Wie Liebende gewöhnlich von ihrer Leidenschaft verblendet werden, so erging es auch Vetter Karln. Sie wünschen den Besitz eines einzigen Gutes, und wähnen alles übrige dagegen entbehren zu können. Stand, Glücksgüter, alle Verhältnisse scheinen in Nichts zu verschwinden, indem das gewünschte Gut zu Einem zu Allem wird. Eltern, Verwandte und Freunde werden uns fremd indem wir uns etwas zueignen, das uns ganz ausfüllt und uns alles übrige fremd macht." UA 997.

45. Carl's boundless and essentially extrasocial love connects him to Werther. From here, one would have to reconstruct Goethe's treatment of the French Revolution in terms of his self-critique of a model of subjectivity first developed in his

writings from the Sturm und Drang period. For an older discussion of Goethe's entire work along these lines, see Baioni's magisterial *Classicismo e revoluzione.*

46. Verhaeghe, *Beyond Gender,* 56.

47. "Besonders mußte Fräulein Luise, die älteste Tochter der Baronesse, ein lebhaftes, heftiges und in guten Tagen herrisches Frauenzimmer sehr vieles leiden, da von ihr behauptet wurde, daß sie bei dem ersten Schrecken ganz aus der Fassung geraten sei, in Zerstreuung, ja in einer Art von völligen Abwesenheit die unnützesten Sachen mit dem größten Ernste zum Aufpacken gebracht, ja sogar einen alten Bedienten für ihren Bräutigam angesehn habe.
Sie verteidigte sich so gut sie konnte, nur wollte sie keinen Scherz der sich auf ihren Bräutigam bezog, dulden, indem es ihr schon Leiden genug verursachte, ihn bei der alliierten Armee, in täglicher Gefahr, zu wissen, und eine gewünschte Verbindung durch die allgemeine Zerrüttung aufgeschoben und vielleicht gar vereitelt zu sehen." UA 996.

48. This suggestion occurs in the context of the discussion concerning the content of the novellas, which, according to the Old Man deal with the relation between the sexes. To Luise's criticism that the stories might be just "a collection of lascivious jokes," the Old Man replies: "[Y]ou will be learning nothing [i.e., from my love stories] you did not know before, especially since for some time now I have observed that you never fail to read a certain kind of review in the journals." CR 27.

49. Freud, *Beyond the Pleasure Principle,* in *SE* 17: 29; *GW* 12: 29.

50. Quoted in *Goethes Werke,* ed. Trunz, 6: 726 (conversation with Eckermann, January 29, 1827).

51. Wellbery, "Afterword," 294.

52. Friedrich Schlegel, "Nachricht von den poetischen Werken des Johannes Bocccaccio" (1801), in Polheim, *Theorie und Kritik,* 12.

53. See the narrator's multiple explanations of the plague as fate, divine punishment, natural phenomenon, and moral test in the Introduzione: "pervenne la mortifera pestilenza: la quale, per operazion de' corpi superiori o per le nostre inique opere da giusta ira di Dio a nostra corrrenzione mandata sopra I mortali . . . ; alquanti anni davanti nelle parti orientali incominciata, quelle d'inumerabile quantità de' viventi avendo private, senza ristare d'un luogo in uno altro continuandosi, verso l'Occidente miserabilmente s'era ampliata." Boccaccio, *Decameron,* 15.

54. On the erotic and aggressive aspects of storytelling in nineteenth-century narratives, see also Brooks, *Reading for the Plot,* 216–38.

55. Todorov, *Grammaire du Décaméron,* 77–78.

56. Bosse, "Geschichten," 314.

57. For a similar argument, see Pavel, "Il romanzo alla ricerca di se stesso," 45–46.

58. Lacan, *Ethics of Psychoanalysis,* 139.

59. For Kafka, see my "Lessons of the Cryptograph."

60. I owe the idea of connecting Luhmann's theory of structural coupling with a notion of genre as medium to David Wellbery's unpublished manuscript "Luhmann's Conceptual Design."

61. Luhmann, "How Can the Mind Participate in Communication?" 170. German version: "Wie ist Bewußtsein an Kommunikation beteiligt?"

62. Luhmann, "Wie ist Bewußtsein an Kommunikation beteiligt?" 885; my trans.

63. Luhmann, "How Can the Mind Participate in Communication?" 172.

64. Ibid., 176–77.

65. Undated letter to Schiller quoted in Goethe, *Sämtliche Werke,* pt. 1, 9: 1514.

66. "Nach einiger Zeit verlor sich auch dieser Klang und verwandelte sich in angenehmere Töne. Sie waren zwar nicht eigentlich melodisch, aber unglaublich angenehm und lieblich. . . . Es war als wenn ein himmlischer Geist durch ein schönes Präludium aufmerksam auf eine Melodie machen wollte, die er eben vorzutragen im begriff sei. Auch dieser Ton verschwand endlich und ließ sich nicht mehr hören, nachdem die ganze wunderbare Geschichte etwa anderthalb Jahre gedauert hatte." UA 1026–27.

67. Jürgen Söring, "Verwirrung und das Wunderbare" makes a similar point. But while Söring reads the ghost stories only as signs of a "radical unsettling [*radikale Verunsicherung*]" (557), I stress that they function also as therapeutic antidote to this *Verunsicherung.*

68. "And certainly the sound was incredibly frightening. Its long resounding vibrations had lingered in everyone's ears, indeed in our very limbs." CR 33; UA 1023.

69. "[G]riff der Hausherr zu einem strengen Mittel, nahm seine größte Hetzpeitsche von der Wand und schwur, daß er das Mädchen bis auf den Tod prügeln wolle, wenn sich noch ein einzigmal das Pochen hören ließe. Von der Zeit an ging sie ohne Anfechtung im ganzen Hause herum, und man vernahm von dem Pochen nichts weiter." UA 1029.

70. "[D]as gute Kind zehrte sich über diesen Vorfall beinah völlig ab, und schien einem traurigen Geiste gleich, da sie vorher frisch, munter und die Heiterste im ganzen Hause gewesen." UA 1029.

71. "Überhaupt . . . scheint mir: daß jedes Phänomen, so wie jedes Factum an sich eigentlich das Interessante sei. Wer es erklärt oder mit andern Begebenheiten zusammenhängt, macht sich gewöhnlich eigentlich nur einen Spaß." UA 1032.

72. "Sie verließ ihn, nachdem sie ihm drei Geschenke . . . für seine drei rechtmäßigen Töchter verehrt und ihm die größte Sorgfalt für diese Gaben anbefohlen hatt. Man hub sie sorgfältig auf und die Abkömmlinge dieser drei Töchter glaubten die Ursache manches glücklichen Ereignisses in dem Besitz dieser Gabe zu finden." UA 1036.

73. Jocelyn Holland, "Singularität und ihre Verdoppelung," also stresses the importance of generational continuity. Holland argues that Goethe's novella cycle,

and the Bassompierre anecdotes in particular, explores the question of continuity on two interrelated levels: on the level of desire and genealogy, and on the level of event and repetition. The story of the veil is said to rearticulate, in a more poetic register, the inequality between lovers already structuring the third novella, thus transforming the latter retroactively into a *type* of story (350). The question of genealogy posed *within* the story is thus extended into the relation *between* stories, biological procreation connected to poetic creation. Situating this intriguing reading in a discussion of the relationship between novelistic novelty and the marvelous, Holland suggests that Goethe develops textual genealogies that provide aesthetic solutions to a social reality marked by political (aristocracy-bourgeoisie) and sexual (man-woman) inequalities (353).

74. "Ich habe ihn in späteren Jahren kennen lernen, umgeben von einer zahlreichen wohlgebildeten Familie . . . Selbst als Mann und Hausvater pflegte er sich manchmal etwas das ihm Freude würde gemacht haben, zu versagen, um nur nicht aus der Übung einer so schönen Tugend zu kommen, und seine ganze Erziehung bestand gewissermaßen darin, daß seine Kinder sich gleichsam aus dem Stehgreife etwas mußten versagen können.

"Auf eine Weise, die ich am Anfang nicht billigen konnte untersagte er, zum Beispiel, einem Knaben bei Tische von einer beliebten Speise zu essen. Zu meiner Verwunderung blieb der Knabe heiter, und es war als wenn weiter nichts geschehen wäre.

"Und so ließen die Ältesten aus eigener Bewegung manchmal ein edles Obst oder sonst einen Leckerbissen vorbeigehen. . . . Er schien über alles gleichgültig zu sein und ließ ihnen eine fast unbändige Freiheit; nur fiel es ihm die Woche einmal ein, daß alles auf die Minute geschehen mußte, alsdann wurden des Morgens gleich die Uhren reguliert, ein jeder erhielt seine Ordre für den Tag, Geschäfte und Vergnügungen wurden gehäuft und niemand durfte eine Sekunde fehlen." UA 1079–80.

75. Humboldt, letter to Goethe, February 9, 1796, in Goethe, *Sämtliche Werke,* pt. 1, 9: 1529.

76. For a concise overview of the discussion on allegory and symbol in German classicism, see Todorov, *Theories of the Symbol,* chap. 6.

77. Goethe, letter to Humboldt, May 27, 1796, in *Sämtliche Werke,* pt. 1, 9: 1531.

78. Goethe, letter to Schiller, August 17, 1795, in *Sämtliche Werke*, pt. 2, 4: 106. See also Kittler, *Geburt des Partisanen,* 159: "Der Erlösungsweg, den das Märchen beschreibt, ist eine Resymbolisierung allegorischer Gestalten."

79. For a clear analysis of the connection between *Märchen* and the politics of German classicism, see Baioni, "*Märchen,*" 73. See also Kittler, *Geburt des Partisanen,* who reads the tale in the context of Goethe's monetary policy at Weimar and sees the end of the fairy tale, like that of *Wilhelm Meister,* as an attempt to reconcile political, economic, and erotic relations (150–62). Witte, "Opfer der

Schlange," argues that Goethe radicalizes Schiller's aesthetic program, in that he construes the work of art as self-expression of an ultimately ineffable subjectivity.

Chapter 3. Border Narratives

1. "Man darf seine Erzeugnisse zwar überhaupt nicht streng nach den Regeln der Kunst beurtheilen, am allerwenigsten aber sie an das Muster des nach der feinen Umgangssprache geglätteten Erzählungston halten." Grimm in the *Hallesche Allgemeine Literatur-Zeitung,* October 14, 1812, cited in Heinrich von Kleist, *Sämtliche Werke,* 3: 702.

2. Brooks, "Tale vs. the Novel," 303.

3. For an insightful reading of Kleist's framing and its relation to the genre of the novella and the problem of social self-description, see Theisen, "Gerahmte Rahmen." Theisen shows how Kleist's strategies of framing undermine the tendency of traditional novellas to distinguish, through the structure of the framed tale, between inside and outside, or fiction and nonfiction. If, traditionally, the community of storytellers and commentators located in the frame served as an imagined reality from which the narrated fictional events were evaluated, in Kleist's *Marquise von O . . . ,* the relation between the two sides is inverted: the seemingly nonfictional newspaper ad becomes the truly incomprehensible event, whereas the fictional narrative consists of commentaries and explanations that only beg more commentaries. As a result of this inversion, Kleist's story claims to be both fiction and nonfiction, or rather: it presents the distinction between fiction and nonfiction as itself fictional, i.e., as the product of an act of distinguishing. While Theisen is above all interested in the paradoxes of observation and reading Kleist's textual strategies evince, I argue that this hyper-self-referentiality is still intimately connected with a pragmatic intention, with the conception of signs radiating beyond the bounds of the text. However, I agree with Theisen that Kleist's fundamental move consists in undermining the distinction between fiction and nonfiction, inside and outside, and thus in complicating the very act of reading.

4. "Hier endigt die Geschichte vom Kohlhaas. Man legte die Leiche unter einer allgemeinen Klage des Volks in einen Sarg; und während die Träger sie aufhoben, um sie anständig auf den Kirchhof der Vorstadt zu begraben, rief der Kurfürst die Söhne des Abgeschiedenen herbei und schlug sie, mit der Erklärung an den Erzkanzler, daß sie in seiner Pagenschule erzogen werden sollten, zu Rittern. Der Kurfürst von Sachsen kam bald darauf, zerrissen an Leib und Seele, nach Dresden zurück, wo man das Weitere in der Geschichte nachlesen muß. Vom Kohlhaas aber haben noch im vergangenen Jahrhundert, im Mecklenburgischen, einige frohe und rüstige Nachkommen gelebt." MK 141–42.

5. From the comments by Klaus Müller-Salget in Heinrich von Kleist, *Sämtliche Werke,* 3: 768.

6. My argument throughout this chapter runs counter to that of Christa Bürger in "Statt einer Interpretation," for whom the lack of frame in Kleist's novellas is indicative of the autonomization of art around 1800. Kleist's technique of isolating his texts from any context—Bürger speaks of the "solipsism" of Kleist's novellas (108)—is supposedly symptomatic of the decay of the literary public sphere as the institutional frame for the dialogic mediation of art and everyday life, aesthetics and morality. In her attempt to read—or to my mind, misread—Kleist's novellas in conjunction with the classicist concept of the symbol (98) and as yet another instance of aesthetic self-referentialization, Bürger overlooks the fact that Kleist explicitly situates his novellas within a referential horizon. That his framing defines the relation between text and "context," novella and historiography, in terms of conflict, rather than of dialogue, does not (dis)qualify his novellas as solipsistic texts, unless one restricts the notion of communication to agreement.

7. On historical medieval genres, see Odilo Engel's article "Geschichte" in *Geschichtliche Grundbegriffe,* 2: 612–13. Contrary to Engel's contention that the proper subject of the chronicle is always impersonal (typically, it is a state or a region), Hayden White writes: "The chronicle also has a central subject—the life of an individual, town, or region; some great undertaking, such as a war or a crusade; or some institution, such as a monarchy, episcopacy, or monastery" (*Content of the Form,* 16). White's disregarding of the institutional restrictions imposed on chronicles is indicative of his purely formalistic approach, which ignores the pragmatic dimension of text production.

8. D. A. Miller, *Narrative and Its Discontents,* ix.

9. "The conflict that interests me here occurs not between the novel and its referent, but, within the novel, between the principles of production and the claims of closure to a resolved meaning," Miller writes (ibid., xi).

10. Ibid., ix.

11. "Dieser außerordentliche Mann würde, bis in sein dreißigstes Jahr für das Muster eines guten Staatsbürgers habe gelten können. Er besaß in einem Dorfe, das noch von ihm den Nahmen führt, einen Meierhof, auf welchem er sich durch sein Gewerbe ruhig ernährte; die Kinder, die ihm sein Weib schenkte, erzog er, in der Furcht Gottes, zur Arbeitsamkeit und Treue; nicht Einer war unter seinen Nachbarn, der sich nicht seiner Wohltätigkeit, oder seiner Gerechtigkeit, erfreut hätte; kurz, die Welt würde sein Andenken haben segnen müssen, wenn er in einer Tugend nicht ausgeschweift hätte. Das Rechtgefühl aber machte ihn zum Räuber und Mörder." MK 13.

12. "Kohlhaasenbrück, der Ort, nach welchem der Roßhandler heiße, im Branderburgischen liege." MK 114.

13. Foucault, "Life of Infamous Men," 79–80. See also id., "Tales of Murder."

14. Whether or not it is directly authored by the state, the chronicle betrays its dependence on power through its very principle of selection—the code that it uses

to sift out the events it records from reality. On the importance of interpretative codes for the creation of historical facts, see Lotman, *Universe of the Mind,* 217–20.

15. Starobinski, *Blessings in Disguise,* 203.

16. Ibid.

17. "Er ritt einst, mit einer Koppel junger Pferde, wohlgenährt alle und glänzend, ins Ausland, und überschlug *eben,* wie er den Gewinst, den er auf den Märkten damit zu machen hoffte, anlegen wolle: teils, nach Art guter Wirte, auf neuen Gewinst, teils aber auch auf den *Genuß der Gegenwart: als* er an die Elbe kam, und bei einer stattlichen Ritterburg, auf sächsischem Gebiete, einen Schlagbaum traf, den er sonst auf diesem Wege nicht gefunden hatte." MK 13; emphases added.

18. Narratology defines an event as the transition from one state into another. The element of instability implied in this definition is usually mitigated by the arrangements of events into a sequential order, however, the sequence creating an effect of logical necessity that neutralizes the disquieting effect of transitoriness. In contrast, the toll gate scene depicts such a transition in its essential form: as a break.

19. Kittler, *Geburt des Partisanen,* has shown that the success of Kohlhaas's military actions depends in large measure on his capacity to surprise his enemies.

20. In an essay on Shakespeare, Cavell's *Must We Mean What We Say?* reminds us that in early modern societies, the state's existence depends on the life of its sovereign, whose "legitimate succession is the only promise of continued life to his state" (343). Kohlhaas's attempt to kill the Elector of Saxony thus signifies an assault on the very principle on which the state bases its survival; the end, which celebrates Kohlhaas's generative power and suggests the elector's impending decline, corroborates this reading.

21. "Was gibt's hier Neues? fragte er, da der Zöllner, nach einer geraumen Zeit, aus dem Hause trat. Landesherrliches Privilegium, antwortete dieser, indem er aufschloß: dem Junker Wenzel von Tronka verliehen.—So, sagte Kohlhaas. Wenzel heißt der Junker? und sah sich das Schloß an, das mit glänzenden Zinnen über das Feld blickte. Ist der alte Herr tot?—Am Schlagfluß gestorben, erwiderte der Zöllner, indem er den Baum in die Höhe ließ.—Hm! Schade! versetzte Kohlhaas. Ein würdiger alter Herr, der seine Freude am Verkehr der Menschen hatte, Handel und Wandel, wo er nur vermogte, forthalf, und einen Steindamm einst bauen ließ, weil mir eine Stute, draußen, wo der Weg ins Dorf geht, das Bein gebrochen. . . . 'Ja, Alter,' setzte er noch hinzu, da dieser: hurtig! hurtig! murmelte, und über die Witterung fluchte: 'wenn der Baum im Walde stehen geblieben wäre, wärs besser gewesen, für mich und euch.' " MK 15.

22. This comes out clearly in the Dresden episode. See the discussion below.

23. "You ask what I understand by the 'nothingness of revelation'? I understand by it a state in which revelation appears to be without meaning, in which it still asserts itself, in which it has *validity* but *no significance* [*in dem sie gilt, aber*

nicht bedeutet]." Gershom Scholem, letter to Benjamin, September 20, 1934. Scholem, *Correspondence of Benjamin and Scholem,* 142.

24. See Agamben, *Homo Sacer,* and more recently, *Stato di eccezione.*

25. The historical documents are reprinted in Bogdal, *Heinrich von Kleist: Michael Kohlhaas,* 76–87. For a comparison between the historical Kohlhase and Kleist's Kohlhaas, see also Müller-Salget's comments in Kleist, *Sämtliche Werke,* 3: 709–13.

26. Michael Kohlhaas, this avenging "angel from heaven" (MK 63), distributes "the money among his supporters" (66), whereas his followers, an undifferentiated "bunch" (66) of "riffraff" (68), are "stimulated by the prospect of plunder" (66).

27. Schiller, "Gedanken über den Gebrauch des Gemeinen und Niedrigen," *Werke und Briefe,* 8: 455.

28. Schiller, "Über den Grund des Vergnügens," in *Werke und Briefe,* 8: 244.

29. Ibid.

30. Here my argument overlaps with that of Maurer, "Gerechtigkeit," who distinguishes between chthonic and symbolic justice and suggests that the former nullifies the elements of distance and difference upon which the latter is based, thus nullifying the symbolic order itself. Kohlhaas, Maurer argues, attempts to establish a new legal order based on the principle of identity, but this project necessarily fails, because it cannot but establish itself in symbolic terms. See also Maurer's incisive discussion of the Dresden episode in terms of the problem of contingency in law (133–36) and his remarks about the status of chance in Kleist's narratives (136–44).

31. Starting out as a "shiny-coated string" (MK/G 89), the horses appear on Kohlhaas's return from Dresden as "scrawny, worn-out nags" (MK/G 92). Months later, they have lost even more of their vitality and value; emaciated and shabby "objects of ridicule for the ragamuffins and the idlers" (MK/G 143), they are declared symbolically dead, only to reappear in Berlin restored to their original beauty, "sleek with health and pawing the ground with their hooves" (MK/G 181).

32. On the comic effect, see Baudelaire's comment: "And since laughter is essentially human, it is, in fact, essentially contradictory; that is to say that it is at once a token of an infinite grandeur and an infinite misery. . . . It is from the perpetual collision of these two infinities that laughter is struck" ("Essence of Laughter," 153–54).

33. See Derrida, "Force of Law," 26.

34. Criticism of Kohlhaas's excess or violence tends to be restricted in the secondary literature to his later acts. Fischer, *Ironische Metaphysik,* 67, for instance, reads Kohlhaas's "patience, politeness and self-constraint" in his quarrel with the Junker as proof of the horse dealer's immaculate *Rechtgefühl* (sense of what is right). Similarly, Kuhns, *Tragedy,* 103, praises Kohlhaas's "even-tempered nature, his tranquillity when first challenged, and the impulse to see good wherever he looks."

35. According to Grimm, *allgemein* means "universal" and carries with it a negative index of excessive abstraction. In the examples cited by Grimm, the term denotes disregard for the concrete and particular. This tone is emphasized by the *genitivus subiectivus* of "Not der Welt," which suggests a world in need rather than specific problems in the world. The phrase assumes even greater weight when read in conjunction with similar formulations in the novella ("Zerbrechlichkeit der Welt" [MK 27] and "ungeheuren Unordnung" [MK 47]) and in other texts by Kleist (*Marquise von O . . .* , 186; *Penthesilea*, l. 2854).

36. For a brilliant discussion of melodrama as a literary mode, see Brooks, *Melodramatic Imagination*. Kleist's excessive rhetoric is often mentioned in the critical literature, but there have been few attempts to analyze it systematically. Breuer, "Schauplätze," has recently drawn attention to the visual and theatrical character of Kleist's texts, linking it to the tradition of the novelistic *historia,* with its insistence on factual evidence and visual proof, which Kleist is said to radicalize by showing that "evidence" and "factuality" are themselves rhetorically constructed and subject to imaginary distortions (218ff.). This is why I speak of Kleist's "rhetoric of factuality."

37. " . . . wo sie eben, unter den schändlichsten Mißhandlungen, zu Boden sinken wollte, als, von dem Zetergeschrei der Dame herbeigerufen, ein russischer Offizier erschien, und die Hunde, die nach solchem Raub lüstern waren, mit wütenden Hieben zerstreute. Der Marquise schien er ein Engel des Himmels zu sein. Er stieß noch dem letzten viehischen Mordknecht, der ihren schlanken Leib umfaßt hielt, mit dem Griff des Degens ins Gesicht."

38. "Don Fernando, dieser göttlicher Held, stand jetzt, den Rücken an die Kirche gelehnt; in der Linken hielt er die Kinder, in der Rechten das Schwert. Mit jedem Hiebe wetterstrahlte er Einen zu Boden; ein Löwe wehrt sich nicht besser."

39. "Gustav legte die Hände vor sein Gesicht. Oh! rief er, ohne aufzusehen, und meinte, die Erde versänke unter seinen Füßen: ist das, was ihr mir sagt, wahr? Er legte seine Arme um ihren Leib und sah ihr mit jammervoll zerrissenem Herzen ins Gesicht. 'Ach,' rief Toni, und dies waren ihre lezten Worte: 'du hättest mir nicht mißtrauen sollen!' Und damit hauchte sie ihre schöne Seele aus."

40. "Er fiel auch, mit diesem kleinen Haufen, schon, beim Einbruch der dritten Nacht, den Zollwärter und Torwächter, die im Gespräch unter dem Tor standen, niederreitend, in die Burg, und während, unter plötzlicher Aufprasselung aller Baracken im Schloßraum, die sie mit Feuer bewarfen, Herse, über die Windeltreppe, in den Turm der Vogtei eilte, und den Schloßvogt und Verwalter, die, halb entkleidet, beim Spiel saßen, mit Hieben und Stichen überfiel, stürzte Kohlhaas zum Junker Wenzel ins Schloß. Der Engel des Gerichts fährt also vom Himmel herab."

41. Brooks, *Melodramatic Imagination,* 14–15.

42. Ibid., 15.

43. "Er nannte sich in dem Mandat, das er, bei dieser Gelegenheit, ausstreute,

'einen Statthalter Michaels, des Erzengels, der gekommen sei, an Allen, die in dieser Streitsache des Junkers Partei ergreifen würden, mit Feuer und Schwert, die Arglist, in welcher die ganze Welt versunken sei, zu bestrafen.' Dabei rief er, von dem Lützner Schloß aus, das er uberrumpelt, und worin er sich festgesetzt hatte, das Volk auf, sich, zur Errichtung einer besseren Ordnung der Dinge, an ihn anzuschließen; und das Mandat war, mit einer Art von Verrückung, unterzeichnet: 'Gegeben auf dem Sitz unserer provisorischen Weltregierung, dem Erzschlosse zu Lützen.'" MK 73.

44. " . . . daß sie an einem Morgen, da er ein Paar Knechte, die in der Gegend, wider seinen Willen, geplündert hatten, aufknüpfen lassen wollte, den Entschluß faßten, ihn darauf aufmerksam zu machen. Eben kam er, während das Volk von beiden Seiten schüchtern auswich, in dem Aufzuge, der ihm, seit seinem letzten Mandat, gewöhnlich war, von dem Richtplatz zurück: ein großes Cherubsschwert, auf einmen rotledernen Kissen, mit Quasten von Gold verziert, ward ihm vorangetragen, und zwölf Knechte, mit brennenden Fackeln folgten ihm." MK 76.

45. Brooks, *Melodramatic Imagination,* 16.

46. "Bare sovereignty" displays the violent essence of sovereignty in much the same way that Kleist's treatment of war strips the latter of all legal measures intended to restrain its violence. On Kleist's treatment of war and violence, see Manfred Schneider, "Welt im Ausnahmezustand."

47. See Dotzler, "Federkrieg."

48. Kittler, *Geburt des Partisanen,* seems to have first linked Schmitt's exploration of legal violence to Kleist. See now also Manfred Schneider, "Welt im Ausnahmezustand."

49. Schmitt, *Begriff des Politischen,* 26 (Schmitt's emphasis).

50. Ibid., 33.

51. See Schmitt, *Political Theology.*

52. In Kleist's drama *Prinz Friedrich von Homburg,* the prince is subjected to an educational program that seeks to purge his aggression of any personal motivation in order to employ it more forcefully in the state's war against "alle Feinde Brandenburgs"; and in his *Die Hermannschlacht,* the master propagandist Hermann produces the image of the "total foe" in order to mobilize, indeed generate, the people's affective investment in their war. See Kittler, *Geburt des Partisanen,* 218–56.

53. It should be remembered that the Dresden episode is entirely Kleist's invention and has no parallel in the historical sources he was using.

54. In the preceding sequences, only Kohlhaas and the Tronkas influenced the course of events; in the Dresden episode, three additional agencies appear (Nagelschmidt, the mob, Count Wrede).

55. Mehigan, *Text as Contract,* 299, makes a similar observation: "The demise of the second principal contractual form in the story, the amnesty, coincides with the envisaged death of one of the contracting parties, the protagonist. He is sen-

tenced to death as one dispossessed of the right to language or, in the conduct of communities, to rely upon it."

56. See also Maurer, "Gerechtigkeit," 134–35.

57. "Bei diesen Worten trat der Kämmerer, mit einem raschen, seinen Helmbusch erschütternden Schritt zu dem Abdecker heran, und warf ihm einen Beutel mit Geld zu; and während dieser sich, den Beutel in der Hand, mit einem bleiernen Kamm die Haare über die Stirn zurückkämmte, und das Geld betrachtete, befahl er einem Knecht, die Pferde abzulösen und nach Hause zu führen! Der Knecht, der auf den Ruf des Herrn, einen Kreis von Freunden und Verwandten, die er unter dem Volke besaß, verlassen hatte, trat auch, in der Tat, ein wenig rot im Gesicht, über eine große Mistpfütze, die sich zu ihren Füßen gebildet hatte, zu den Pferden heran." MK 96.

58. "Johan Nagelschmidt nämlich, einer von den durch den Roßhändler zusammengebrachten, und nach Erscheinung der kurfürstlichen Amnestie wieder abgedankten Knechten, hatte für gut befunden, wenige Wochen nachher, . . . einen Teil dieses zu allen Schandtaten aufgelegten Gesindels von neuem zusammenzuraffen, und das Gewerbe, auf dessen Spur ihn Kohlhaas geführt hatte, auf seine eigne Hand fortzusetzen. Dieser nichtsnutzige Kerl nannte sich, teils um den Häschern von denen er verfolgt ward, Furcht einzuflößen, teils um das Landvolk, auf die gewohnte Weise, zur Teilhahme an seinen Spitzbübereien zu verleiten, einen Statthalter des Kohlhaas; . . . dergestalt, daß in Plakaten, die den Kohlhaasischen ganz ähnlich waren, sein Mordbrennerhaufen als ein zur bloßen Ehre Gottes aufgestandener Kriegshaufen erschien. . . . Alles, wie schon gesagt, keineswegs zur Ehre Gottes, noch aus Anhänglichkeit an den Kohlhaas, dessen Schicksal ihnen völlig gleichgültig war, sondern um unter dem Schutz solcher Vorspiegelungen desto ungestrafter und bequemer zu sengen und zu plündern." MK 100.

59. Note that when the narrator criticizes the amorality of the "scoundrel" Nagelschmidt who "styled himself Kohlhaas' *Statthalter*," he repeats his own earlier description of the horse dealer, who, we were told, "called himself 'a Statthalter of the Archangel Michael, come to punish . . . for the wickedness into which the whole world was sunk, all those who should take the side of the Junker'" (MK 121).

60. Derrida, *Dissemination*, 109: "As soon as the supplementary outside is opened, its structure implies that the supplement itself can be 'typed,' replaced by its own double, and that a supplement to the supplement, a surrogate for the surrogate, is possible and necessary."

61. Increasing the void because now not only the official representatives of justice but also their unofficial surrogates are completely discredited.

62. "Kaum hatte der Kerl diese Antwort dem Schloßhauptmann überbracht, als der Großkanzler abgesetzt, der Präsident, Graf Kallheim, an dessen Stelle zum Chef des Tribunals ernannt, und Kohlhaas, durch einen Kabinettsbefehl des Kur-

fürsten arretiert, und schwer mit Ketten beladen in die Stadttürme gebracht ward. Man machte ihm auf den Grund dieses Briefes, der an alle Ecken der Stadt angeschlagen ward, den Prozeß; und da er vor den Schranken des Tribunals auf die Frage, ob er die Handschrift anerkenne, dem Rat, der sie ihm vorhielt, antwortete: 'ja!' zur Antwort aber auf die Frage, ob er zu seiner Verteidigung etwas vorzubringen wisse, indem er den Blick zur Erde schlug, erwiderte, 'nein!' so ward er verurteilt, mit glühenden Zangen von Schinderknechten gekniffen, geviertelt, und sein Körper, zwischen Rad und Galgen, verbrannt zu werden." MK 112–13.

63. See Bookman, "Mittelalterliches Recht bei Kleist."

64. "Es traf sich daß der Kurfürst von Sachsen auf die Einladung des Landdrosts, Grafen Aloysius von Kallheim, der damals *an der Grenze von Sachsen* beträchtlichte Besitzungen hatte, . . . zu einem großen Hirschjagen, das man, um ihn zu erheitern, angestellt hatte, nach Dahme gereist war; dergestalt, daß unter dam Dach bewimpelter Zelte, die quer über die Straße auf einem Hügel erbaut waren, die ganze Gesellschaft vom Staub der Jagd noch bedeckt unter dem Schall einer heitern vom Stamm einer Eiche hershcallenden Musik, von Pagen bedient und Edelknaben, an der Tafel saß, als der Roßhändler langsam mit seiner Reuterbedeckung die Straße von Dresden daher gezogen kam. Denn die Erkrankung eines der kleinen, zarten Kinder des Kohlhaas, hatte den Ritter von Malzahn, der ihn begleitete, genötigt, drei Tage lang in Herzberg zrückzubleiben; . . . Der Kürfurst, der mit halboffener Brust . . . saß, . . . sagte . . . : 'Lasset uns hingehen, und dem Unglücklichen, wer es auch sei, diesen Becher mit Wein reichen!' . . . und schon hatte, mit Erquickungen jeglicher Art, die ganze Gesellschaft wimmelnd das Zelt verlassen, als der Landdrost ihnen mit einem verlegenen Gesicht entgegen kam, und sie bat zurückzubleiben. Auf die betretene Frage des Kurfürsten was vorgefallen wäre . . . antwortete der Landdrost, . . . daß der Kohlhaas im Wagen sei; auf welche jedermann unbegreifliche Nachricht, indem weltbekannt war, daß derselbe bereits vor sechs Tagen abgereist war, der Kämmerer, Herr Kunz, seinen Becher mit Wein nahm, und ihn . . . in den Sand schüttete. . . und während der Ritter Friedrich von Malzahn, unter ehrfurchtsvoller Begrüßung der Gesellschaft, die er nicht kannte, langsam *durch die Zeltleinen, die über die Straße liefen, nach Dahme weiter zog,* begaben sich die Herrschaften . . . ohne weiter davon Notiz zu nehmen, ins Zelt zurück." MK 115–17.

65. Cited in Kleist, *Sämtliche Werke und Briefe,* 3: 715. Breger, *Ortlosigkeit des Fremden,* 302–24, shows the persistence of this line of criticism and its connection to the reading of the gypsy as a kind of interpretative linchpin in the scholarship.

66. Brooks, *Reading for the Plot,* 97. See also Culler, "Story and Discourse."

67. Breuer, "Schauplätze," interprets Kleist's method of "drastische Überbietung . . . von Verhaltens- und Erzählkonventionen" (224) against the background of the close link between *historia* and fiction in traditional novellas. See esp. 223–24.

68. Barthes, "Introduction to the Structural Analysis of Narrative," 94.

69. The claim of Lützeler, "Heinrich von Kleist," 221, that the gypsy's function in the novella is to provide a vivid historical background completely overlooks the figure's complex engagement with questions of referentiality and mimeticism.

70. See also Reuß, "'Michael Kohlhaas' und 'Michael Kohhaas,'" 38–39.

71. See Menninghaus, *Unendliche Verdoppelung.*

72. On the "literarization" of the gypsy, see Trumpener, "Time of the Gypsies" and Breger, *Ortlosigkeit des Fremden,* esp. 868–69. Breger's claim that the gypsy is above all a foil onto which Kleist's readers can project their own interpretative fantasies might be factually correct but underdetermines the function of the soothsayer and its relation to the novella's anti-referentialism.

73. " . . . daß der Kurfürst und ich, am dritten Tage der Zusammenkunft, die wir in Jüterbock hielten, auf eine Zigeunerin trafen; und da der Kurfürst, aufgeweckt wie er von Natur ist, *beschloß, den Ruf diese abenteuerlichen Frau, von deren Kunst, eben bei der Tafel, auf ungebührliche Weise die Rede gewesen war, durch einen Scherz im Angesicht alles Volks zu nichte zu machen:* so trat er mit verschränkten Armen vor ihren Tisch, und forderte, der Weissagung wegen, die sie ihm machen sollte, ein Zeichen von ihr, das sich noch heute erproben ließe, vorschützend, daß er sonst nicht, und wäre sie auch die römische Sybille selbst, an ihre Worte glauben könne."

74. Koselleck, *Futures Past,* 10 (trans. modified, since Keith Tribe translates "anhaltenden Kampf" as "sporadic struggle," one of his many glaring mistakes).

75. "Die Frau, indem sie uns flüchtig von Kopf zu Fuß maß, sagte: das Zeichen würde sein, daß uns der große, gehörnte Rehbock, den der Sohn des Gärtners im Park erzog, auf dem Markt, worauf wir uns befanden, bevor wir ihn noch verlassen, entgegenkommen würde. Nun mußt du wissen, daß dieser, für die Dresdner Küche bestimmte Rehbock, in einem mit Latten hoch verzäunten Verschlage, den die Eichen des Parks beschatteten, hinter Schloß und Riegel aufbewahrt ward, dergestalt, daß, da überdies anderen kleineren Wildes und Geflügeltes wegen, der Park überhaupt und obenein der Garten, der zu ihm führte, in sorgfältigem Beschluß gehalten ward, schlechterdings nicht abzusehen war, wie uns das Tier, diesem sonderbaren Vorgeben gemäß, bis auf dem Platz, wo wir standen, entgegen kommen würde; gleichwohl schickte der Kurfürst aus Besorgnis vor einer dahinter steckenden Schelmerei, nach einer kurzen Abrede mit mir, entschlossen, auf unabänderliche Weise, Alles was sie noch vorbringen würde, des Spaßes wegen, zu Schanden zu machen, ins Schloß, und befahl, daß der Rehbock augenblicklich getötet, und für die Tafel, an einem der nächsten Tage, zubereitet werden sollte. Hierauf wandte er sich zu der Frau, vor welcher dieser Sache laut verhandelt worden war, zurück, und sagte: nun, wohlan! was hast du mir für die Zukunft zu entdecken?" MK 128–29.

76. "'Nun trat, zu meinem in der Tat herzlichen Trost, in eben diesem Augenblick der Ritter auf, den der Kurfürst ins Schloß geschickt hatte, und meldete ihm,

mit lachendem Munde, daß der Rehbock getötet, und durch zwei Jäger, vor seinen Augen, in den Küche geschleppt worden sei. Der Kurfürst, indem er seinen Arm munter in den meinigen legte, in der Absicht, mich von dem Platz hinwegzuführen, sagte: nun, wohlan! so war die Prophezeiung eine alltägliche Gaunerei, und Zeit und Gold, die sie uns gekostet nicht wert! Aber wie groß war unser Erstaunen, da sich, noch während dieser Worte, ein Geschrei rings auf dem Platze erhob, und aller Augen sich einem großen, von Schloßhof herantrabenden Schlächterhund zuwandten, der in der Küche den Rehbock als gute Beute beim Nacken erfaßt, und das Tier drei Schritte von uns, verfolgt von Knechten und Mägden, auf den Boden fallen ließ: dergestalt, daß in der Tat die Prophezeiungdes Weibes, zum Unterpfand alles dessen, was sie vorgebracht, erfüllt, und der Rehbock uns bis auf den Markt, obschon allerdings tot, entgegen gekommen war. Der Blitz, der an einem Wintertag von Himmel fällt, kann nicht vernichtender treffen, als mich dieser Anblick, und meine erste Bemühung, sobald ich der Gesellschaft in der ich mich befand, überhoben, war gleich, den Mann mit dem Federhut, den mir das Weib bezeichnet hatte, auszumitteln . . . und jetz, Freund Kunz, vor wenig Wochen, in der Meierei zu Dahme, habe ich den Mann mit meinen eigenen Augen gesehn.'—Und damit ließ er die Hand des Kämmerers fahren; und während er sich den Schweiß abtrocknete, sank er wieder auf das Lager zurück." MK 130–31.

77. "Als er auf dem Richtplatz ankam, fand er den Kurfürsten von Brandenburg mit seinem Gefolge, worunter sich auch der Erzkanzler, Herr Heinrich von Geusau befand, unter einer unermeßlichen Menschenmenge, daselbst zu Pferde halten: ihm zur Rechten der Kaiserliche Anwalt Franz Müller, eine Abschrift des Todesurteils in der Hand; ihm zur Linken, mit dem Conclusum des Dresdner Hofgerichts, sein eigener Anwalt, der Rechtsgelehrte Anton Zäuner; ein Herold *in der Mitte des halboffenen Kreises, den das Volk schloß,* mit einem Bündel Sachen, und den beiden, von Wohlsein glänzenden, die Erde mit ihren Hufen stampfenden Rappen. . . . Demnach sprach der Kurfürst, als Kohlhaas von der Wache begleitet, auf den Hügel zu ihm heranschritt: Nun, Kohlhaas, heut ist der Tag, an dem dir dein Recht geschieht! Schau her, *hier liefere ich dir Alles, was du auf der Tronkenburg gewaltsamer Weise eingebüßt,* und was ich, als dein Landesherr, dir wieder zu verschaffen, schuldig war, zurück: Rappen, Halstuch, Reichsgulden, Wäsche, bis auf die Kurkosten sogar für deinen bei Mühlberg gefallenen Knecht Herse. Bist du mit mir zufrieden?—Kohlhaas, während er das, ihm auf den Wink des Erzkanzlers eingehändigte Conclusum, mit großen, funkelnden Augen überlas, setzte die . . . Kinder . . . nieder; und da er auch einen Artikel darin fand, in welchem der Junker Wenzel zu zweijähriger Gefängnisstrafe verurteilt ward: so ließ er sich, aus der Ferne, ganz überwältigt von Gefühlen, mit kreuzweis auf die Brust gelegten Händen, vor dem Kurfürsten nieder. . . . Der Kurfürst rief: 'nun, Kohlhaas, der Roßhandler, du, dem solchergestalt Genugtuung geworden, mache dich bereit, kaiserlicher Majestät, deren Anwalt hier steht, wegen des Bruchs ihres

Landfriedens, deinerseits Genugtuung zu geben!' Kohlhaas, indem er seinen Hut abnahm, und auf die Erde warf, sagte: daß er bereit dazu wäre! übergab die Kinder, nachdem er sie noch einmal vom Boden erhoben, und an seine Brust gedrückt hatte, dem Amtmann von Kolhaasenbrück, und trat, während dieser sie unter stillen Tränen, vom Platz hinwegführte, an den Block." MK 139–41.

78. As Klaus Bogdal has shown, the execution scene both cites and inverts the scene of mass unrest in Dresden. Both scenes figure a triangular constellation consisting of Kohlhaas, the masses, and official representatives; both are centered around the issue of "justice"; both are set in the open, in public places situated in the political-geographical centers of Saxony (marketplace in Dresden) and Brandenburg (execution site in Berlin); and both foreground the physicality of Kohlhaas's horses—this material emblem of the conflict—thus emphasizing the importance of materiality and the visible for the fantasy of satisfaction they enact. But these structural similarities only serve as a backdrop that throws into relief the difference between the two scenes. The horses, emaciated and shabby "objects of ridicule for the ragamuffins and the idlers" in Dresden (MK/G 143), reappear in Berlin "fattened" and shiny, visible signs of renewed symbolic plenitude; the disorder in the marketplace contrasts with the geometrical symmetry of the public execution, the lack of "satisfaction" with the fulfillment of Kohlhaas's "dearest wish on earth." Most important, the masses, which in Dresden were an active and aggressive force, are in Berlin mere observers, passive witnesses to an official spectacle organized for, not by, them. In sum, the ending recasts the scene of mass unrest from the perspective of power. Bogdal, *Heinrich von Kleist*, 58–62.

79. See also Mehigan, *Text as Contract*, 307: "No longer is the administration of the law characterized by paper bureaucracy, the seemingly endless delegation of authority and the underlying threat of violence." Of course, the violence is not underlying and illegal but open and legal.

80. This is why those who read the text's observation of the elector's instrumental behavior as proof of Kleist's critique are misguided. See Wittkowski, "Is Kleist's Michael Kohlhaas a Terrorist?" 478–79.

81. "[E]ine Gemeinschaft, deren Dasein keine deutsche Brust überleben, und die nur mit Blut, vor dem die Sonne erdunkelt, zu Grabe gebracht werden soll." *Sämtliche Werke*, 3: 479. On Kleist's propagandistic writings, see Kittler's powerful study *Geburt des Partisanen*.

82. The text casts the Elector of Saxony from the very beginning under the sign of pathological weakness. Here is how the elector's first political action, his decision concerning the state's take on Kohlhaas, is framed: "Apparently the preliminary step contemplated by the Prince [to issue a warrant for the arrest of Kunz von Tronka on charges of abuse of authority] had killed all desire in the Elector's heart, which was highly receptive in matters of friendship, to go ahead with the military campaign against Kohlhaas, for which all the preparations were already made" (MK 86). The elector's decision to grant Kohlhaas amnesty, a decision that

will be of huge narrative and political consequence, is motivated not by political or military considerations but by his juvenile love for Heloise, Kunz's wife. Such rule of the heart, the novella suggests, weakens the political realm by centering it on a sexual object: the *sublime* idea of nation is supplanted by the body of a woman. As the elector himself puts it: "Folly, you rule the world, and your throne is a pretty feminine mouth" (MK 118).

The significance of the elector's constant blushing, fainting, and sweating becomes clear against the background of contemporary aesthetics, which classifies these signs under the register of the *sentimental,* the polar opposite of the sublime, categories gendered feminine and masculine respectively. Moreover, these bodily signs mark him quite literally as a *pathological* subject in the Kantian sense of the word, that is, as a self bound to the pleasure principle (body and passions) and therefore incapable of sacrificing himself for an idea, whether it be freedom, *Gemeinschaft,* or justice. By contrast, what qualifies the Elector of Brandenburg as a great political leader is not any moral superiority to the Elector of Saxony but his total and uncompromising willingness to subordinate everyone and everything—individuals (e.g., Kohlhaas) as well as extrapolitical concerns (ethics)—to a single purpose: the formation and strengthening of the unified political body that is represented in the final spectacle of power. The Elector of Brandenburg, while not sacrificing himself (this, we saw, is Kohlhaas's symbolic function), nonetheless demonstrates what for Kleist is *the* central political virtue: the ability to cancel out the passions of the self in the interest of the political community. Undeterred by personal as well as moral considerations, he is—like the elector in *Prinz Friedrich von Homburg*—the embodiment of a total and totalitarian will to politics and power. The showdown between Kohlhaas and the Elector of Saxony in the last paragraph juxtaposes the sublime with the sentimental body: while the horse dealer, in serenely accepting his execution, asserts his power *over his* body, the fainting elector becomes the victim of *his* body. The end, then, figures the confrontation between two political economies of the self and two potential German futures: between the sacrificial self of the warrior capable of meeting the Napoleonic challenge and the suffering self of the feminized German facing political decline and extinction (the soothsayer's prediction).

83. "Der Kurfürst rief: 'nun, Kohlhaas, der Roßhandler, du, dem solchergestalt Genugtuung geworden, mache dich bereit, kaiserlicher Majestät, deren Anwalt hier steht, wegen des Bruchs ihres Landfriedens, deinerseits Genugtuung zu geben!' Kohlhaas, indem er seinen Hut abnahm, und auf die Erde warf, sagte: daß er bereit dazu wäre! . . . Eben knüpfte er sich das Tuch vom Hals ab und öffnete seinen Brustlatz: als er, mit einem flüchtigen Blick auf den Kreis, den das Volk bildete, in geringer Entfernung von sich, zwischen zwei Rittern, die ihn mit ihren Leibern halb deckten, den wohlbekannten Mann mit blauen und weißen Federbüschen wahrnahm. Kohlhaas löste sich, indem er mit einem plötzlichen, die Wache, die ihn umringte, befremdenden Schritt, dicht vor ihn trat, die Kapsel von

der Brust; er nahm den Zettel heraus, entsiegelte ihn, und überlas ihn: und das Auge unverwandt auf den Mann mit blauen und weißen Federbüschen gerichtet, der bereits süßen Hoffnungen Raum zu geben anfing, steckte er ihn in den Mund und verschlang ihn. Der Mann mit blauen und weißen Federbüschen sank, bei diesem Anblick, ohnmächtig, in Krämpfen nieder. Kohlhaas aber, während die bestürzten Begleiter desselben sich herabbeugten, und ihn vom Boden aufhoben, wandte sich zu dem Schafott, wo sein Haupt unter dem Beil des Scharfrichters fiel. Hier endigt die Geschichte des Kohlhaas . . . Der Kurfürst von Sachsen kam bald darauf, zerrissen an Leib und Seele, nach Dresden zurück, wo man das Weitere in der Geschichte nachlesen muß. Von Kohlhaas aber haben noch im vergangenen Jahrhundert, im Mecklenburgischen, einige frohe und rüstige Nachkommen gelebt." MK 141–42.

84. "Worauf er sich, selbst zufrieden auf einen Stuhl niedersetzte.—Wenn man an den Zeremoniemeister denkt, so kann man sich ihn bei diesem Auftritt nicht anders, als in einem völligen Geistesbankerott vorstellen, nach einem ähnlichen Gesetz, nach welchem in einem Körper, der von dem elektrischen Zustand Null ist, wenn er in eines elektrisierten Körpers Atmosphäre kommt, plötzlich die entgegengesetzte Elektrizität erweckt wird. Und wie in dem elektrischen dadurch, nach einer Wechselwirkung, der ihm inwohnende Elektrizitäts-Grad wieder verstärkt wird, so ging unseres Redners Mut, bei der Vernichtung seines Gegners zur verwegensten Begeisterung über." AV 537.

Conclusion. The Big Either

1. For a reading of the modern novella along these lines, see my "La forma e il caso."

2. Marx, *Grundrisse*, 165–66.

3. On Kierkegaard's (non)concept of chatter, see Fenves, *"Chatter,"* esp. 191–243, on *Two Ages*.

4. See Kierkegaard's theater metaphors and his discussion of spectatorship, 72–73.

5. This is the title of chapter 39 of Musil's novel, but similar formulations can be found throughout the text.

6. On Kafka, see my "Lessons of the Cryptograph." This crisis of culture and meaning also affects the symbolic form of the bildungsroman, whose narratives increasingly center around trauma and other experiences that resist integration into narratives of growth and individuation. See Moretti, "'A useless longing for myself.'" Given my earlier argument about the bifurcation of the novella and the novel around 1800, Moretti's claim that in the early decades of the twentieth century the form of the bildungsroman increasingly approximates that of the novella (he speaks of "bildungsnovelle" [49]) may be taken to support my argument that

the novella form articulates the dark underside and paradoxes intrinsic in earlier notions of progress.

7. In mathematics, by Hilbert and Frege; in scientific methodology, by Hempel; and in philosophy, by Husserl and Carnap, to name only the most important figures in this regard. On Frege, Husserl, and the problem of foundation in modern German philosophy, see Roberts, *Logic of Reflection*.

8. Schmitt, *Political Theology*, 15.

9. Ibid., 5.

10. "The legal prescription, as the norm of decision, only designates how decisions should be made, not who should decide" (ibid., 32–33).

11. See Schmitt, "Wendung zum totalen Staat." See also the incisive comments by Schmidt-Biggemann, *Geschichte als absoluter Begriff*, 65–75.

12. Benjamin, "Critique of Violence."

13. Benjamin, *Illuminations*, 252: "The tradition of the oppressed teaches us that the 'state of emergency' in which we live is not the exception but the rule" ("Theses on the Philosophy of History," Thesis VIII).

14. Benjamin, "Critique of Violence," 300.

References

Agamben, Giorgio. *Homo Sacer: Sovereign Power and Bare Life*. Translated by Daniel Heller-Roazen. Stanford, Calif.: Stanford University Press, 1998.

———. *Stato di eccezione*. Turin: Bollati Boringhieri, 2003. Translated by Kevin Attel as *State of Exception* (Chicago: University of Chicago Press, 2005).

Allison, Henry E. *Kant's Theory of Freedom*. Cambridge: Cambridge University Press, 1990.

———. *Idealism and Freedom*. Cambridge: Cambridge University Press, 1996.

Anderson, Benedict. *Imagined Communities: Reflections on the Origin and Spread of Nationalism*. New York: Verso, 1983.

Arendt, Hannah. *On Revolution*. New York: Penguin Books, 1963.

Aris, Reinhold. *Political Thought in Germany*. London: G. Allen & Unwin, 1936.

Aust, Hugo. *Novelle*. Stuttgart: Metzler, 1990.

Austin, J. L. *Philosophical Papers*. Oxford: Clarendon Press, 1961.

———. *How to Do Things with Words*. Cambridge, Mass.: Harvard University Press, 1975.

Baioni, Giuliano. *Classicismo e revoluzione: Goethe e la revoluzione francese*. Naples: Guida, 1969.

———. "*Märchen—Wilhelm Meisters Lehrjahre—Herman und Dorothea*: Zur Gesellschaftsidee der deutschen Klassik." *Goethe-Jahrbuch* 92 (1975): 73–127.

Baker, Keith. *Inventing the French Revolution*. Cambridge: Cambridge University Press, 1990.

———. "Sovereignty." In *A Critical Dictionary of the French Revolution*, ed. François Furet and Mona Ozouf, trans. Arthur Goldhammer, 844–59. Cambridge, Mass.: Harvard University Press, 1989.

Bakhtin, M. M. *The Dialogic Imagination*. Edited and translated by Michael Holquist. Austin: University of Texas Press, 1981.

Balke, Friedrich. *Der Staat nach seinem Ende: Die Versuchung Carl Schmitts*. Munich: Wilhelm Fink, 1996.

Barthes, Roland. "La Bruyère." In *Critical Essays*, trans. Richard Howard, 221–39. Evanston, Ill.: Northwestern University Press, 1972.

———. "Introduction to the Structural Analysis of Literature." In id., *Image-Music-Text*, trans. Stephen Heath, 74–124. New York: Hill & Wang, 1977.

————. *The Rustle of Language.* Translated by Richard Howard. Berkeley: University of California Press, 1989.

Baudelaire, Charles. "On the Essence of Laughter." In *The Painter of Modern Life and Other Essays,* ed. and trans. Jonathan Mayne, 147–65. New York: Phaidon Press, 1964.

Beck, Lewis White. *A Commentary on Kant's Critique of Practical Reason.* Chicago: University of Chicago Press, 1960.

Beiser, Frederick C. *Enlightenment, Revolution, and Romanticism.* Cambridge, Mass.: Harvard University Press, 1992.

Benjamin, Walter. *Illuminationen: Ausgewählte Schriften.* Frankfurt a/M: Suhrkamp, 1955. Reprint, 1980. Translated by Harry Zohn as *Illuminations*, ed. Hannah Arendt (New York: Schocken Books, 1969).

————. *Zur Kritik der Gewalt und andere Aufsätze.* Frankfurt a/M: Suhrkamp, 1965. Reprint, 1981.

————. *Reflections: Essays, Aphorisms, Autobiographical Writings.* Translated by Edmund Jephcott. Edited by Peter Demetz. New York: Schocken Books, 1978. Reprint, 1986.

Benveniste, Emile. *Problems in General Lingustics.* Translated by Mary Elizabeth Meek. Coral Gables, Fla.: University of Miami Press, 1971.

Best, Otto F. "Schuld und Vergebung." *Germanisch-Romanische Monatsschrift* 20 (1970): 180–93.

Blamberger, Günther. "Agonalität und Theatralität: Kleists Gedankenfigur des Duells im Kontext der europäischen Moralistik." *Kleist Jahrbuch,* 1999: 25–41.

Blanning, T. C. W. *The French Revolution in Germany.* Oxford: Clarendon Press, 1983.

Boccaccio, Giovanni. *Decameron.* Edited by Vittore Branca. Turin: Einaudi, 1980.

Böckenförde, Ernst-Wolfgang. "Verfassungsgebende Gewalt des Volkes—Ein Grenzbegriff des Verfassungsrechts." In *Zum Begriff der Verfassung,* ed. Ulrich K. Preuß, 58–82. Frankfurt a/M: Fischer, 1994.

Bogdal, Klaus-Michael. *Heinrich von Kleist: Michael Kohlhaas.* Munich: Wilhelm Fink, 1981.

Bookman, Hartmut. "Mittelalterliches Recht bei Kleist: Ein Beitrag zum Verständnis des 'Michael Kohlhaas'." *Kleist-Jahrbuch,* 1985: 84–108.

Bosse, Heinrich. "The Marvelous and Romantic Semiotics." *Studies in Romanticism* 14 (Summer 1975): 211–37.

————. "Geschichten." In *Literaturwissenschaft: Einführung in ein Sprachspiel,* ed. Heinrich Bosse and Ursula Renner, 299–320. Freiburg: Rombach, 1999.

Bräutigam, Bernd. "Die ästhetische Erziehung der deutschen Ausgewanderten." *Zeitschrift für deutsche Philologie* 96 (1977): 508–39.

Breger, Claudia. *Ortlosigkeit des Fremden: "Zigeunerinnen" und "Zigeuner" in der deutschsprachigen Literatur um 1800.* Cologne: Böhlau, 1998.

Brentano, Margherita von. "Kant's Theorie der Geschichte und der bürgerlichen

Gesellschaft." In *Spiegel und Gleichnis,* ed. N. W. Bolz and W. Hübener, 205–14. Würzburg: Könighausen & Neumann, 1983.

Breuer, Ingo. "'Schauplätze jämmerlicher Mordgeschichte': Tradition der Novelle und Theatralität der Historia bei Heinrich von Kleist." *Kleist-Jahrbuch,* 2001: 196–225.

Brooks, Peter. *The Melodramatic Imagination: Balzac, Henry James, Melodrama, and the Mode of Excess.* New York: Columbia University Press, 1984.

———. *Reading for the Plot: Design and Intention in Narrative.* New York: Vintage Books, 1984.

———. "The Tale vs. the Novel." In *Why the Novel Matters,* ed. Mark Spilka and Caroline McCracken-Flesher. Bloomington: Indiana University Press, 1990.

Brown, Jane K. "Introduction." In *Conversations of German Refugees;* [and] *Wilhelm Meister's Journeyman Years, or, The Renunciants,* by Johann Wolfgang von Goethe, ed. Jane K. Brown, 1–10. New York: Suhrkamp, 1989.

Burg, Peter. *Kant und die Französische Revolution.* Berlin: Duncker & Humbolt, 1974.

———. "Die Französische Revolution als Heilsgeschehen." In *Materialien zu Kants Rechtsphilosophie,* ed. Zwi Batscha, 237–69. Frankfurt a/M: Suhrkamp, 1976.

Bürger, Christa. "Statt einer Interpretation: Anmerkungen zu Kleists *Das Erdbeben in Chili.*" In *Positionen der Literaturwissenschaft: Acht Modellanalysen am Beispiel von Kleist "Das Erdbeben in Chili,"* ed. David Wellbery, 88–110. Munich: C. H. Beck, 1985.

Butler, Judith. *Bodies That Matter: On the Discursive Limits of "Sex."* New York: Routledge, 1993.

———. *Excitable Speech: A Politics of the Performative.* New York: Routledge, 1997.

———. "Afterword." In Shoshana Felman, *The Scandal of the Speaking Body: Don Juan with J. L. Austin, or Seduction in Two Languages*, trans. Catherine Porter, 113–25. Stanford, Calif.: Stanford University Press, 2003.

Cavell, Stanley. *Must We Mean What We Say?* New York: Scribner, 1969.

Caygill, Howard. *A Kant Dictionary.* Oxford: Blackwell, 1995.

Craig, Gordon Alexander. *The Politics of the Prussian Army, 1640–1945.* New York: Oxford University Press, 1955.

Culler, Jonathan. "Story and Discourse in the Analysis of Narrative." In *The Pursuit of Signs. Semiotics, Literature, Deconstruction,* 169–88. Ithaca, N.Y.: Cornell University Press, 1981.

Dammann, Günter. "Goethes *Unterhaltungen deutscher Ausgewanderten* als Essay über die Gattung der Prosaerzählung im 18. Jahrhundert." In *Der deutsche Roman der Spätaufklärung,* ed. Harro Zimmermann, 1–24. Heidelberg: Carl Winter, 1990.

Davis, Lennhard J. *Factual Fictions: The Origins of the English Novel.* New York: Columbia University Press, 1983.

References

Delekat, Friedrich. *Immanel Kant: Historisch-Kritische Interpretation der Hauptschriften.* Heidelberg: Quelle & Meyer, 1969.

Deleuze, Gilles, and Félix Guattari, *What Is Philosophy?* Translated by Hugh Tomlinson and Graham Burchell. New York: Columbia University Press, 1994.

De Man, Paul. "Aesthetic Formalization: Kleist's *Über das Marionettentheater.*" In id., *The Rhetoric of Romanticism,* 263–90. New York: Columbia University Press, 1984.

Derrida, Jacques. *Of Grammatology.* Translated by Gayatri Chakravorty Spivak. Baltimore: Johns Hopkins University Press, 1974.

———. *Dissemination.* Translated by Barbara Johnson. Chicago: University of Chicago Press, 1981.

———. *Limited Inc.* Translated by Alan Bass and Samuel Weber. Evanston, Ill.: Northwestern University Press, 1988.

———. "Force of Law: The 'Mystical Foundation of Authority.'" In *Deconstruction and the Possibility of Justice,* ed. Drucilla Cornell, M. Rosenfeld, and D. G. Carlson, 3–67. New York: Routledge, 1992. Published in French as *Force de Loi: Le "Fondement mystique de l'autorité"* (Paris: Galilée, 1994).

———. "Mochlos; or, The Conflict of the Faculties." In *Logomachia: The Conflict of the Faculties,* ed. Richard Rand. Lincoln: University of Nebraska Press, 1992.

Descombes, Vincent. *The Barometer of Modern Reason.* Translated by Stephen Adam Schwartz. New York: Oxford University Press, 1993.

Dotzler, Bernhard. "'Federkrieg': Kleist und die Autorschaft des Produzenten." *Kleist-Jahrbuch,* 1998: 37–61.

Ellis, John M. *Narration in the German Novelle.* Cambridge: Cambridge University Press, 1974.

Engel, Odilo. "Geschichte." In *Geschichtliche Grundbegriffe,* ed. Otto Brunner, W. Conze, and R. Koselleck, 2: 610–24. Stuttgart: Klett, 1975.

Fehér, Ferenc. *The Frozen Revolution: An Essay on Jacobinism.* Cambridge: Cambridge University Press, 1987.

———. "Practical Reason in the Revolution: Kant's Dialogue with the French Revolution." In *The French Revolution and the Birth of Modernity,* ed. Ferenc Fehér, 201–19. Berkeley: University of California Press, 1990.

Felman, Shoshana. *The Scandal of the Speaking Body: Don Juan with J. L. Austin, or Seduction in Two Languages.* Translated by Catherine Porter. Stanford, Calif.: Stanford University Press, 2003.

Fenves, Peter. *A Peculiar Fate: Metaphysics and World-History in Kant.* Ithaca, N.Y.: Cornell University Press, 1991.

———. *"Chatter": Language and History in Kierkegaard.* Stanford, Calif.: Stanford University Press, 1993.

Fineman, Joel. "The History of the Anecdote: Fiction and Fiction." In *The New Historicism,* ed. H. Aram Veeser, 49–77. New York: Routledge, 1989.

Fischer, Bernd. *Ironische Metaphysik: Die Erzählungen Heinrich von Kleists.* Munich: Wilhelm Fink Verlag, 1988.

Fischer, Gottfried, and Peter Riedesser. *Lehrbuch der Psychotraumatologie.* Munich: Ernst Reinhardt Verlag, 1999.

Fish, Stanley. *Doing What Comes Naturally.* Durham, N.C.: Duke University Press, 1989.

Forrester, John. *The Seductions of Psychoanalysis: Freud, Lacan and Derrida.* Cambridge: Cambridge University Press, 1990.

Förster, Eckart. "Die Bedeutung von §§ 76, 77 der *Kritik der Urteilskraft* auf die Entwicklung der nachkantischen Philosophie." *Zeitschrift für philosophische Forschung* 56 (2002): 169–90, 321–45.

Foucault, Michel. "Tales of Murder." In *I, Pierre Rivière, having slaughtered my mother, my sister and my brother . . . : A Case of Parricide in the Nineteenth Century,* ed. id., trans. Frank Jellinek, 199–212. 1975. Reprint, Lincoln: University of Nebraska Press, 1982. Originally published as *Moi, Pierre Rivière, ayant égorgé ma mère, ma soeur et mon frère . . . un cas de parricide au XIXe siècle,* ed. Michel Foucault (Paris: Gallimard, 1973).

———. "The Life of Infamous Men." In *Power, Truth, Strategy,* ed. Meaghan Morris and Paul Patton, 76–91. Sydney: Feral Publications, 1979.

———. *The Politics of Truth.* Edited by Sylvère Lotringer and Lysa Hochroth. New York: Semiotext(e), 1997.

France, Peter. *Politeness and Its Discontents: Problems in French Classical Culture.* New York: Cambridge University Press, 1992.

Freud, Sigmund. *Gesammelte Werke.* London: Imago, 1940. Cited as GW.

———. *The Standard Edition of the Works of the Complete Psychological Works.* General editor, James Strachey. London: Hogarth Press and Institute of Psychoanalysis, 1953–74. Cited as SE.

Furet, François. *Interpreting the French Revolution.* Translated by Elborg Forster. Cambridge: Cambridge University Press, 1981.

———. *Revolutionary France, 1770–1880.* Translated by Antonia Nevill. Oxford: Blackwell, 1992.

Gaier, Ulrich. "Soziale Bildung gegen ästhetische Erziehung: Goethes Rahmen der *Unterhaltungen deutscher Ausgewanderten* als satirische Antithese zu Schillers *Ästhetischen Briefen* I–IX." In *Poetische Autonomie? Zur Wechselwirkung von Dichtung und Philosophie in der Epoche Goethe und Hölderlins,* 207–72. Stuttgart: Klett, 1987.

Gailus, Andreas. "Of Beautiful and Dismembered Bodies: Art as Social Discipline in Schiller's *On the Aesthetic Education of Man.*" In *Impure Reason: Dialectic of Enlightenment in Germany,* ed. W. Daniel Wilson and Robert C. Holub, 146–65. Detroit: Wayne State University Press, 1992.

———. "A Case of Individuality: K. Ph. Moritz and the *Magazine for Empirical Psychology.*" *New German Critique* 79 (2000): 67–105.

———. "Lessons of the Cryptograph: Revelation and the Mechanical in Kafka's 'In the Penal Colony.'" *Modernism/Modernity* 8, no. 2 (2001): 295–303.

———. "La forma e il caso: La novella tedesca dell'Ottocento." In *Il romanzo,* ed. Franco Moretti, 505–36. Turin: Einaudi, 2002.

Gallas, Helga. *Das Textbegehren des "Michael Kohlhaas": Die Sprache des Unbewußten und der Sinn der Literatur.* Reinbek: Rowohlt, 1981.

Giddens, Anthony. *Social Theory and Modern Sociology.* Stanford, Calif.: Stanford University Press, 1987.

Gillespie, Gerald. "Kleist's Hypotheses of Affective Expression: Acting-out in Language." *Seminar* 17 (1981): 275–83.

Goethe, Johann Wolfgang von. *Werke.* Edited on behalf of the Großherzogin Sophie von Sachsen. Weimar: Böhlau, 1895.

———. *Werke.* Edited by Erich Trunz. 14 vols. Munich: C. H. Beck, 1981.

———. "On Epic and Dramatic Poetry." In id., *Essays on Art and Literature,* trans. Elleen von Nardroff and Ernest H. von Nardroff, ed. John Gearey, 192–94. New York: Suhrkamp, 1986. Vol. 3 of *Goethe's Collected Works.* Cited as EDP.

———. *Collected Works.* Edited by Viktor Lange, Eric A. Blackall, and Cyrus Hamlin. New York: Suhrkamp, 1988–.

———. *Scientific Studies.* Edited and translated by Douglas Miller. New York: Suhrkamp, 1988. Vol. 12 of *Goethe's Collected Works.* Cited as SS.

———. *Sämtliche Werke: Briefe, Tagebücher und Gespräche.* Edited by Friedmar Apel et al. Frankfurt a/M: Deutscher Klassiker Verlag, 1989–.

———. *Zur Morphologie.* In id., *Sämtliche Werke nach Epochen seines Schaffens,* vol. 12: *Zur Naturwissenschaft überhaupt, besonders zur Morphologie,* ed. Hans J. Becker et al., 9–386. Munich: Carl Hanser, 1989. Cited as M.

———. *Conversations of German Refugees.* Translated by Jan van Heurck in cooperation with Jane K. Brown. Edited by Jane K. Brown. New York: Suhrkamp, 1991. Vol. 10 of *Goethe's Collected Works.* Cited as CR.

———. *Unterhaltungen deutscher Ausgewanderten.* In id., *Sämtliche Werke: Briefe, Tagebücher und Gespräche,* part 1, vol. 9: *Wilhelm Meisters theatralische Sendung; Wilhelm Meisters Lehrjahre; Unterhaltungen deutscher Ausgewanderten,* ed. Wilhelm Voßkamp and Herbert Jaumann, 993–1114. Frankfurt a/M: Deutscher Klassiker Verlag, 1992. Cited as UA.

———. *Campagne in Frankreich.* In id., *Sämtliche Werke: Briefe, Tagebücher und Gespräche,* part 1, vol. 16: *Campagne in Frankreich; Belagerung von Mainz; Reiseschriften,* ed. Klaus-Detlef Müller, 386–573. Frankfurt a/M: Deutscher Klassiker Verlag, 1994. Cited as CAF.

———. "Reise der Söhne Megaprazons." In id., *Sämtliche Werke: Briefe, Tagebücher und Gespräche,* part 1, vol. 8: *Die Leiden des jungen Werthers; Die Wahlverwandtschaften; Kleine Prosa; Epen,* ed. Waltraud Wiethölter, 578–94. Frankfurt a/M: Deutscher Klassiker Verlag, 1994. Cited as RSM

———. "Über epische und dramatische Dichtung. Von Goethe und Schiller." In id., *Sämtliche Werke: Briefe, Tagebücher und Gespräche*, part 1, vol. 22: *Ästhetische Schriften, 1824–1832*, ed. Anne Bohnenkamp, 295–306. Frankfurt a/M: Deutscher Klassiker Verlag, 1999. Cited as EDD

Graham, Ilse. *Heinrich von Kleist: Wort into Flesh: A Poet's Quest for the Symbol.* Berlin: De Gruyter, 1977.

Greiner, Bernhard. "Mediale Wende des Schönen—'freies Spiel' der Sprache und 'unaussprechlicher Mensch.' 'Über die allmähliche Verfertigung der Gedanken beim Reden.' 'Brief eines Dichters an einen anderen.'" In *Heinrich von Kleist: Neue Wege zur Forschung,* ed. Anton Philipp Knittel und Inka Kording, 163–77. Darmstadt: Wissenschaftliche Buchgesellschaft, 2003.

Gumbrecht, Hans Ulrich. "Outline of a Literary History of the French Revolution." In *Making Sense in Life and Literature,* trans. Glen Burns, 178–225. Minneapolis: University of Minnesota Press, 1992.

Günther, Horst, ed. *Die Französische Revolution: Berichte und Deutungen deutscher Schriftsteller und Historiker.* Frankfurt a/M: Deutscher Klassiker Verlag, 1985.

Guyer, Paul. *Kant and the Experience of Freedom.* Cambridge: Cambridge University Press, 1993.

———. "Absolute Idealism and the Rejection of Kantian Dualism." In *Cambridge Companion to German Idealism,* ed. Karl Ameriks, 37–57. Cambridge: Cambridge University Press, 2000.

Hamacher, Werner. "Das Beben der Darstellung." In *Positionen der Literaturwissenschaft: Acht Modellanalysen am Beispiel von Kleist "Das Erdbeben in Chili,"* ed. David Wellbery, 149–74. Munich: C. H. Beck, 1985.

Hegel, G. W. F. *Phänomenologie des Geistes.* Frankfurt a/M: Suhrkamp, 1970. Vol. 3 of *Werke in zwanzig Bänden.*

———. *Vorlesungen über die Geschichte der Philosophie.* Frankfurt a/M: Suhrkamp, 1971. Vols. 18–20 of *Werke in zwanzig Bänden.*

———. *Werke in zwanzig Bänden.* Edited by Eva Moldenhauer and Karl Markus Michel. Frankfurt a/M: Suhrkamp, 1970–.

Henel, Heinrich. "Anfänge der deutschen Novelle." *Monatshefte* 77 (1985): 433–48.

Henrich, Dieter. "Der Begriff der sittlichen Einsicht und Kants Lehre vom Faktum der Vernunft." In *Kant: Zur Deutung seiner Theorie von Erkennen und Handeln,* ed. Gerold Prauss, 223–52. Cologne: Kiepenheuer & Witsch, 1973.

———. "Kant über die Revolution." In *Materialien zu Kants Rechtsphilosophie,* ed. Zwi Batscha, 359–66. Frankfurt a/M: Suhrkamp, 1976.

———. *Aesthetic Judgment and the Moral Image of the World: Studies on Kant.* Stanford, Calif.: Stanford University Press, 1992.

Hiebel, Hans H. "Das Rechtsbegehren des Michael Kohlhaas: Kleist und Kafkas Rechtsvorstellungen." In *Heinrich von Kleist: Studien zu Werk und Wirkung,* ed. Dirk Grathoff, 282–312. Opladen: Westdeutscher Verlag, 1988.

Holland, Jocelyn. "Singularität und ihre Verdoppelung: Goethes Aufnahme französischer Literatur." In *Singularitäten. Literatur—Wissenschaft—Verant-wortung*, ed. Marianne Schuller and Elisabeth Strowick, 345–61. Freiburg i. B.: Rombach, 2001.

Holz, Hans-Heinz. *Macht und Ohnmacht der Sprache*. Frankfurt a/M: Athenäum, 1962.

Humboldt, Wilhelm von. *Werke*. Edited by Andreas Flitner and Klaus Giel. Stuttgart: Cotta, 1960–64.

Humphrey, Richard. *The Historical Novel as Philosophy of History: Three German Contributions: Alexis, Fontane, Döblin*. London: Institute of Germanic Studies, University of London, 1986.

Hunt, Lynn. *Politics, Culture and Class in the French Revolution*. Berkeley: University of California Press, 1984,

Hunter, Ian. "Aesthetics and Cultural Studies." In *Cultural Studies,* ed. Lawrence Grossberg, C. Nelson, and P. Treichler, 347–72. New York: Routledge, 1992.

Hunter, J. Paul. *Before Novels: The Cultural Contexts of Eighteenth-Century English Fiction*. New York: Norton, 1990.

Jacobson, Roman. *Style in Language*. Edited by Thomas Sebeok. Cambridge, Mass.: MIT Press, 1960.

Joos, Jean-Ernest. *Kant et la question de l'autorité*. Paris: L'Harmattan, 1995.

Julien, Philippe. *Jacques Lacan's Return to Freud*. Translated by Devra Beck Simiu. New York: New York University Press, 1994

Kalweit, Hilmar. "Szenerien der Individualisierung." In *Individualität,* ed. Manfred Frank and Anselm Haverkamp, 384–421. Munich: W. Fink, 1988.

Kant, Immanuel. Kant's gesammelte Schriften. Edited by the Königlich Preußischen Akademie der Wissenschaften. Berlin: De Gruyter, 1922–. Cited as AA.

———. *Religion Within the Limits of Reason Alone*. Translated by Theodore M. Greene and Hoyt H. Hudson. Chicago: Open Court, 1934. Cited as RLR.

———. *Kritik der reinen Vernunft*. Edited by Raymund Schmid. Hamburg: Meiner, 1956. Cited as KrV.

———. *Der Streit der Fakultäten*. Edited by Klaus Reich. Hamburg: Meiner, 1959. Cited as SF.

———. *Observations on the Feeling of the Beautiful and Sublime*. Translated by John T. Goldthwait. Berkeley: University of California Press, 1960. Cited as OBS.

———. "Idea for a Universal History from a Cosmopolitan Point of View." In *On History,* trans. and ed. Lewis White Beck, 11–26. Indianapolis: Bobbs-Merrill, 1963. Cited as IUH.

———. *Groundwork of the Metaphysic of Morals*. Translated by H. J. Paton. New York: Harper & Row, 1964. Cited as GMM.

———. "On the Common Saying: 'This may be true in theory, but it does not apply in practice.'" In *Kant's Political Writings*, trans. H. B. Nisbet, ed. Hans Reiss, 61–92. Cambridge: Cambridge University Press, 1970. Cited as TP.

———. "Perpetual Peace: A Philosophical Sketch." In *Kant's Political Writings,* trans. H. B. Nisbet, ed. Hans Reiss, 93–130. Cambridge: Cambridge University Press, 1970. Cited as PP.

———. *Critique of Judgment.* Translated by Werner Pluhar. Indianapolis: Hackett, 1987. Cited as CJ.

———. *Kritik der praktischen Vernunft.* Edited by Karl Vorländer. Hamburg: Meiner, 1990. Cited as KpV.

———. *Kritik der Urteilskraft.* Edited by Karl Vorländer. Hamburg: Meiner, 1990. Cited as KU.

———. *Die Religion innerhalb der Grenzen der Vernunft.* Hamburg: Meiner, 1990. Cited as RGV.

———. *The Conflict of the Faculties / Der Streit der Fakultäten.* Translated by Mary J. Gregor. Lincoln: University of Nebraska Press, 1992. Cited as CF.

———. *Critique of Practical Reason.* Translated by Lewis White Beck. New York: Macmillan, 1993. Cited as CprR.

———. *Grundlegung zur Metaphysik der Sitten.* Edited by Karl Vorländer. Hamburg: Meiner, 1994. Cited as GMS.

———. *The Metaphysics of Morals.* In *The Cambridge Edition of the Works of Immanuel Kant: Practical Philosophy,* trans. and ed. Mary J. Gregor, 353–605. Cambridge: Cambridge University Press, 1996. Cited as MM.

———. *Critique of Pure Reason.* Translated and edited by Paul Guyer and Allen W. Wood. New York: Cambridge University Press, 1998. Cited as CPR.

Kiefer, Hans. "Species facti. Geschichtserzählung bei Kleist und in Relationen bei preußischen Kollegialbehörden um 1800." *Kleist-Jahrbuch,* 1988/89: 13–40.

Kierkegaard, Søren. *Two Ages.* In *Kierkegaard's Writings,* vol. 14. Edited and translated by Howard V. Hong and Edna Hong. Princeton, N.J.: Princeton University Press, 1978. Cited as TA.

Kittler, Wolf. *Die Geburt des Partisanen aus dem Geist der Poesie: Heinrich von Kleist und die Strategie der Befreiungskriege.* Freiburg: Rombach, 1987.

Kleist, Heinrich von. *The Marquise of O—and Other Stories.* Translated and with an Introduction by Martin Greenberg. New York: Frederick Ungar, 1960.

———. *Michael Kohlhaas.* In id., *The Marquise of O—and Other Stories,* trans. and ed. Martin Greenberg. New York: Frederick Ungar, 1960. Cited as MK/G.

———. *Sämtliche Werke und Briefe.* Edited by Ilse-Marie Barth et al. 4 vols. Frankfurt a/M: Deutscher Klassiker Verlag, 1987–97.

———. *Michael Kohlhaas.* In id., *Sämtliche Werke und Briefe,* vol. 3: *Erzählungen. Anekdoten. Gedichte. Schriften,* ed. Klaus Müller-Salget, 11–142. Frankfurt a/M: Deutscher Klassiker Verlag, 1990. Cited as MK.

———. "Über die allmähliche Verfertigung der Gedanken beim Reden." In id., *Sämtliche Werke und Briefe,* vol. 3: *Erzählungen; Anekdoten; Gedichte; Schriften,* ed. Klaus Müller-Salget, 534–40. Frankfurt a/M: Deutscher Klassiker Verlag, 1990. Cited as AV.

———. "On the Gradual Production of Thoughts Whilst Speaking." In id., *Selected Writings*, trans. David Constantine, 405–9. London: J. M. Dent, 1997. Cited as GP.

———. *Selected Writings*. Translated by David Constantine. London: J. M. Dent, 1997.

Kommerell, Max. *Geist und Buchstabe der Dichtung*. Tübingen: Laupp, 1944.

Korsgaard, Christine. "Taking the Law into Our Own Hands: Kant on the Right to Revolution." In *Reclaiming the History of Ethics,* ed. Andrew Reath, B. Herman, and C. Korsgaard, 297–328. Cambridge: Cambridge University Press, 1997.

Koselleck, Reinhart. *Preußen zwischen Reform und Revolution*. Stuttgart: Klett, 1967.

———. "Geschichte." In *Geschichtliche Grundbegriffe: Historisches Lexikon zur politisch-sozialen Sprache in Deutschland,* ed. Otto Brunner, W. Conze, and R. Koselleck, 2: 647–717. Stuttgart: Klett, 1975.

———. "Krise." In *Geschichtliche Grundbegriffe: Historisches Lexikon zur politisch-sozialen Sprache in Deutschland,* ed. Otto Brunner, W. Conze, and R. Koselleck, 3: 617–50. Stuttgart: Klett-Cotta, 1982.

———. *Futures Past: On the Semantics of Historical Time*. Translated by Keith Tribe. Cambridge, Mass.: MIT Press, 1985.

Kowalik, Jill Ann. "Kleist's Essay on Rhetoric." *Monatshefte* 81 (1989): 434–46.

Kuhns, Richard. *Tragedy: Contradiction and Repression*. Chicago: University of Chicago Press, 1991.

Kunz, Josef, ed. *Novelle*. Darmstadt: Wissenschaftliche Buchgesellschaft, 1977.

Lacan, Jacques. *The Ethics of Psychoanalysis, 1959–1960*. Translated by Dennis Porter. Book 7 of *The Seminars of Jacques Lacan*. New York: Norton, 1992.

Laplanche, Jean. *Life and Death in Psychoanalysis*. Translated by Jeffrey Mehlman. Baltimore: Johns Hopkins University Press, 1976.

Larmore, Charles. "Hölderlin and Novalis." In *Cambridge Companion to German Idealism,* ed. Karl Ameriks, 141–60. Cambridge: Cambridge University Press, 2000.

Lotman, Yuri M. *Universe of the Mind*. Translated by Ann Shukman. Bloomington: Indiana University Press, 1990.

Luhmann, Niklas. "Interaktion in Oberschichten: Zur Transformation ihrer Semantik im 17. und 18. Jahrhundert." In *Gesellschaftsstruktur und Semantik: Studien zur Wissenssoziologie der modernen Gesellschaft,* 1: 72–161. Frankfurt a/M: Suhrkamp, 1980.

———. *The Differentiation of Society*. Translated by Stephen Holmes and Charles Larmore. New York: Columbia University Press, 1982.

———. "Wie ist Bewußtsein an Kommunikation beteiligt?" In *Materialität der Kommunikation,* ed. Hans Ulrich Gumbrecht and K. Ludwig Pfeiffer, 884–913. Frankfurt a/M: Suhrkamp, 1988.

————. *Das Recht der Gesellschaft.* Frankfurt a/M: Suhrkamp, 1993.

————. *Social Systems.* Translated by John Bednarz Jr. Stanford, Calif.: Stanford University Press, 1995.

————. *Die Gesellschaft der Gesellschaft.* Frankfurt a/M: Suhrkamp, 1997.

————. *Die Realität der Massenmedien.* Opladen: Westdeutscher Verlag, 1996.

————. "How Can the Mind Participate in Communication?" In Niklas Luhmann, *Theories of Distinction: Redescribing the Descriptions of Modernity,* ed. William Rasch, 169–84. Stanford, Calif.: Stanford University Press, 2002.

Lützeler, Paul Michael. "Heinrich von Kleist: Michael Kohlhaas." In *Romane und Erzählungen der deutschen Romantik: Neue Interpretationen,* ed. id., 213–39. Stuttgart: Reclam, 1981.

Lyotard, Jean-François. *L'Enthousiasme: La Critique kantienne de l'histoire.* Paris: Galilée, 1986.

Marquard. Odo. "Kant und die Wende zur Ästhetik." *Zeitschrift für philosophische Forschung* 16 (1962): 231–43, 363–74.

Marx, Karl. *Grundrisse: Foundations for a Critique of Political Economy (Rough Drafts).* Translated by Martin Nicolaus. Baltimore: Penguin Books, 1973.

Marx, Karl, and Friedrich Engels. *Collected Works.* New York: International Publishers, 1976.

Mathes, Jürg. "Die 'Disproportionen der Kräfte.' Zu einer Buchstabenkonfiguration in Goethes *Unterhaltungen deutscher Ausgewanderten.*" In *Jahrbuch des Freien Deutschen Hochstifts,* 1981: 116–30.

Maurer, Karl-Heinz. "Gerechtigkeit zwischen Differenz und Identität in Heinrich von Kleists Michael Kohlhaas." *Deutsche Vierteljahreszeitschrift für Literaturwissenschaft und Geistesgeschichte* 75 (2001): 123–44.

McKeon, Michael. *The Origins of the English Novel, 1660–1740.* Baltimore: Johns Hopkins University Press, 1987.

Mehigan, Timothy J. *Text as Contract: The Nature and Function of Narrative Discourse in the Erzählungen of Heinrich von Kleist.* Frankfurt a/M: Peter Lang, 1988.

————, ed. *Heinrich von Kleist und die Aufklärung.* Rochester, N.Y.: Camden House, 2000.

Meier, Christian. *The Greek Discovery of Politics.* Translated by David McLintock. Cambridge, Mass.: Harvard University Press, 1990.

Menninghaus, Winfried. *Unendliche Verdoppelung: Die frühromantische Grundlegung der Kunsttheorie im Begriff absoluter Selbstreflexion.* Frankfurt a/M: Suhrkamp, 1987.

Miller, D. A. *Narrative and Its Discontents: Problems of Closure in the Traditional Novel.* Princeton, N.J.: Princeton University Press, 1981.

Miller, J. Hillis. "Laying Down the Law in Literature: The Example of Kleist." *Cardozo Law Review* 11 (1990): 1491–1514.

Moretti, Franco. *The Way of the World: The Bildungsroman in Europe.* London: Verso, 1987.

References

──────. *Signs Taken for Wonders: Essays in the Sociology of Literary Form.* Rev. ed. Translated by Susan Fischer, D. A. Forgacs, and D. A Miller. London: Verso, 1988.

──────. "'A useless longing for myself': The Crisis of the European Bildungsroman." In *Studies in Historical Change,* ed. Ralph Cohen, 43–59. Charlottesville: University Press of Virginia, 1992.

──────. *Atlas of the European Novel, 1800–1900.* London: Verso, 1998.

Mücke, Dorothea von. *Virtue and the Veil of Illusion: Generic Innovation and the Pedagogical Project in Eighteenth-Century Literature.* Stanford, Calif.: Stanford University Press, 1991.

Müller-Sievers, Helmut. *Self-Generation: Biology, Philosophy, and Literature around 1800.* Stanford, Calif.: Stanford University Press, 1997.

Nagel, Thomas. *The View from Nowhere.* New York: Oxford University Press, 1986.

Nagy, Gregory. *Greek Mythology and Poetics.* Ithaca, N.Y.: Cornell University Press, 1990.

Negri, Antonio. *Il potere costituente: Saggio sulle alternative del moderno.* Carnago: SugarCo, 1992.

Neumann, Gerhard. "Die Anfänge deutscher Novellistik: Schillers 'Verbrecher aus verlorener Ehre' und Goethes *Unterhaltungen deutscher Ausgewanderten.*" In *Unser Commercium. Goethes und Schillers Literaturpolitik,* ed. Wilfried Barner, E. Lämmert, and N. Oellers, 433–60. Stuttgart: Klett, 1984.

──────. "Das Stocken der Sprache und das Straucheln des Körpers: Umrisse von Kleists kultureller Anthropologie." In *Heinrich von Kleist: Kriegsfall-Rechtsfall-Sündenfall,* ed. Gerhard Neumann, 13–31. Freiburg: Rombach 1994.

Patton, Paul. "The World Seen From Within: Deleuze and the Philosophy of Events." *Theory and Event* 1 (1997): 1–9.

Paulin, Roger. *The Brief Compass: The Nineteenth-Century German Novelle.* Oxford: Clarendon Press, 1985.

Pavel, Thomas. "Il romanzo alla ricerca di se stesso: Saggio di morfologia storica." In *Il romanzo,* vol. 2: *Le forme,* ed. Franco Moretti, 36–66. Turin: Einaudi, 2002.

Peters, John Durham. *Speaking into the Air: A History of the Idea of Communication.* Chicago: University of Chicago Press, 1999.

Pinkard, Terry. *German Philosophy, 1760–1860.* Cambridge: Cambridge University Press, 2002.

Pippen, Robert. "Hegel's Practical Philosophy: The Realization of Freedom." In *Cambridge Companion to German Idealism,* ed. Karl Ameriks, 180–200. Cambridge: Cambridge University Press, 2000.

Polheim, Karl Konrad. *Novellentheorie und Novellenforschung.* Stuttgart: Metzler, 1965.

──────, ed. *Theorie und Kritik der deutschen Novelle von Wieland bis Musil.* Tübingen: Max Niemeier, 1970.

Redfield, James M. *Nature and Culture in the Iliad.* Chicago: University of Chicago Press, 1975.

Reich, Klaus. "Einleitung des Herausgebers." In Immanuel Kant, *Der Streit der Fakultäten,* ed. Klaus Reich, ix–xxvi. Hamburg: Meiner, 1959.

Reiss, Hans. "Introduction." In Immanuel Kant, *Political Writings,* 1–41. Cambridge: Cambridge University Press, 1970.

Reuß, Roland. "'Michael Kohlhaas' und 'Michael Kohlhaas.'" In Heinrich von Kleist, *Sämtliche Werke,* vol. 2.1, *Michael Kohhaas.* Supplement, Berliner Kleist Blätter 3, 3–43. Berlin: Stroemfeld / Roter Stern, 1990.

Riedel, Manfred. "Epoche. Epochenbewußtsein." In *Historisches Wörterbuch der Philosophie,* ed. Joachim Ritter et al., 2: 596–99. Basel: Schwabe, 1971–.

———. "Einleitung." In Immanuel Kant, *Schriften zur Geschichtsphilosphie,* ed. Manfred Riedel, 3–20. Stuttgart: Reclam, 1974.

———. *Urteilskraft und Vernunft: Kants ursprüngliche Fragestellung.* Frankfurt a/M: Suhrkamp, 1989.

Ritter, Joachim. *Hegel and the French Revolution: Essays on the Philosophy of Right.* Translated by Richard Dien Winfield. Cambridge, Mass.: MIT Press, 1982.

Roberts, Julian. *Logic of Reflection: German Philosophy in the Twentieth Century.* New Haven, Conn.: Yale University Press, 1992.

Rogozinski, Jacob. "It Makes Us Wrong: Kant and Radical Evil." In *Radical Evil,* ed. Joan Copjec, 30–46. New York: Verso, 1996.

Rohrwasser, Michael. "Eine Bombenpost: Über die allmähliche Verfertigung der Gedanken beim Schreiben." In *Heinrich von Kleist,* ed. Heinz-Ludwig Arnold, 151–63. Munich: Text + Kritik , 1993.

Russo, Elena. "Editor's Preface." In "Exploring the Conversible World," ed. id., special issue, *Yale French Studies* 92 (1997): 1–7.

Santner, Eric L. *My Own Private Germany: Daniel Paul Schreber's Secret History of Modernity.* Princeton, N.J.: Princeton University Press, 1996.

Sauerwein, Herbert. "Die 'Omnipotenz' des pouvoir constituant: Ein Beitrag zur Staats- und Verfassungstheorie." Diss., Johann-Wolfgang-Goethe-Universität, Frankfurt a/M, 1960.

Schaub, Mirjam. *Gilles Deleuze im Wunderland: Zeit- als Ereignisphilosophie.* Munich: Wilhelm Fink, 2003.

Schiller, Friedrich. *Sämtliche Werke.* Edited by Gerhard Fricke and Herbert G. Göpfert. Munich: Hanser, 1960.

———. *On the Aesthetic Education of Man in a Series of Letters.* Translated by Elizabeth M. Wilkinson and L. A. Willoughby. Oxford: Clarendon Press, 1967.

———. *Werke und Briefe,* vol. 8: *Theoretische Schriften,* ed. Rolf Peter Janz et al. Frankfurt a/M: Deutscher Klassiker Verlag, 1992.

Schlaffer, Hannelore. *Poetik der Novelle.* Stuttgart: Metzler, 1993.

Schleiermacher, Friedrich Daniel Ernst. "Versuch einer Theorie des geselligen

Betragens." In *Kritische Gesamtausgabe*, vol. 2, ed. Hans-Joachim Birkner et al., 165–84. Berlin: Walter de Gruyter, 1984.

Schmidt-Biggemann, Wilhelm. *Theodizee und Tatsachen*. Frankfurt a/M: Suhrkamp, 1988.

———. *Geschichte als absoluter Begriff: Der Lauf der neueren deutschen Philosophie*. Frankfurt a/M: Suhrkamp, 1991.

Schmitt, Carl. *Verfassungslehre*. Berlin: Duncker & Humblot, 1928. Reprint, 1983.

———. *Der Begriff des Politischen*. Berlin: Duncker & Humblot, 1933. Reprint, 1963.

———. "Die Wendung zum totalen Staat." In *Positionen und Begriffe im Kampf mit Weimar-Genf-Versailles, 1923–1939*, 146–55. Hamburg: Hanseatische Verlagsanstalt, 1940.

———. *Political Theology: Four Chapters on the Concept of Sovereignty*. Translated by George Schwab. Cambridge, Mass.: MIT Press, 1985.

Schneewind, J. B. "Autonomy, Obligation, and Virtue: An Overview of Kant's Moral Philosophy." In *The Cambridge Companion to Kant,* ed. Paul Guyer, 309–41. New York: Cambridge University Press, 1992.

Schneider, Helmut. "Deconstruction of the Hermeneutical Body." In *Body and Text in the Eighteenth Century,* ed. Veronica Kelly and Dorothea von Mücke, 209–29. Stanford, Calif.: Stanford University Press, 1994.

Schneider, Manfred. "Die Welt im Ausnahmezustand: Kleists Kriegstheater." *Kleist-Jahrbuch,* 2001: 104–20.

Scholem, Gershom, ed. *The Correspondence of Walter Benjamin and Gershom Scholem, 1932–1940*. Translated by Gary Smith and Andre Lefevre. New York: Schocken Books, 1989.

Schulze-Jahde, Karl. "Kohlhaas und die Zigeunerin." *Jahrbuch der Kleist-Gesellschaft* 17 (1933–37): 108–35.

Sheehan, James J. *German History, 1770–1866*. Oxford: Clarendon Press, 1989.

Sieyès, Emmanuel-Joseph. *What Is the Third Estate?* Translated by M. Blondel. Edited by S. E. Finer. New York: Praeger, 1964.

Simmel, Georg. "Soziologie der Geselligkeit." In *Verhandlungen des ersten deutschen Soziologentages,* 1–16. Tübingen: J. C. B. Mohr, 1911.

———. *Soziologie: Untersuchungen über die Formen der Vergesellschaftung*. Edited by Otthein Rammstedt. Vol. 11 of *Gesamtausgabe*. Frankfurt a/M: Suhrkamp, 1992.

Söring, Jürgen. "Die Verwirrungen und das Wunderbare in Goethes *Unterhaltungen deutscher Ausgewanderten*." *Zeitschrift für deutsche Philologie* 100 (1981): 544–59.

Srbik, Heinrich, Ritter von. *Metternich: Der Staatsmann und der Mensch*. 3 vols. Munich: F. Bruckmann, 1925–54.

Starobinski, Jean. *Blessings in Disguise; or, the Morality of the Evil*. Translated by Arthur Goldhammer. Cambridge: Polity Press, 1993.

Stephan, Inge. *Literarischer Jakobinismus in Deutschland, 1789–1806.* Stuttgart: Metzler, 1976.

Stephens, Anthony. "Das nenn ich menschlich nicht verfahren: Skizze zu einer Theorie der Grausamkeit im Hinblick auf Kleist." In *Heinrich von Kleist: Studien zu Werk und Wirkung,* ed. Dirk Grathoff, 10–39. Opladen: Westdeutscher Verlag, 1988.

Swales, Martin. *The German Novelle.* Princeton, N.J.: Princeton University Press, 1977.

Theisen, Bianca. *Bogenschluss. Kleists Formalisierung des Lesens.* Freiburg i. B.: Rombach, 1996.

———. "Gerahmte Rahmen. Kommunikation und Metakommunikation in Kleists 'Marquise von O . . . '" In *Heinrich von Kleist und die Aufklärung,* ed. Tim Mehigan, 158–68. Rochester, N.Y.: Camden House, 2000.

Todorov, Tzvetan. *Grammaire du Décaméron.* The Hague: Mouton, 1969.

———. *Theories of the Symbol.* Translated by Catherine Porter. Ithaca, N.Y.: Cornell University Press, 1982.

Trumpener, Katie. "The Time of the Gypsies: A 'People Without History' in the Narrative of the West." *Critical Inquiry* 18, no. 4 (Summer 1992): 843–84.

Valjavec, Fritz. *Entstehung der politischen Strömungen.* Munich: R. Oldenburg, 1951.

Verhaeghe, Paul. *Beyond Gender: From Subject to Drive.* New York: The Other Press, 2001.

Veyne, Paul. *Writing History.* Translated by Mina Moore-Rinvolucri. Middletown, Conn.: Wesleyan University Press, 1971.

Vorländer, Karl. *Immanuel Kant: Der Mann und das Werk.* Hamburg: Meiner, 1977.

Weber, Samuel. *Institution and Interpretation.* Minneapolis: University of Minnesota Press, 1987.

Wiese, Benno von. *Novelle.* Stuttgart: Metzler, 1963.

Wellbery, David. "Afterword." In *Goethe's Collected Works,* vol. 11, ed. David Wellbery, trans. Judith Ryan and Viktor Lange, 283–96. New York: Suhrkamp, 1988.

———. "Contingency." In *Neverending Stories,* ed. Ann Fehn et al., 237–57. Princeton, N.J.: Princeton University Press, 1992.

———. "Die Enden des Menschen. Anthropologie und Einbildungskraft im Bildungsroman." In *Das Ende: Figuren einer Denkform,* ed. Karlheinz Stierle and Rainer Warning, 600–639. Munich: Wilhelm Fink, 1996.

———. "Luhmann's Conceptual Design." MS.

White, Hayden. *The Content of the Form.* Baltimore: Johns Hopkins University Press, 1987.

Wild, Rainer. "Einleitung." In Johann Wolfgang Goethe, *Sämtliche Werke nach Epochen seines Schaffens,* vol. 4.1, ed. Rainer Wild, 1040–53. Munich: Hanser, 1988.

References

Wittkowski, Wolfgang. "Is Kleist's Michael Kohlhaas a Terrorist? Luther, Prussian Law Reforms and the Accountability of Government." *Historical Reflections / Reflexions Historiques* 26 (2000): 471–86.

Witte, Bernd. "Das Opfer der Schlange: Zur Auseinandersetzung Goethes mit Schiller in den 'Unterhaltungen deutscher Ausgewanderten' und im 'Märchen.'" In *Unser Commercium: Goethes und Schillers Literaturpolitik*, ed. Wilfried Barner, E. Lämmert, and N. Oellers, 461–84. Stuttgart: Klett, 1984.

Wittgenstein, Ludwig. *Philosophische Untersuchungen / Philosophical Investigations.* Translated by G. E. M. Anscombe. New York: Macmillan, 1963.

Yovel, Yirmiyahu. *Kant and the Philosophy of History.* Princeton, N.J.: Princeton University Press, 1980.

Žižek, Slavoj. "The Limits of the Semiotic Approach to Psychoanalysis." In *Psychoanalysis and . . .* , ed. Richard Feldstein and Henry Sussman, 89–113. New York: Routledge, 1990.

———. *For They Know Not What They Do: Enjoyment as a Political Factor.* New York: Verso, 1991.

———. *The Plague of Fantasies.* New York: Verso, 1997.

Index

accident, 7, 17, 19, 38, 136, 137
aesthetics: idealistic, 1, 15, 16, 84–86, 117; of sublimation, 75, 101, 102, 105–6; Weimar, 84, 105–6
affect, 12, 77–78, 92, 93, 94, 99, 123. *See also* passion
Agamben, Giorgio, xv, 116, 172n48
Allison, Henry E., 167n5, 171n26
Althusser, Louis, 12–13
Arendt, Hannah, 51, 54–55, 172n48
Aris, Reinhold, 169n10
Aristotle, 59–60, 137, 173n53
art: as energetic sign, 135, 141; integral part of politics, in *Michael Kohlhaas*, 26–27, 109, 128, 135, 141–45. *See also* aesthetics
Austin, John L., 12, 13
authority, xiv, 82–83, 84, 85, 101, 104–5, 115

Baioni, Guiliano, 179n45, 181n79
Baker, Keith, 162n14, 171n33
Bakhtin, M. M., 176n13, 177nn27,28&32
Balke, Friedrich, 62
Barthes, Roland, 136, 176n19, 190n68
Baudelaire, Charles, 185n32
Beiser, Frederick C., 164n31, 168–69n10
Benjamin, Walter, 27, 44, 157–58, 170n17
Berliner Abendblätter (Kleist), 160n1
"Betrothal in St. Domingo, The" (Kleist), 123, 174n66
Beyond the Pleasure Principle (Freud), 77, 92–93, 175n9
Bildung, 14–21, 23, 24, 79, 147
bildungsroman. See *Wilhelm Meister's Apprenticeship* (Goethe)
Blamberger, Günther, 159n1
Blanning, T. C. W., 169n10

Boccaccio, Giovanni, 24, 26, 75, 79, 87, 94–96, 107, 179n53
body: extrapersonal character of, 14; and gesture, 14, 124; and historical change, 148; and incorporation of the sign, 145–49; melodramatic, 124–26; role of, in speech, 7–8, 13–14, 21; speaking, 13–14; transcending consciousness, 14
Bogdal, Klaus-Michael, 185n25, 192n78
Bookmann, Hartmut, 189n63
border/boundary, xiv; and aesthetic distance, 22, 40, 41, 42, 59–60; of communication, 90–91; of concept, 22; in *Conversations of German Refugees*, 21, 75, 76; crossing, 113–15; of the ego, 79; and form, 76, 112; between France and Germany, 21, 22, 41; genre, novella as, 25; geographic, 21, 22, 41, 42, 113; as historical threshold, 22; of law, 111; of meaning, 76, 77, 78, 79; in *Michael Kohlhaas*, 21–22, 107–15; of narrativity, 22, 110–11; and paradox of exteriority, 11; as protective shield, 77–78; in sociability, 80–81; of social codes, 79; of systems, 76–77; of text, 107–12; topography of, 11, 21–22, 24–25
Bosse, Heinrich, 177n34, 179n56
Breger, Claudia, 189n65, 190n72
Breuer, Ingo, 166n56, 186n36, 189n67
Brooks, Peter, 124–25, 135, 179n54, 182n2, 186n36
bureaucracy: as force of devitalization, 10, 27, 111–12, 128, 129, 130, 152; and formless differences, 115–16; in *Michael Kohlhaas*, 111–12, 115–16, 128, 130, 143; in Prussia, 10, 111
Burg, Peter, 169n15, 172n46

Index

Burke, Edmund, 168n10
Butler, Judith, 12–13

Carnap, Rudolf, 195n7
categorical imperative, 46, 50, 57, 120
Cavell, Stanley, 184n20
Cervantes, Miguel de, 24, 94
chatter, 154
Charles V, Emperor, 108
chronicle, 109–10, 112, 116, 135–37, 147, 183–84n14
communication: aesthetic, crisis of, 82–86; and community, 4, 63–66, 154; and consciousness, 97–98; dialogue and diffusion as paradigmatic models of, 88–89; driven by passion, 11, 74, 91, 96–98; and enthusiasm, 63–67; impersonal, 71, 86, 87, 154; in modern novella, 79, 86–90, 95–96; and newness, 79, 86–90; opposed to speech, 4, 154; paradox of exteriority in, 97, 98; riddle of desire in, 99–100; of rumor, 72; in sociability, 80–82; temporality of, 3, 4, 154; unconscious, 64
community, 4, 10, 63–66, 80–82, 154
compulsion to repeat, 77
Concept of the Political, The (Schmitt), 127–28
Conflict of the Faculties (Kant), 22, 25–26, 120; alliance between philosophy and power in, 33, 70–71, 72–73; and communication, 63–66; enthusiasm in, 25, 28–29, 37, 38, 39, 47–50, 56–63, 66–67; exclusion of people as political actor, 32–33, 71; French Revolution as spectacle, 40, 41, 42, 47–48, 50, 59–60, 71, 173n53; importance of institutional mediation in, 29, 33, 70–73, 120, 167n6; and paradox of exteriority, 28, 70, 167n6; philosophical prediction in, 34–38; and repetition, 67–69; as response to revolutionary violence, 26, 50, 55–56, 61–63; role of philosophy in, 25–26, 28, 31–33, 35–38, 38–40, 41–42, 70–72; and shift from action to reception, 26, 40, 41, 50, 59–60, 63; struc-

ture of argument in, 37; and structure of university, 29–33, 70; subject to censorship, 29; tension between principle and emotion in, 26, 57, 120. See also enthusiasm; sign, of history
Conrad, Joseph, 96, 156
consciousness, 97–98, 99
constative language, 135, 137, 138, 139, 145, 148
constituting power, 50–56
contingency, 11, 12, 17, 19, 22–24. See also accident
Conversations of German Refugees (Goethe): aesthetics of sublimation in, 101, 105–6; breakdown of sociability in, 26, 74–75, 86–88, 90–91, 95–96; compared to Decameron, 26, 87, 94–96; depiction of French Revolution in, 74–79, 91–94; desire as unruly force in, 74–79, 92–94; ethics of renunciation in, 75, 101, 102–6; and Fairy Tale, 75, 105–6; feminity in, 100, 103; and invention of modern novella, 26, 74, 95–97; model of communication in, 86, 87–89, 95, 96; new model of subjectivity in, 79, 86, 94; news in, 86–90; opposed to epic narrative, 82–86; and paradox of exteriority, 96; paternity and authority in, 76, 82–83, 104; and plague of subjectivity, 26; role of boundary in, 21, 75, 76; storytelling in, 75, 86, 97, 98, 102; and trauma, 26, 76, 78–79, 92, 93, 94, 99; typography in, 85, 86
conversible world, 80–82
Craig, Gordon, 169n10
crisis, 161n11; of aesthetic communication, 82–86; evacuation of passion as, 151–56; foundational, xiv, 21, 125, 157; French Revolution as, in Goethe, 78–79; of medium, 98; in psychoanalysis, 77, 78; of sovereignty, 8–10, 21; and speech, 5–10; of symbolization, 77–79, 90, 95–96; of system, 75–79; in systems theory, 77, 78; and temporality of novella, 25; valorization of, 157–58